MAKING MAGIC IN ELIZABETHAN ENGLAND

THE MAGIC IN HISTORY SERIES

The Magic in History series explores the role magic and the occult have played in European culture, religion, science, and politics. Titles in the series bring the resources of cultural, literary, and social history to bear on the history of the magic arts, and they contribute to an understanding of why the theory and practice of magic have elicited fascination at every level of European society. Volumes include both editions of important texts and significant new research in the field.

MAGIC in HISTORY

MAKING MAGIC
IN ELIZABETHAN ENGLAND

TWO EARLY MODERN VERNACULAR

BOOKS OF MAGIC

EDITED BY FRANK KLAASSEN

THE PENNSYLVANIA STATE UNIVERSITY PRESS
UNIVERSITY PARK, PENNSYLVANIA

Library of Congress Cataloging-in-Publication Data

Names: Klaassen, Frank F., editor.
Title: Making magic in Elizabethan England : two early modern vernacular books
    of magic / edited by Frank Klaassen.
Other titles: Magic in history.
Description: University Park, Pennsylvania : The Pennsylvania State University
    Press, [2019] | Series: Magic in history | Includes bibliographical references
    and index.
Summary: "Examines two anonymous manuscripts of magic produced in
    Elizabethan England: the Antiphoner Notebook and the Boxgrove Manual.
    Explores how scribes assembled these texts within wider cultural developments
    surrounding early modern forms of magic"—Provided by publisher.
Identifiers: LCCN 2019007013 | ISBN 9780271083681 (cloth : alk. paper)
Subjects: LCSH: Magic—England—Early works to 1800. | Antiphoner notebook.
    | Boxgrove manual. | Magic—England—History—16th century.
Classification: LCC BF1622.E5 M35 2019 | DDC 133.4/30942—dc23
LC record available at https://lccn.loc.gov/2019007013

For Sharon, who shares my enduring fascination with the shadowy people behind old and grotty bits of parchment.

CONTENTS

ACKNOWLEDGMENTS

Knowledge adequate to produce an edition seldom rests in a single mind. Perhaps more than any other form of writing, it demands contributions and advice from a wide number of people. These editions began as a project in an undergraduate course at the University of Saskatchewan in which a group of Classical, Medieval, and Renaissance Studies students produced the initial transcriptions of the Antiphoner Notebook. Without their hunger for learning, questions about specific details of the text, and genuinely hard work this project might never even have been conceived. As the project became a dedicated edition, the assistance and wisdom of Margaret Dore, Claire Fanger, John Haines, Richard Kieckhefer, Yin Liu, Laura Mitchell, Brent Nelson, Lea Olsan, Joseph Peterson, Chris Philips, Maria Segol, Jason Underhill, Mihai Vartejaru, and Sharon Wright have been crucial to bringing it to completion. Laurel Beyer, David Greenfield, Ian Hampton, Ruth and Walter Klaassen, Mark Stanley, and James Wiebe offered the perspective and wisdom of intelligent lay readers. Elise Jensen labored long and hard to produce hand-drawn versions of the characters and images that she then converted to digitally useable files. I am grateful to copy editors Nicholas Taylor and Jess Klaassen-Wright and to the latter for preparing the index. Thanks are also due to the helpful staff at the British Library and the Bodleian Library. Financial support from the University of Saskatchewan and the Social Sciences and Humanities Research Council of Canada made it all possible.

Particular thanks are due to my brother, Michael Klaassen, and Claire Fanger for their generous guidance in sorting out some of the finer details of the Latin passages, and to Margaret Dore, for her invaluable assistance with the Hebrew names in the Boxgrove Manual. Any remaining errors are certainly my own.

ABBREVIATIONS

Basel 1578   Agrippa von Nettesheim, Heinrich Cornelius. *Opera*. Basel: Thomas Guarin, 1578. VD16 ZV 263

DIMEV   Mooney, Linne R., Daniel W. Mosser, Elizabeth Solopova, Deborah Thorpe, and David Hill Radcliffe. "The *DIMEV*: An Open-Access, Digital Edition of the *Index of Middle English Verse*. Based on the *Index of Middle English Verse* (1943) and Its *Supplement* (1965)." http://www .dimev.net/.

DOP   Agrippa von Nettesheim, Heinrich Cornelius. *De occulta philosophia libri tres*. Edited by V. Perrone Compagni. Leiden: Brill, 1992.

Heptameron   Peter of Abano, pseud. *Heptameron, seu elementa magica*. In *Opera*, by Heinrich Cornelius Agrippa von Nettesheim, 527–61. Basel: Thomas Guarin, 1578. VD16 ZV 263.

Liber quartus   Agrippa von Nettesheim, Heinrich Cornelius. *Liber quartus de occulta philosophia seu de cæremoniis magicis*. In *Opera*, by Heinrich Cornelius Agrippa von Nettesheim, 562–83. Basel: Thomas Guarin, 1578. VD16 ZV 263.

Turner   Agrippa von Nettesheim, Heinrich Cornelius. *Henry Cornelius Agrippa HIS Fourth BOOK of Occult Philosophy. Of Geomancy. Magical Elements of Peter de Abano. Astronomical Geomancy. The Nature of Spirits. Arbatel of Magick*. Translated by Robert Turner. London, 1655.

VD 16   Verzeichnis der im deutschen Sprachbereich erschienenen Drucke des 16. Jahrhunderts. http://www.bsb-muenchen.de/sammlungen/historische -drucke/recherche/vd-16/.

GENERAL INTRODUCTION:
THE DEVIL IN THE DETAILS

The most significant corpus of European magic manuscripts surviving from the early modern period, in terms of its influence on modern traditions, maybe even raw numbers, was produced in England. Occultists and historians of medieval magic looking for witnesses to earlier works have long recognized this fact, but historians of the early modern period have begun only in recent decades to pay closer attention to this considerable body of evidence as a whole and the complex culture of magic that produced it.[1] In her effort to emphasize the centrality of hermetic and kabbalistic traditions, Frances Yates quietly overlooked this literature, which she regarded as the magic of a past age. She painted England as a stagnant intellectual backwater, which eventually took up the stylish continental trends in magic, beginning with John Dee, whom she represents as a great hermetic mage. Work on John Dee has freed him from this straightjacket, but in turn, *he* has come to dominate the study of early modern English magic.[2] The incredible richness of his surviving works, their intellectual sophistication and influence on modern magic, his intimate associations with the great monarchs and intellectuals of his day, and, perhaps most of all, the intriguing ambiguities and drama of his story have made him both compelling and also very much worthy of study. At the same time, these qualities make him *unrepresentative* of the culture of magic practice, most of which was pursued in less sophisticated ways and further from the halls of power. In fact, Dee's magic itself was to a significant degree the product of an ambient culture of magic, one more accurately represented by the likes of his skryer, Edward Kelly, than Dee himself.[3] Where scholars have tentatively dipped into the wider literature of practical magic it has tended to be tangential to their work on other projects. So it remains that not a great deal is known about this significant body of evidence and the intellectual world in which it was produced.

In opposition to the Enlightenment view of magic as a disappearing and therefore irrelevant relic of a superstitious past, Yates painted a picture of an attractive and intellectually sophisticated tradition of high magic that lay at the core of the Renaissance and the scientific revolution. This was critical to redeeming magic and establishing it as a legitimate topic for scholarly investigation. Understandably, later scholars of early modern magic have tended to follow her in this strategy and have shied away from a body of evidence that does not have this kind of sheen but is, in raw statistical terms, overwhelmingly more representative of sixteenth-century magic.[4] They have also been legitimately leery of it. Until recently, little was known about the medieval traditions that fill sixteenth-century magic manuscripts. As a result, there has been no clear way to get a handle on this substantial library of texts: what aspects of the older traditions their scribes preserved, how they transformed them, and how their activities reflect the peculiar circumstances of the period. But this has changed.

In the past two decades scholars have made significant progress in coming to terms with the literature and intellectual culture of medieval learned magic.[5] It is now possible to see that, although sixteenth-century scribes worked with a substantially medieval set of traditions, the story is not merely one of continuity. A good deal of subtle experimentation took place at this time in which we can see scribes conceptualizing magic on a basic level. The new trends in science and the religious upheavals of the period brought new perspectives to medieval traditions, including magic. These influences were compounded by the vernacularization and popularization of medieval learned magic, the reconfiguration and reframing of magic in the hands of renaissance intellectuals, and the increasing body of printed works on magic. All of these were clearly in the minds of scribes as they copied and reimagined the magic literature they had inherited. The result was not a coherent body of magic literature, much less one that changed in predictable ways. Whereas some scribes carefully preserved and duplicated earlier texts, others significantly transformed them. Some simplified; some experimented with new forms or synthesized old ones. Some preserved the Catholic elements; some carefully edited them out. In short, sixteenth-century England had its own distinctive, rich, and lively subculture of magic that we are now uniquely positioned to explore. And the devil, as it were, is in the details.

It is my contention that in these manuscripts of deceiving rogues and true believers, middlebrow conjurers and Latinate mages, as much as in the dizzying esoteric traditions of renaissance high magic, we may see the origins of modern European magic. This volume seeks to correct the imbalance in our understanding of sixteenth-century magic by exploring two manuscripts representative of this broad and largely unexplored body of evidence. The Antiphoner Notebook, written on blank parchment that once formed the margins of a large monastic manuscript, is preserved in the Bodleian Library at Oxford University. A late sixteenth-century scribe who was interested in magic, charms, and the old religion filled its pages with material from at least three sources: a medieval conjuring manual, one or more collections of medieval charms, and Scot's *Discoverie of Witchcraft*. The Boxgrove Manual is an attempt by an English magician writing sometime after 1578 to synthesize at least two late medieval conjuring texts with two pseudonymous printed works on ritual magic and materials from the great Renaissance magus Henry Cornelius Agrippa of Nettesheim. It is now preserved in the British Library. While they certainly do not represent the entire spectrum of magic practice in late sixteenth-century England, these two texts evince many important dimensions of that period in the history of magic, in particular how two scribes went about assembling or *making* a book of magic.[6] To do this the scribes did not simply copy from old books; they collected various sources, then weighed, adapted, and blended them for their own purposes. In turn, this process of scribal authorship reveals a good deal about their reading habits, motivations, and ideas, all of which were expressions of the social and intellectual upheavals of the sixteenth century and the wider intellectual culture of magic in the early modern period. Only by examining the manuscripts of contemporary magicians and by firmly situating the authors in their intellectual worlds—in the books they read and how they transformed them—may we begin to reframe our approach to magic in the early modern period.

Medieval Ritual Magic and Charms: Sources and Continuities

The texts in this volume derive material from two principal genres of medieval magic: charms and ritual magic. The Antiphoner Notebook contains examples of both, while the Boxgrove Manual draws solely on the latter. Knowing where these forms of magic came from can help us understand why they look the way they do, the ways they reflect continuity with their medieval sources, and ultimately the changes they underwent at the hands of their Elizabethan scribes and authors. Our discussion will begin with the tradition of ritual magic before turning briefly to charms.

The term "ritual magic" commonly designates practices involving lengthy ritual operations. Works in this genre written in the Latin West were based in significant measure on the Christian liturgy and framed in Christian terms but also drew in part on Hebraic and Arabic magic traditions. Although this form of magic generally requires the observance of astrological conditions, particularly the phases of the moon, planetary hours, and days of the week, the texts make clear that the most important elements are the preparatory ritual observances and the spiritual condition or character of the operator. For example, the magician must be a Christian in a state of grace (having confessed and taken communion and having avoided sources of corruption, such as sex, for a period of at least three days), be blameless in his comportment, with a clean body and clothes, and often have observed a lengthy regime of prayer, fasting, and religious devotion. European ritual magic also tends to seek direct experience of the numinous or the infusion of spiritual gifts. If the number of surviving manuscripts is any indication, the most significant premodern work of this genre was undoubtedly the *Ars notoria*, which sought the infusion of knowledge and spiritual gifts following the performance of complex rituals, prayers, and contemplative exercises. Other examples include the *Liber iuratus Honorii, Clavicula Salomonis, Thesaurus spirituum,* and *Liber consecrationum,* which were supplemented by a significant variety of anonymous texts. These works seek direct experience of spirits or the divine, although the purported nature of those spirits and the manner of approaching them varies somewhat. They situate their rituals in a variety of mythologies. Some trace their lineage to mythical medieval authors such as Honorius of Thebes, others to Old Testament figures like Adam or Solomon.[7]

Scribes of ritual magic in the Latin West regularly adapted and transformed the magic books that they had inherited. In fact, the mythology of these texts encouraged this tendency by valorizing the role and agency of the practitioner. Works of ritual magic represented the great magician as a kind of divinely guided practitioner-editor whose long experience in magic was crucial to uncovering the truths in obscure and ancient magic books intended only for the chosen few. Numerous rituals reinforce these ideas by offering concourse with spirits for the express purpose of attaining information or guidance regarding the practice of magic. As they confronted these often fragmentary and difficult texts, it seems likely that many imagined themselves in the role of an elect inheritor and interpreter of primordial secrets. One of the byproducts of this culture was what Julien Véronèse has called the author-magician, the practitioner who created new works of magic to which they attached their name.[8] But this was only the most dramatic expression of a wider culture in which scribes actively took up the challenge of interpreting their obscure source texts, expanded and explicated them, and/or compiled their own new magic books from them.[9] For example, scribes wrote explanatory additions to the original *Ars notoria* in order to make it more understandable, and later ones abbreviated and simplified it in various versions. Similarly, the fourteenth-century monk John of Morigny created a new system of intellectual magic based on the *Ars notoria* that he combined with Benedictine contemplative traditions and the affective Marian piety.[10] The changes that scribes made to the texts were sometimes minor, but they were certainly regular, giving rise to a textually chaotic and shifting body of literature that reflects in fascinating ways the changing intellectual, religious, and social world around it. At the same time, until the latter decades of the fifteenth century the literature remained relatively coherent in its self-conception and form, particularly its heavy endorsement of, and reliance on, conventional religion. This general stability was in part assured by the stability of the intellectual and social environment in which it was transmitted.

Medieval ritual magic was generally the preserve of male clerics, both regular and secular, and also more broadly of those associated with the universities, who had adopted clerical sensibilities. Unsurprisingly, it reflects their worldview. The goals promised by the texts suggest a largely male audience, but more crucially the rules of operation uniformly assume male practitioners, ban undue concourse with women, and often specifically forbid revealing the secrets of magic to them.[11] The procedures not only required Latinity, but the operations reflect an extensive knowledge of the liturgy difficult to perform by those not well versed in it. By demanding learning, a high level of self-control, fasting, sexual abstinence, regular participation in rites of the Church, knowledge of the liturgy, and homosocial surroundings, they not only made a virtue of the clerical lifestyle, but also turned it into a source of cosmic power. That the texts were written in Latin made them inaccessible to most people and tended to reinforce their claims to being high secrets fit only for the learned few. The rituals drew heavily from the liturgy and were represented as both holy and thoroughly Christian. In other words, despite being illicit and despite their promotion of some theologically problematic ideas, they tended simultaneously to reinforce the religious and intellectual status quo in significant ways.[12]

During the course of the fifteenth century, however, the readership of these texts began to expand as scribes increasingly transmitted learned magic of various kinds into vernacular languages, placing it in the hands of people with different sensibilities and who did not have the language skills to understand the original Latin texts.[13] This process accelerated considerably in the sixteenth century and a considerable body of vernacular ritual magic literature developed alongside the older Latin literature. New readers and transmitters of magic increasingly did not have university training or an extensive knowledge of the liturgy, were not the products or inhabitants of the same homosocial world as their predecessors, and did not lead even superficially clerical lives. Predictably the texts began to change. They tended to shed many of the complex liturgical elements in favor of greater simplicity. They also began to draw in elements from popular magic or to create new ones that did not reflect the sensibilities of the original medieval texts. This is particularly visible in this volume in the ritual magic sections of the Antiphoner Notebook, which are shorter and quite different from their medieval models. The scribe's inability in Latin rendered some of the prayers and invocations nonsensical and also drove him to use Scot's *Discoverie of Witchcraft* as a sourcebook. Scot not only provided translations of medieval texts but also collected vernacular material which had already been simplified and transformed.[14] A parallel process is also visible in the tradition of books of secrets in which Latinate scribes became cultural brokers providing materials to a non-Latinate audience, while simultaneously systematizing popular knowledge in written form.[15] As we shall see, the Boxgrove Manual also translated and digested magic from a variety of medieval and early modern Latin sources. Although medieval in conception it incorporated materials from sixteenth-century printed works on magic, excised Catholic elements, and privatized the magic by removing the requirement of priestly assistance from the rituals. The result was a subtly transformed sort of magic that was in turn made available to a vernacular audience. At the same time, the fact that it was copied for a priest demonstrates that learned magic also continued to be the preserve of an educated and even clerical elite.

Scholars often give the impression that the Renaissance brought about a profound and widespread rewriting and revision of magic from the 1480s onward. This is a gross oversimplification, if not a genuine misrepresentation of the culture of magic in the sixteenth century in which medieval ritual magic was preserved and transmitted in its original form with tremendous enthusiasm. The great Renaissance writers, starting with Marsilio Ficino and Pico della Mirandola, and followed later by Cornelius Agrippa and Giordano Bruno, produced striking and original new works on or involving magic that were profoundly influential in the development of Western esoteric traditions. However, the impact of these writers was sporadic and slow to take root, in significant measure because of the arcane nature of their works. In 1533 the Oxford necromancer Richard Jones expressed frustration with Agrippa's *De occulta philosophia*, saying that it was "of very small effect."[16] Although this might be taken as the bravado of a middlebrow conjurer, the comment reflects the attitude of many sixteenth-century scribes of magic. Jones evidently regarded it as important and acquired a copy in the very year it was first published. But unlike the highly scripted ritual magic texts Jones was used to, Agrippa was more concerned to make larger arguments about the nature of magic and the cosmos and actually provided very little concrete information on *what* to do with all the materials he provided or *how* to do it. In fact, Agrippa's project sought to reformulate magic in the original and proper form practiced by ancient Hebrew prophets and patriarchs. His whole point—which was very much the same among the other Renaissance writers—was that contemporary magic got it wrong and should be entirely reformulated. As a result, the works of the great Renaissance mages did not accord well with the needs, inclinations, and sensibilities of most practicing magicians, who saw no need to build a different system of practical magic from obscure sources in ancient Greek and Hebrew.

Predictably, most sixteenth-century scribes, even those who were educated enough to read Latin or other ancient languages, filled the pages of their books with the highly scripted works of medieval ritual magic. In fact, most important medieval ritual magic texts are known primarily through copies made in the sixteenth century by scribes eager to preserve these older traditions. Ironically, the printed works pseudonymously attributed to Agrippa and the other works bound with them were far more influential in sixteenth-century books of magic than his legitimate works because they reflect these earlier forms of scripted ritual magic.[17] By contrast, Agrippa's *De occulta philosophia* took up a role as the premier magic sourcebook or encyclopedia of magic, one that it has consistently played to the present day. From it scribes drew scattered elements that they inserted into magic that otherwise retained its old forms in most respects. In all this, other writers like Pico, Ficino, and Bruno, who were significantly *less* accessible than Agrippa, were all but irrelevant. As we shall see, the Latinate author of the Boxgrove Manual reflects this situation. He employed Agrippa both for nuggets of information and also for some framing cosmological concepts as he constructed a system based in significant measure on medieval ritual magic manuscripts and new printed works of practical magic, themselves based largely on medieval sources.

Although it contains some ritual magic material, another form of scripted magic fills most of the pages of the Antiphoner Notebook. Charms and protective amulets constituted what may be the most common genre of magic in the later Middle Ages. They were certainly the most ubiquitous, as charms may be found not only in medical works and dedicated collections, but scattered throughout the library in margins, flyleaves, and elsewhere. Unlike ritual magic, charms were practiced as part of a conventional regimen of healing and protection from misfortune by a much wider demographic including both clerical and lay, wealthy and poor, educated and illiterate. Also, unlike ritual magic with its complex liturgical rituals and cosmologies, charms are quite simple and short and based on the conservative bedrock of conventional and everyday religious practices. They employ basic prayers such as the Pater Noster and Ave Maria, formulae like the Credo, the invocation of saints, divine names, religious historiola, and gestures like the sign of the cross for healing and protection. As a kind of lay liturgy, these changed very little over time except in minor textual ways. Many charms have long textual histories spanning numerous centuries and were very broadly transmitted in Europe.[18] Even the Reformation, which had been attacking the "superstition" of Catholic practices for decades by the time the Antiphoner

Notebook was written, had little effect on the attractiveness of this aspect of the old religion. Many of the charms the scribe copied are almost identical to ones found in fourteenth-century manuscripts. A fuller discussion of this genre may be found in the introduction to that work below.

Although I have argued that magic texts changed as they were transmitted to vernacular and nonclerical contexts and that this process accelerated in the sixteenth century, I have on balance emphasized continuity with the past. The older traditions were preserved in their medieval forms, and when scribes copied magic texts they were overwhelmingly medieval in origin. Even if they were simplified the general outlines of the magic remained more or less consistent. To emphasize these forms of continuity through the sixteenth century in medieval ritual magic and charms, however, is only part of the picture. The sixteenth century brought with it a host of dramatic changes that had a direct impact on magic. By comparison, from the mid-thirteenth to the fifteenth century the broader intellectual and social conditions that informed the conception and practice of magic were relatively stable in England. Most importantly, theology and religious practice did not change in any significant way. The rise and persecution of the Lollards certainly inspired a more conservative attitude toward heresy, but the continental habit of associating heresy with magic and apostasy was never strong in England and, in any event, Lollards were not associated with magic. This being said, magic consistently was understood as a matter for Church rather than secular courts, except in highly unusual cases. Scholastic culture dominated the intellectual world without significant challenges, and the universities remained the center of intellectual life. If intellectual condemnations of magic became more sophisticated in their awareness of magic texts, the basic message of those condemnations did not change. Unsurprisingly, although the textual traditions were fluid and the manuscripts of magic often highly individual, the basic nature of magic remained fairly stable to the end of the fifteenth century, particularly in its close relationship with conventional religion. The same could not be said for the sixteenth century.

The Changing Conditions of the Sixteenth Century

There have been many attempts to sketch out broad narratives to make sense of what happened to magic in sixteenth-century England. These divide into three main currents. The first, epitomized by the work of Keith Thomas, has its conceptual roots in Reformation and Enlightenment rhetoric and claims to trace a process of disenchantment initiated by Protestant theology and the new science. In the second—by no means limited to the discredited Yates thesis—Renaissance intellectual historians have sought to understand sixteenth-century magic as the product of new continental currents in magic and more widely in natural philosophy. Finally, historians of the witch trials have attempted, with varying degrees of success, to construct narratives in which growing forces, including building social pressures, increasing institutional paranoia, and the feminization of magic culminated in the witch trials after 1560. There is a measure of truth in all of these, but by addressing only one facet of a set of complicated and interrelated changes they tend to obscure as much as they reveal.

The history of magic in sixteenth-century England cannot be reduced to a simplistic narrative. At this time, new currents began to spread in the literature and culture of science (often including an interest in magic),[19] which explicitly attacked scholastic method, insisting on the importance of experience over authority in establishing truth. Institutional religion underwent significant transformation during the Reformation, and religious factions vied for control, often employing accusations of magic in their rhetorical attacks on one another, although this was more typically a Protestant strategy. Popular fear of, fascination with, and attraction to magic grew simultaneously, encouraged by popular literature on the subject, either in the form of books of secrets on the one hand or sensational tracts about cases of witchcraft and magic on the other. During this century magic first became a crime (at least in some of its forms) as the Tudor state attempted on two occasions to shift the prerogative to prosecute it from Church to secular courts. Extensive witch trials erupted for the first time starting in 1563. Finally, as we have seen, medieval magic literature was transmitted to a substantially larger non-Latinate and nonclerical audience in manuscript and print, and new continental ideas about magic and witchcraft flowed into England. The effects of this sudden maelstrom of forces were predictably unpredictable and might be best described as a diverse set of experimental responses to a world in flux. This is certainly the case in the manuscripts of magic in which we find that the once-discrete streams of medieval magic practice began to bleed into one another and were transformed in a variety of unprecedented ways that would not stabilize until the latter half of the seventeenth century. So let us begin by describing these destabilizing conditions in somewhat more detail.

The traditional response of the English institutional church to magic, in its usual form divorced from treason, was on balance a kind of aggrieved, de facto tolerance, punctuated by occasional presentments at church courts.[20] This does not seem to have changed significantly in the sixteenth century. The church courts, where we find most cases of magic tried prior to 1560, occasionally treated it as a significant religious crime by probing for evidence of idolatry or heresy, but in most cases they treated it as a minor misdemeanor of superstition or simply as fraud. A mid-century canon written by reforming bishops called for the gravest penalties (*poenas gravissimas*) for a widely defined set of magical practices including illicit prayers. That it was never promulgated made it little more than a controlled expression of exasperation, and in any event, the gravest penalty the church could inflict on its own remained public penance.[21] Moreover, at least half of the cases involving magic found their way into the church courts not because of magic per se but rather the social disruption it had caused, and more often the clients of cunning folk were presented rather than the cunning folk themselves.[22] For example, those who found themselves accused of theft by a diviner or a diviner's client often sought redress for false accusations. In other words, there is little evidence the church courts went looking for magic; instead, they dealt with it when it fell into their laps.

The situation in the secular courts was similar. Despite legislation by Henry VIII and Elizabeth I, the English secular courts were generally disinclined to prosecute people for crimes of magic in itself, especially before 1560. Henry's legislation made even the common practices of treasure hunting and thief identification capital crimes. The extreme and unforgiving nature of this law no doubt discouraged its use, but it also seems that the long-standing institutional habit of regarding magic as a matter for the church courts persisted. No one was ever prosecuted under it. The Elizabethan legislation may have been motivated by perceived magical threats to the crown from Catholic forces or by embarrassment over not being able to prosecute dramatic cases of non-treasonous magic. In any case, it was not intended in the first instance as part of a sweeping campaign to extirpate magic (as much as some parties might have liked this). Curiously, it was only ever employed in witch trials, a use for which it was certainly not intended.[23] Although magic became a capital crime under Henry's legislation and for repeat offenders under Elizabeth's, very few executions of actual magic practitioners took place. It was just as common for magicians to walk free having been subject only to periods of incarceration or public penance if they had been tried in church courts. The actions against John Dee (who was certainly engaging in dubious forms of astrological prediction surrounding the future of the monarchy in England under Mary) resulted in little more than damage to his reputation.[24] Robert Allen, a cunning man who performed a variety of magical services in London, was accused of foretelling the death of Edward VI and evidently caught red-handed. He spent a year or two in the Tower of London before being released. This could easily have been nudged into a treason trial but never was.[25] Despite having seduced a young Harry Lord Neville into various forms of magic practice and skulduggery, the magician-conman Gregory Wisdom not only escaped serious punishment but went on to be accepted as a medical practitioner by the College of Physicians.[26] John Prestall, a high-profile repeat offender involved in all sorts of magic and magical treason, managed to walk away from several trials for magic.[27] The large number of surviving magic manuscripts and the large estimated numbers of practicing cunning folk suggest that the overwhelming majority of practitioners never even came to the attention of the courts.[28] When the attentions of some secular courts turned to common malefic witchcraft after 1563, the trials that resulted were episodic and localized, the number of presentments outweighed convictions by a rate of four to one, and relatively speaking the numbers of executions were quite low. More to the point, these did not tend to target people who were actual magic practitioners.

All this being said, the legislation and the institutional concern that motivated it certainly had an impact on magic. For a start, although legislators had entirely different intentions for the law, the witch trials *were* made possible by Elizabeth's Act of 1563. The Tudor state was also quite clearly concerned about learned magic and magical treason and communicated this clearly in its legislative efforts and its numerous trials or investigations of treasonous magic, real or imagined.[29] More significantly, the magic practitioners with whom this volume is centrally concerned were aware of the law, weighed their own practices in relation to it, and sometimes adjusted them accordingly. In 1510 a group of Yorkshire treasure hunters appeared in the archbishop's court at York for employing necromantic magic to locate and retrieve a hoard of gold at Mixindale Head.[30] In their confessions, they recount assuring each other that, by compelling demons to bring them the gold, they were not breaking the king's law. They were at least partially correct in this. At that point there was no law against magic as such. Their claim that they had not dug for it would certainly not have stood up in court since buried treasure was by definition the property of the crown.[31] Similarly, when Robert Allen was arrested for predicting Edward VI's death, he complained that Edward's repeal of Henry's legislation meant that he had done nothing illegal.[32] Naturally, as those arresting him knew, it was quite possible to prosecute him under other laws, particularly if his actions could be deemed treasonous. Finally, accounts of court cases actually found their way into magic literature itself. As we shall see, instructions for a protective talisman in the Antiphoner Notebook (item 39) include an account of the hanging of Robert Tresilian in which he reportedly used magic to protect himself from harm. Although the Antiphoner Notebook got the story wrong, the case was real. These examples demonstrate that magic practitioners were concerned about their legal status and operated in awareness not only of the law but also of the actions of the state. Although it is not clear *how* this awareness may have affected their behavior, there is no question that it probably did, if only to make them more cautious and to emphasize the antisocial nature of their activities. As we

shall see, the numerous pamphlets on trials for magic and witchcraft that circu-
lated in this period made known the new laws, the concerns of the state, and its
actions against magic to a wider audience and in a more rapid fashion than in
previous centuries.

The Reformation did not produce new and original attacks on magic so
much as it revitalized them and added significant new levels of complexity.
Protestant theology tended to paint a much more stark and one-way relationship between the divine and the physical world in which there was less room
for unofficial ways to seek the benefits of divine power. Although this theological turn resulted in frequent attacks on Catholic practice and theology as
magical, it did not necessarily translate into a rejection of the idea that magic
might in fact work. Protestant antimagic writing was (perhaps tellingly) slow to
develop. From the 1560s onward, a number of printed tracts recounted trials for
crimes of magic or witchcraft, but these were largely sensational accounts,
more concerned with communicating lurid details than offering incisive critiques of magic.[33] The first and most influential Protestant antimagic work in
England, Scot's *Discoverie of Witchcraft*, was not written until 1583. It took the
position that magic invoking higher spiritual powers, which it rhetorically
elided with Catholicism, was entirely fraudulent and inefficacious. Certainly,
Protestant critiques of Catholicism would have heightened concerns with
magic and superstition after 1583, but given the halting and inconsistent progress of the English Reformation and the lack of significant innovation in antimagic arguments by Protestants, the basic messaging from the church to the
laity on magic probably did not change a great deal during most of the sixteenth
century.

In two other respects, however, the Reformation was a real game changer.
First, significant portions of the magic library, including ritual magic and charms,
were inherently Catholic in form simply by having been produced in the Middle
Ages. They reflected the Catholic worldview in which mechanisms for drawing
on divine power were available in the world to humans. They also allied themselves with the institutional church through their use of its rituals and hagio-
graphic mythologies. Thus in a Protestant state they not only lost the principal
sources of power and legitimization, they also became doubly illicit and problematic by virtue of being magic *and* Catholic. Second, the negative association
between magic and Catholicism was constructed not only on theological grounds,
but also by an increasing association of magic with foreign-sponsored Catholic
efforts to overthrow the Protestant state, an association that grew through the
century as a result of numerous public investigations and trials for treasonous
magic. As a result magic was illicit on a number of new political and theological levels. The Catholic elements in ritual magic such as the invocations of

saints, particularly the Virgin Mary or the use of Catholic liturgy, were now regarded as illicit in themselves but also could suggest that a practitioner had Catholic sympathies and belonged to a politically subversive group. In short, the old magic was now illicit not only by virtue of being magic, but also by association with Catholicism and the forces aligned against the English crown.

The Reformation did not so much disenchant as break apart the old consensus about what magic should be like or how to make it. Richard Kieckhefer has described magic in the medieval world as the reverse side of the tapestry of conventional religion. The metaphor captures the significant integration of conventional religious practice into medieval magic without lessening the distinctiveness of the magic practices or their generally illicit nature. But in the sixteenth century the competing tapestries of Protestantism, Catholicism, and various streams of the Radical Reformation produced their own forms and views of magic. That is to say, practitioners who identified with these different streams each engaged with the old magic literature in new and distinctive ways. Perhaps more significantly, in the resulting disorder and particularly in Protestant regions like England, *all forms* of magic became increasingly disengaged from conventional religion. The author of the Boxgrove Manual and the priest who paid to have it copied were both Protestants. The author had carefully removed all the explicitly Catholic elements from his sources creating, superficially at least, a Protestant magic book, but one that had substantially fewer threads connecting it to conventional religion than its medieval models did in their period. Aside from its use of Protestant translations of the Bible, there was nothing *inherently* Protestant about the magic. It was Protestant only by subtraction. The removal of rituals conducted in public space from the operations (such as particular masses and confession) and the relegation of the rituals of consecration entirely to private spaces only further drove this disconnection. The scribe of the Antiphoner Notebook superficially did the opposite, but the results were more or less the same. He was clearly nostalgic for the old religion, and his unexpurgated Catholic magic was doubly illicit in Elizabeth's England both by virtue of being magic and through its apparent alliance with a rejected, competing, and even seditious religious faction. Perhaps most curiously, other variations were also possible, once again with the same results. In the Antiphoner Notebook the ritual for the "wastecote of proof" invokes only the name of the devil for its power. In this profoundly un-medieval form of magic (comparable to the seventeenth-century Faustian grimoires of the Germanic context), the text makes no attempt to forge an alliance with conventional religion of any kind and seems self-consciously to establish magic as something genuinely opposed to it. In short, no matter what a magician did, magic was no longer what it had been in the Middle Ages.

The notion that modernity is distinguished by a process of disenchantment has been justifiably challenged in recent decades. Magic persisted at all levels of society long after the sixteenth century and, far from declining, enchantment has simply taken on diverse and peculiarly modern forms in the subsequent centuries, incorporating elements of Enlightenment and Romantic thought, modern psychology, science, secularism, and even postmodernism. The sources in this volume make clear that this recognition should not drive us to reject the influence of the Reformation and other forces peculiar to the sixteenth century as important elements in the history of magic. Instead of initiating a decline, these forces were responsible for provoking one undeniable feature of modernity—that its magic commonly defines itself in *opposition* to conventional religion or Christianity in general. That the early stages of this disengagement may be seen only through a close examination of the manuscripts is perhaps the strongest apology for this edition of two obscure magic books from late sixteenth-century England.

Notes

1. Although the outlines of this literature have long been known and a significant number of editions produced by occult presses, no general assessment of this body of evidence (including ritual magic, astral or astrological magic, books of secrets, experiments, recipes, and the vast array of divinatory techniques) has been made. More focused studies include Jean-Patrice Boudet, "Les who's who démonologiques de la Renaissance et leurs ancêtres médiévaux," *Médiévales* 44 (Spring 2003): 117–39; Stephen Clucas, "'Non est legendum sed inspicendum solum': Inspectival Knowledge and the Visual Logic of John Dee's Liber Mysteriorum," in *Emblems and Alchemy*, ed. Alison Adams and Stanton J. Linden, Glasgow Emblem Studies 3 (Glasgow: Glasgow Emblem Studies, 1998), 109–32; Clucas, "Regimen animarum et corporum: The Body and Spatial Practice in Medieval and Renaissance Magic," in *The Body in Late Medieval and Early Modern Culture*, ed. Darryll Grantley and Nina Taunton (Aldershot, U.K.: Ashgate, 1999), 113–29; Clucas, "John Dee's Angelic Conversations and the *Ars Notoria*," in *John Dee: Interdisciplinary Studies in English Renaissance Thought*, ed. Stephen Clucas (Dordrecht: Springer, 2006), 231–73; Mordechai Feingold, "The Occult Tradition in the English Universities of the Renaissance: A Reassessment," in *Occult and Scientific Mentalities in the Renaissance*, ed. Brian Vickers (Cambridge, U.K.: Cambridge University Press, 1984), 73–94; Deborah E. Harkness, *John Dee's Conversations with Angels: Cabala, Alchemy, and the End of Nature* (Cambridge, U.K.: Cambridge University Press, 1999); Lauren Kassell, "Reading for the Philosopher's Stone," in *Books and the Sciences in History*, ed. Marina Frasca-Spada and Nicholas Jardine (Cambridge, U.K.: Cambridge University Press, 2000), 13–34; Kassell, "The Economy of Magic in Early Modern England," in *The Practice of Reform in Health, Medicine, and Science, 1500–2000: Essays for Charles Webster*, ed. Margaret Pelling and Scott Mandelbrote (Aldershot, U.K.: Ashgate, 2005), 43–57; Kassell, *Medicine and Magic in Elizabethan London: Simon Forman: Astrologer, Alchemist, and Physician*, Oxford Historical Monographs (Oxford, U.K.: Clarendon Press, 2005); Kassell, "'All This Land Full Fill'd of Faerie,' or Magic and the Past in Early Modern England," *Journal of the History of Ideas* 67, no. 1 (2006): 107–22; Frank Klaassen, "Three Magic Rituals to Spoil Witches," *Opuscula: Short Texts of the Middle Ages and Renaissance* 1 (2011): 1–10; Klaassen, "Ritual Invocation and Early Modern Science: The Skrying Experiments of Humphrey Gilbert,"

in *Invoking Angels*, ed. Claire Fanger (University Park: Pennsylvania State University Press, 2011), 341–66; Klaassen, *The Transformations of Magic: Illicit Learned Magic in the Later Middle Ages and Renaissance* (University Park: Pennsylvania State University Press, 2013); Frances Timbers, *Magic and Masculinity: Ritual Magic and Gender in the Early Modern Era* (London: Taurus, 2014); Julien Véronèse, *L'Ars notoria au Moyen Âge: Introduction et édition critique*, Micrologus Library (Florence: SISMEL edizioni del Galluzzo, 2007); Francis Young, *The Cambridge Book of Magic: A Tudor Necromancer's Manual* (Ely, U.K.: Francis Young, 2015). Joseph Peterson also deserves recognition for his high-quality popular scholarship on early modern magic. Of particular note for sixteenth-century England is Daniel Harms, James R. Clark, and Joseph H. Peterson, *The Book of Oberon: A Sourcebook of Elizabethan Magic* (Woodbury, Mich.: Llewellyn Publications, 2015).

2. Clucas, "Non Est Legendum Sed Inspicendum Solum"; Clucas, "*Regimen Animarum Et Corporum*"; Clucas, "John Dee's Angelic Conversations and the *Ars Notoria*"; Nicholas H. Clulee, *John Dee's Natural Philosophy: Between Science and Religion* (London: Routledge, 1988); Harkness, *John Dee's Conversations with Angels*; G. J. R. Parry, *The Arch-Conjuror of England: John Dee* (New Haven, Conn.: Yale University Press, 2011); Benjamin Wooley, *The Queen's Conjurer: The Science and Magic of Dr. John Dee, Adviser to Queen Elizabeth I* (New York: Henry Holt, 2001).

3. It is illustrative of the current imbalance in scholarship on sixteenth-century magic that a focused study of Edward Kelly has not yet been done.

4. Frank Klaassen, "Medieval Ritual Magic in the Renaissance," *Aries* 3, no. 2 (2003): 166–99.

5. I cite only the major collections, book-length editions, and monographs: Jean-Patrice Boudet, *Entre science et nigromance: Astrologie, divination et magie dans L'Occident Médiéval, xiie–xve siècle* (Paris: Publications de la Sorbonne, 2006); Jan N. Bremmer and Jan R. Veenstra, *The Metamorphosis of Magic from Late Antiquity to the Early Modern Period* (Leuven: Peeters, 2002); Charles Burnett, *Magic and Divination in the Middle Ages: Texts and Techniques in the Islamic and Christian Worlds* (Aldershot, U.K.: Variorum, 1996); Charles Burnett and W. F. Ryan, *Magic and the Classical Tradition* (London: Warburg Institute, 2006); Claire Fanger, *Conjuring Spirits: Texts and Traditions of Medieval Ritual Magic*, Magic in History (University Park: Pennsylvania State University Press, 1998); Fanger, ed., *Invoking Angels: Theurgic Ideas and Practices, Thirteenth to Sixteenth Centuries* (University Park: Pennsylvania State University Press, 2012); Fanger, *Rewriting Magic: An Exegesis of the Visionary Autobiography of a Fourteenth-Century French Monk*, Magic in History (University Park: Pennsylvania State University Press, 2015); John of Moringy, *Liber Florum Celestis Doctrine: The Flowers of Heavenly Teaching*, ed. Claire Fanger and Nicholas Watson (Toronto: Pontifical Institute of Mediaeval Studies, 2015); Richard Kieckhefer, *Forbidden Rites: A Necromancer's Manual of the Fifteenth Century* (Stroud, U.K.: Sutton, 1997); Klaassen, *Transformations of Magic*; Sophie Page, *Magic in the Cloister: Pious Motives, Illicit Interests, and Occult Approaches to the Medieval Universe* (University Park: Pennsylvania State University Press, 2013); Véronèse; Nicolas Weill-Parot, *Les "images astrologiques" au Moyen Âge et à la Renaissance* (Paris: Honoré Champion, 2002).

6. For a similar examination of the process of assembling materials on esoteric topics in sixteenth-century England, see Kassell, "Reading for the Philosopher's Stone."

7. For a discussion of the genre of ritual magic in general see Claire Fanger, "Medieval Ritual Magic: What It Is and Why We Need to Know More About It," in *Conjuring Spirits: Texts and Traditions of Medieval Ritual Magic*, ed. Claire Fanger (Stroud, U.K.: Sutton, 1998), vii–xx. See also Klaassen, *Transformations of Magic*, 81–159.

8. See Julien Véronèse, "La notion d''auteur-magicien' à la fin du Moyen Âge: Le cas de l'ermite Pelagius de Majorque," *Médiévales* 51 (2006): 119–38. See also Klaassen, *Transformations of Magic*, 89–114.

9. On the mythology of the divinely guided editor and the transmission of ritual magic texts see Klaassen, *Transformations of Magic*, 89–155.

10. John of Morigny, "Prologue to *Liber visionum*," ed. and trans. Claire Fanger and Nicholas Watson, *Esoterica* 3 (2001): 108–217. See also Claire Fanger, "Divine Dreamwork: Confluence of Visionary Traditions in John of Morigny's *Flowers of Heavenly Teaching*," *Magic, Ritual, and Witchcraft* 13, no. 1 (2018): 1–39.

11. In the few known cases where women were involved in ritual magic operations, they tended to be adjuncts to male operators. See Frank Klaassen, "Learning and Masculinity in Manuscripts of Ritual Magic of the Later Middle Ages and Renaissance," *Sixteenth Century Journal* 38, no. 1 (2007): 55. See also Lyndal Roper, "Stealing Manhood: Capitalism and Magic in Early Modern Germany," *Gender & History* 3 (March 1991): 4–22. This appears to change by the seventeenth century, when more women began to take up this literature and were more commonly employed as skryers.

12. Klaassen, "Learning and Masculinity in Manuscripts of Ritual Magic."

13. Although the earliest vernacular versions of ritual magic texts are from thirteenth-century Castile, it was not until the fifteenth century that translation began across European languages. See Sebastià Giralt, "Magic in Romance Languages," in *The Routledge History of Medieval Magic*, ed. Sophie Page and Catherine Rider (Turnhout: Routledge, forthcoming). A veritable explosion of magic texts written in the vernacular took place in the sixteenth century, and there would be little profit in attempting to give citations of all these works. An example of fifteenth-century English vernacular invocation magic may be found in Oxford, Bodleian Library, Rawlinson D. 252. London, British Library, Sloane 3849, fols. 7r–16r and 23r–29v, is the earliest surviving conjuring manual written entirely in English and dates to the second quarter of the sixteenth century, sometime after 1534. For a fifteenth-century German example see Jan R. Veenstra, "The Holy Almandal," in *The Metamorphosis of Magic*, ed. Jan N. Bremmer and Jan R. Veenstra (Leuven: Peeters, 2006).

14. The initial treasure-hunting operations (nos. 2 and 3) are quite short. For a transformed text see the diabolic "wastecote of proof," which the scribe drew from Scot. See Reginald Scot, *The Discouerie of Witchcraft* (London: W. Brome, 1584), bk. 12, chap. 9. See also below, Antiphoner Notebook, item 49.

15. William Eamon, *Science and the Secrets of Nature: Books of Secrets in Medieval and Early Modern Culture* (Princeton, N.J.: Princeton University Press, 1994), 105.

16. NA SP 1/72/176v.

17. See for example Heinrich Cornelius Agrippa von Nettesheim, pseud., *Liber quartus de occulta philosophia, seu de cerimoniis magicis. Cui accesserunt, elementa magica Petri De Abano, Philosophi* (Marburg, [1559?]).

18. See for example Lea Olsan, "The Three Good Brothers Charm: Some Historical Points," *Incantatio* 1 (2011): 48–78.

19. I use the imprecise and potentially anachronistic term "science" as opposed to "natural philosophy" to signal currents that the latter term does not capture, such as the informal lay communities of inquiry and forms of social interaction described in recent scholarship. See Eric H. Ash, *Power, Knowledge, and Expertise in Elizabethan England* (Baltimore: Johns Hopkins University Press, 2004); Deborah E. Harkness, *The Jewel House: Elizabethan London and the Scientific Revolution* (New Haven, Conn.: Yale University Press, 2007).

20. Owen Davies, *Cunning-Folk: Popular Magic in English History* (London: Hambledon and London, 2003), 1–16; Francis Young, *Magic as a Political Crime in Early Modern England* (London: Taurus, 2018), 24–26.

21. *Reformatio legum ecclesiasticarum, ex authoritate primum regis Henrici. 8. inchoata: Deinde per regem Edouardum 6. prouecta, adauctaque in hunc modum, atque nunc ad pleniorem ipsarum reformationem in lucem ædita* (London, 1641), 33. Cited in Young, *Magic as a Political Crime in Early Modern England*, 79–80.

22. Davies, *Cunning-Folk*, 1–16.

23. Michael Devine, "Treasonous Catholic Magic and the 1563 Witchcraft Legislation: The English State's Response to Catholic Conjuring in the Early Years of Elizabeth I's Reign," in *Supernatural and Secular Power in Early Modern England*, ed. Marcus K. Harmes (Burlington, Vt.: Ashgate, 2015), 67–91; Young, *Magic as a Political Crime in Early Modern England*.

24. Parry, *Arch-Conjuror of England*, 30–35.

25. See also Young, *Magic as a Political Crime in Early Modern England*, 79.

26. On Wisdom's career see Alec Ryrie, *A Sorcerer's Tale: Faith and Fraud in Tudor England* (Oxford, U.K.: Oxford University Press, 2008), esp. 49 (on his receipt of a license from the College of Physicians).

27. Young, *Magic as a Political Crime in Early Modern England*, 91–145; Michael Devine, "John Prestall: A Complex Relationship with the Elizabethan Regime" (master's thesis, Victoria University of Wellington, 2010).

28. Based on MacFarlane's data from Essex, Davies has suggested there was roughly one cunning person per 2,500–3,000 in the general population. He emphasizes the likelihood of temporal and geographical variation. Davies, *Cunning-Folk*, 67–81; Alan MacFarlane, *Witchcraft in Tudor and Stuart England: A Regional and Comparative Study* (London: Routledge & K. Paul, 1970), 115–30.

29. Young, *Magic as a Political Crime in Early Modern England*, 55–150.

30. For a largely accurate transcription of this case see James Raine, "Proceedings Connected with a Remarkable Charge of Sorcery, Brought Against James Richardson and Others, in the Diocese of York, AD 1510," *Archaeological Journal* 16 (1859): 71–81.

31. Ibid., 78.

32. London, British Library, Harley 425, fol. 98v; John Gough Nichols, ed., *Narratives of the Days of the Reformation: Chiefly from the Manuscripts of John Foxe the Martyrologist* (London: Camden Society, 1859), 172–75.

33. *The Examination of John Walsh before Maister Thomas Williams, Commissary to the Reuerend Father in God William Bishop of Excester, Vpon Certayne Interrogatories Touchyng Wytchcrafte and Sorcerye, in the Presence of Diuers Ge[n]tlemen and Others. The .Xxiii. of August. 1566* (London: Iohn Awdely, 1566). On pamphlets and their relationship to witchcraft prosecutions see MacFarlane, *Witchcraft in Tudor and Stuart England*, 81–91.

Introduction

Manuscripts are seldom one-dimensional artifacts, but this odd little book contains an unusually complex set of archaeological layers. After the closure of the monasteries and the abandonment of the old liturgy, works describing Roman monastic rites became moribund and valueless. The generous margins of one such liturgical book were cut off and folded in half to make this portable oblong notebook. The once magnificent remainder was thrown away, stuffed in bindings or used wherever bits of thin rawhide might be handy. The maker of the new notebook evidently sought to squeeze as much writing space as possible from the offcut scraps, and so the neumes, the marginal tracery surrounding its initials, and even scribal doodles of the original volume intrude into the writing space from time to time. The collation is very irregular and artless, so it was doubtlessly assembled by an amateur, and it does not appear ever to have had more than a simple parchment cover. The scribe began writing in a relatively formal hand but quickly descended to cursive on the third folio and to dense informal cursive on the tenth. If initially conceived in more grandiose terms, the volume became an informal notebook, a work in progress that the scribe never entirely filled, leaving folios 26v–43v blank. In the early part of the seventeenth century a second scribe, probably a subsequent owner, added an additional three charms (items 69–71) on folio 45v and one on the bottom of folio 25r (item 63). The physical construction and writing of the manuscript thus spanned three centuries.

The process by which the contents were found and copied was similarly complex. It falls roughly into two sections. The first (items 1–3) contains works of ritual magic, which were probably derived from one or two dedicated necromantic manuals. Prior to 1550, necromantic operations tended to travel in discrete volumes and certainly not with the material found in the second section. The scribe did not compose the first ritual himself since it is in Latin and, as we shall see, he did not have adequate ability to write in that language. He may, however, have translated the subsequent ritual magic operations (nos. 2–3) from a Latin original.[1] After this the scribe began by copying a range of relatively conventional charms and magical experiments (nos. 4–47 and 64–68). Charms appear in all sorts of medieval and early modern books and so these could have been collected from a variety of sources, but the consistency of the hand and the uniformity of contents suggest that a dedicated collection of charms was one of the sources.[2] Most of the remaining material (nos. 48–62) was drawn from quite a different and unlikely book, Reginald Scot's *Discoverie of Witchcraft*, a work of antimagic and anti-Catholic invective printed in London in 1583. The way the book came together was thus complex and involved a typically sixteenth-century blend of manuscript and print, Latin and vernacular sources.

The scribe appears to have had enough Latin to more or less understand the Latin passages that he copied and perhaps even to have translated some of it. At one point (item 56) he writes "*radix Iesse*" (i.e., the root or stem of Jesse), in place of the phrase "*radix David*," which was actually written in his source text. He no doubt did this because the former is a biblical phrase that would have been repeated often in the Roman liturgy, while the latter is relatively unusual. His instinctual use of the liturgical commonplace suggests he was from the last generation of common people in Britain who learned Latin (or some at least) by hearing it in church, in this scribe's case, presumably, under Mary but not inconceivably under Henry VIII.[3] He was also part of a growing group of literate commoners who began to claim as their own the learned magic of the Middle Ages, which had once been the preserve of those with some level of higher learning, usually clerics. At the same time, he did not have adequate Latinity to assure that he had the grammar right. He would have had particular difficulty in expanding abbreviated words, and as a result there are times when the Latin passages make no sense at all. No doubt because he did not entirely understand the language and associated it with the rituals of the church, Latin was for him a language of numinous power and therefore, despite the difficulties it presented, important to preserve as part of the magic.

The contents suggest that the scribe was possibly a cunning man. The contents focus on the three common areas of activity in this group: healing, thief identification, and treasure hunting. Davies distinguishes between charmers and cunning folk, so the fact that a significant portion of the contents are charms might suggest that the owner was not a cunning man. However, the variety of other materials make clear the practitioner was more than a simple charmer.[4] Although it could conceivably have been copied by a woman, legal records from the period suggest that treasure hunting by conjuring was an almost uniformly male activity.[5] The fact that these three forms of magic do not typically travel together in medieval manuscripts meant that the scribe had to intentionally collect this particular configuration of magic from different sources. Thus it seems likely that professional interests lay behind his choices. The collection contains a reasonably broad battery of healing magic, which would have assisted the owner in responding to a wide range of client problems. Its shape and size made it portable and easy to use. Although cunning folk are mythically understood to have been female purveyors of traditional, orally transmitted healing techniques, evidence suggests that they were more commonly men and that literacy actually made them more attractive to clients.[6] Even if he never used this book in his practice, it would have served as a powerful marker of his abilities. The more carefully executed early pages, particularly the first ones written in Latin, would have been impressive to his non-Latinate and potentially illiterate clients.

We will begin by examining in more detail the relationship between this collection and its medieval sources before turning to a brief analysis of its significance to sixteenth-century magic.

Charms, Amulets, and Cures

Charms are found commonly in medieval medical and recipe collections. They are also scattered broadly in the margins and flyleaves of manuscripts of every kind.[7] They are the most broadly distributed and most common form of magic of the premodern period, although they might be said to be on the fringes of the category, somewhere between magic, liturgy, and medicine. Their use of basic Christian prayers, their often sophisticated and poetic use of Christian symbolism and narratives, and their uniformly good goals of healing or protection make them defensible as pious exercises. The implicit assumption that their effects were automatic is simply an extension of the same assumptions made about liturgical performances, particularly the sacraments, or the power of relics. As a result they are just as easily classifiable as popular religion or a kind of lay liturgy. The keepers of orthodoxy had an ambivalent relationship with this literature. They objected when charms were assumed to be automatic or contained unorthodox elements such as mysterious words or signs, but they also often counseled tolerance if they were used in a spirit of humility and true piety. There was no sense in punishing people for practices that effectively reinforced conventional religion. Among the charms in this collection we also find explicit works of popular piety such as a lay indulgence (item 53), demonstrating that for the scribe these were all related activities.

Charms were also a common part of medieval medical practice. The regular appearance of charms in medical works suggests that doctors and other healers regarded them as another instrument of their trade or as a different mode of curing to be used alongside medicines or other treatments.[8] Naturally, for many people who could not afford other sorts of medical care, they were a standard response to illnesses or medical emergencies. The overwhelming majority of the charms in the Antiphoner Notebook are designed to address various particular medical crises or emergencies such as wounds, bleeding, fevers, toothaches, and childbirth. Many of the remainder, such as the protective amulets, include these among the misfortunes they are designed to fend off. Although the scribe had a marked preference for healing that included ritual performance, the recipes commonly include medicines or physical elements which no doubt were key in making them effective. The charm for sleep (item 14), for example, combines a prayer with ingredients known to have soporific qualities (i.e., poppy seeds, lettuce, and beer). The Three Good Brethren Charm (item 31) employs wool as a bandage for a wound. Lanolin, the oil found on wool, is still used as a salve.

The charms of the Antiphoner Notebook demonstrate continuity in the transmission of this medieval genre through the sixteenth century. The charms that were not transcribed from Reginald Scot (items 4–47 and 63–71)—and indeed quite a few that were—are indistinguishable from what one finds in late medieval collections, and many are direct witnesses to those found in such books. Lea Olsan has suggested a number of conventional elements in medieval charms, all of which recur in this collection. They tend to use repeated sound patterns, often in nonsense words, rhyme schemes, words of power (i.e., divine names). They use words and signs indicating that the charm must be ritually performed, such as "I adjure you," and crosses indicating that the charmer should make the sign of the cross. They often include biblical passages, particularly from the Psalms, by citing a single line, and for a religiously literate person these tags were evidently meant to recall the religious resonances of the entire passage.[9] Invocation of the saints also evoked for the reader the broader set of stories associated with them.[10] In addition, charms commonly employ religious narratives or *historiola* from biblical or apocryphal sources.[11] The line between prayer, charm, and amulet is also blurry since many of the prayers were meant to be written on a scrap of parchment and carried about for protection.[12] While I have not reorganized relevant sections of the text in stanza form, patterns of rhyming appear in many of the charms. Item 38, for example, could be presented as follows:

What manner of ill y^t ever thow be
on gods behalf I coniure thee,
wth ye blessed crosse +

y^t Iesus was done on wth force
I coniure ye wth nayles three
y^t Iesus was nayld vpon a tree,
I coniure y^{ee} wth ye crowne of thorne
y^t on Iesus head was done for scorne,
I coniure ye wth ye blissed bloud
that Iesus bledd vpon ye roode
I coniure ye wth woundes .5.
y^t Iesus suffred in his lyfe,
I coniure ye wth ye holy spare,
y^t Longis till his hart cane bare,
I coniure ye nevertheless
wth all the vertues of ye messe.

The intent of such rhymes and alliterations was clearly, as Olsan suggests, to intensify the magical effect, but also to aid memorization. In all these respects the volume evinces considerable continuity with the medieval genre.

The clear preference for charms as a mode for healing was not ubiquitous among local healers. A contemporary work of comparable quality and seemingly also the property of a literate healer contains mostly simple recipes for medicines lacking in performative elements.[13] In the Antiphoner Notebook by contrast, only items 22 and 25 involve no verbal formula, prayer, or ritual performance, and the latter employs the potentially fantastic ingredient of a bee's tongue. So the scribe has a clear preference for cures involving prayers and religious words of power, even when herbs or other ingredients are used. This was, no doubt, reinforced by his attraction to, or nostalgia for, aspects of the old religion, including charms using Latin formulae, Latin prayers (notably Ave Marias), divine names and words, invocations of saints, and a lay indulgence.

Conjurations and Experiments

The conjuring procedures recorded in this book are typical of the genre in terms of their goals but less complex than most medieval and sixteenth-century ritual magic. Treasure hunting and identification of thieves and/or the return of stolen goods are two of the most common uses of spirit conjuring, others being provoking love or lust, creating illusions, influencing superiors, and gaining knowledge or secret information.[14] At the same time they are relatively short. As the Boxgrove Manual illustrates, a typical demon conjuring operation might run to ten or twenty times the length of these ones, and many ritual magic texts take up entire volumes. This simplification of rituals was evidently a function of the transmission of this literature from Latin to vernacular versions, from dedicated necromantic manuals to multipurpose collections, from a clerical to a lay context.

Although it clearly has its roots in medieval necromancy, the first ritual, which seeks to force the return and punishment of thieves with wax images, is the least typical. Despite having a relatively regular presence in legal accusations of magic in which it was associated with conjuring, the use of wax images for harm in necromantic (i.e., demon conjuring) collections is curiously uncommon. Instead this type of magic appears in collections dedicated to astrological magic with Arabic roots and for some reason tended not to find its way into conventional conjuring texts.[15] The apparent compelling of angels in this operation is also somewhat less common in necromancy. As agents of the divine, angels could not (according to conventional theology) be commanded, but only supplicated or their assistance achieved through praying to God, although some ritual magic texts insist that angels of lower orders can be conjured and such sources or ideas might also lie behind the operation.[16] It may also be the result of a lack of clarity in the translation of the Arabic original in which the differences between planetary spirits, demons, and angels were not always clear. Although the initial prayer to God requesting that he command his angels to assist goes some distance to mitigating the stark commands of angels that follow, the result is a ritual that, at least on the surface, lacks theological sophistication.[17]

The next two sections are, by contrast, relatively conventional and the scribe may have intended them to be used together. The use of a crystal for seeing spirits or discovering hidden information (item 2) occurs quite commonly in the later Middle Ages and early modern period. Crystallomantic operations to see spirits or other visions commonly employed a virgin child, but this was by no means universal.[18] Distinctive in this one is the option for seeing spots moving in the crystal as opposed to spirits. This increased the likelihood of subjectively convincing success since such visual phenomena are easier to imagine or provoke than a full-fledged spiritual vision.[19] The experiment seeks quite typical goals (i.e., to answer questions, find secret knowledge, acquire learning or "science," and find treasure), but it may well be that the scribe intended simply to use it for getting information about the location of treasure. This is suggested by the fact that the next piece (item 3) includes only the second stage of treasure hunting, that is, exorcizing the ground around the cache after you have found out where it is. Treasure-hunting rituals commonly assumed that demons protected treasures, although whether the burier put them there or they found the treasure on their own and wanted it for themselves is not clear. Very much like exorcism, this ritual simply seeks to cast a demon out of a certain territory and keep it away for long enough to get the treasure out. Numerous examples of such texts survive, not to mention a good deal of evidence for real treasure-hunting operations.[20] So once again, the continuities with medieval literature are significant despite some simplification and reconfiguration.

Making New Magic: Religious Controversy and Re-enchantment

The scribe of the Antiphoner Notebook drew a substantial amount of material from Reginald Scot's *Discoverie of Witchcraft*. Using a variety of commonsense arguments Scot sought to demonstrate the irrationality of belief in magic and witchcraft. As a Protestant he argued that scripture could not sustain such belief. Instead, magic on the one hand and Catholic religious practice on the other falsely assume that humans can manipulate events that are in fact determined only by divine omnipotence. At first glance, an explicitly anti-Catholic and anti-magic work commonly regarded as a forerunner of Enlightenment rationalism might seem an unlikely place to go to find magic or charms. However, in the process of making his arguments, Scot provides numerous and extensive examples of magic and "popish" superstition. The depth and variety of these examples, found mainly in books 12 and 15, were extensive enough to make the *Discoverie* an attractive sourcebook for magic practitioners. As the Antiphoner Notebook demonstrates, this use had begun already in the late sixteenth century. When new editions were printed in the mid-seventeenth century, one publisher clearly sought to attract this market by substantially expanding the magic sections. The material that the scribe of the Antiphoner Notebook chose from Scot and the editorial changes he made to it reveal a common person struggling with the religious controversy of the sixteenth century and the literature it produced. The result is a book of magic that preserves older elements, adopts features of the new religion, and despite itself, creates entirely new ones.

As we have seen, almost everything in the book reflects the sensibilities of someone who liked the "old religion." The scribe seeks intercession from the saints and clearly liked to use Latin, despite his poor knowledge of the language. Operations and charms begin and conclude with conventional liturgical phrases such as "in nomine patris, et filii, et spiritus sancti (in the name of the Father and of the Son and of the Holy Spirit)" and commonly conclude with the core prayers of medieval Christianity in Latin (the Pater Noster and Ave Maria) and its basic confession of faith, the Apostles' Creed. Others are the sort of thing one finds in late medieval primers and which Eamon Duffy has described as expressing in popular form the core mysteries and rituals of the medieval Church.[21] They rehearse basic biblical stories, core scriptural passages, and basic elements of Roman liturgical and religious practices (e.g., blessings, exorcisms, indulgences, prayers, and intercession of the saints). But how does all this square with the explicitly magic material?

A close look at what the scribe copied, what he edited out, and the mistakes he made while copying make clear he did not regard or wish it to be regarded as magic. At one point (item 51) he follows Scot in almost writing the word "charm" but crosses it out and writes "prayer" instead. This was not magic but due religious practice. In the same way he generally does not copy any of Scot's introductions or conclusions that denigrate Catholic theology. So he was clearly aware of Scot's rhetoric and made steps to change or exclude it, arguably a self-conscious process of *re-enchantment*, as opposed to the disenchantment that writers like Scot are supposed to have brought about. More significantly, the scribe in this way implicitly designated the overwhelming majority of the book's contents as prayers rather than charms, that is, as legitimate religious exercises rather than magic. At the same time, he copies out the experiment for the "wastecote of proof," including Scot's claim that it was written "by the pope, or some such archconiuror" (item 49). If he disagreed with Scot on the question of charms, he evidently was prepared to follow Scot (and the English crown) in antipapal sentiments. In other words, he was not a recusant. Instead he appears to have been a more or less loyal Englishman, prepared to approve the break with Rome, but one who also happened to like the old religion (and evidently magic as well). Evidence suggests such feelings and tendencies were quite common at this time.[22]

Nonetheless it remains that, in one collection and without any divisions between them, he copied what he explicitly regarded as religion together with material that was written by an "arch-conjurer." More to the point, he seems to have fancied he was a kind of conjurer himself since the volume contains explicit demon and angel invocations (items 1–3) that were certainly not defensible extensions of late medieval piety. In fact, the arch-conjurer's operation that he copied from Scot is even *less* defensible than conventional medieval necromancy. The "wastecote of proof" (item 49) is supposed to be made by a virgin girl *in the name of the devil*. Medieval necromancers who styled themselves as devoted Christians would have regarded this unequivocally as bad and diabolic magic. One only ever conjured in the name of Jesus. Thus, taken as a whole, the collection represents a complex set of irreconcilable interests, particularly given that, in his encounter with Scot, the scribe consciously reflected on the differences between religion and magic.

There are a variety of possible explanations for this. He may have copied in a truly haphazard fashion, purely for interest sake. He may have understood the contradictions, but simply did not regard the conventional divisions as important. He may even have followed Scot in regarding medieval religion and magic as contiguous or related practices but did not regard this as a bad thing. It seems most likely that, whatever he may have believed, his choices were informed by the practical requirement of a cunning man's profession. Clients seeking healing would probably have preferred prayers. Clients seeking treasure would have expected conjuring. In this view, the theological distinctions were irrelevant to what he copied, or at least less relevant than practical considerations. Yet, whatever the motivations behind it, the result was a peculiarly early modern intellectual artifact.

Keith Thomas suggested that Protestantism was part of a broader process that led to the decline of magic in the West, and one might well argue that this text is a demonstration of his claim that the religion of the medieval church was inherently magical and encouraged magical beliefs.[23] But the process was more complex. As Robert Scribner has argued, many forms of "Protestant magic" developed after the Reformation, such as the use of the Bible or sermons for apotropaic purposes, even though they could not be supported by a strictly observed Protestant theology that emphasized an exclusively top-down relationship between God and humanity.[24] The Boxgrove Manual and many other sixteenth-century magic texts bear this out. They were clearly written by and for Protestants who had simply removed the more explicitly Roman elements from their sources. The Antiphoner Notebook demonstrates in a very concrete way how people resisted the calls for disenchantment by not only passively preserving the old religion and the old magic but also even by self-consciously *re-creating it*. It also betrays one further and peculiarly early modern complication.

This book was part of another process in which popular beliefs in magic or religion were subtly changed by antimagic or anti-Catholic invective. Scot naturally went out of his way to choose materials of a most extreme nature. A wonderful example is the popular pardon (item 53) that Joseph of Arimathea found written on Jesus's dead body by the hand of God that promises 32,755 years of pardon from purgatory. Although Scot might well have copied it from some late medieval source, it certainly does not represent the majority of lay pardons circulating in the later Middle Ages, which were less extreme in their claims.[25] The problem was that our scribe evidently had no other way of getting this kind of material, not least because a Catholic primer would have been illegal. The only available source offered him something slightly different: an exaggerated caricature of late medieval piety. In a similar way, the overtly diabolic "wastecote of proof," for which there are no medieval antecedents, would have been profoundly unusual in a conjuring book. Scot included it not because it was representative, but because of its very *atypical* diabolic overtones. In this process, magic was turned into a *caricature* of itself or of medieval Catholicism. By copying it, the scribe of the Antiphoner Notebook accepted those anachronisms into the written traditions of magic. This anachronization of magic adds another level of complexity to a process we have already discussed in the general introduction: the shift of magic out of the comfortable embrace of conventional religion and its transformation into something that opposed conventional religion.

The Manuscript

Shelfmark: Oxford, Bodleian Library, MS Additional B. 1.

Date: Written in the second half of the sixteenth century on frag-
                ments from an English liturgical manuscript of the early four-
                teenth century, which could be a missal, breviary, antiphoner,
                or gradual, but does not appear to be a sequentiary or troper.
                (I am indebted to John Haines for this identification.)

Size/Material: 155 × 105 millimeters. Parchment. Made from margins cut
                from a large manuscript probably measuring about 620 milli-
                meters in height.

Foliation: ii (doubled over parchment cover) + 48 + i. Modern foliation.

Collation: 1^{12} 2^{8} 3^{16} (7–16 blank) 4^{12} (1 blank, 2 all but 45 mm cut out, 3–8
                blank, 11–12 blank). No quire numbering. Catchwords on
                folios 3–10, sporadically thereafter (e.g., fol. 21v).

Scripts: Written by two scribes. Working in the last decades of the six-
                teenth century, the principal scribe fills most of the booklet in
                English hands of decreasing formality, beginning with a more
                formal book hand but moving quickly into a more informal
                cursive English secretary hand. The second scribe added a few
                charms and recipes in the seventeenth century (items 67–69)
                on folio 45v and one on the bottom of folio 25r (item 61).

Editorial Principles

This is a semi-diplomatic edition. I have preserved the spellings of the original
text but not the original line endings. Folio breaks are indicated in square brackets in the text. Item numbers and the occasional title (where the scribe does not
provide one) have been inserted for ease of reference and are also indicated in
square brackets. The crowded and informal nature of the manuscript make it
quite difficult to read. As a result, I have occasionally inserted spaces in the text
between sections for visual clarity and ease of analysis.

   Biblical quotations in the notes are from the New Revised Standard Version
and biblical citations employ this version, but given the differences in verse
numbering, I have also occasionally included references to the Latin Vulgate
where appropriate.

English Text

In general the spelling, capitalization, and punctuation of the original have been
preserved. In instances of clear scribal error the text has been changed and this

has been indicated in the notes. On occasion, for the sake of clarity, punctuation has been changed or inserted. Scribal interlinear insertions have been included silently in the text. Scribal expunctuation of errors resulting from duplication of words or phrases have been omitted. Otherwise, they have been retained and are indicated with a strikeout. Where my readings are conjectural due to illegibility or destruction, this has been indicated in the notes.

Latin Text

The Latinity of the scribe was poor and as a result many of the Latin passages are untranslatable as they stand. At the same time it seems likely the scribe was not only attracted to Latin but also had some rudimentary understanding of it. To provide a window into his thinking as well as his Latin sources, the longer passages of Latin have been accompanied with translations in parallel columns.

In the Latin sections, abbreviations have been silently expanded and punctuation and capitalization have occasionally been added for clarity. Otherwise, so as not to gravely misrepresent the original, the Latin is presented as it appears in the manuscript. Suggestions as to what the original Latin text may have been, which help to make sense of it, have been indicated in square brackets. The resulting translations are frequently speculative and something of an abstraction. Where the level of conjecture is particularly high, this fact has been indicated in the notes.

As was common in vernacular magic, the English portions of the manuscript are liberally peppered with short Latin phrases and divine names. The scribe intended these to be recited or written as words of power within the otherwise English text. This character has been preserved in the edition. Divine names have not been translated. The various liturgical formulae (e.g., *In nomine patris et filii et spiritus sancti*) have also been left unchanged, but translations have been provided in the notes at their first occurrence. The abbreviations for prayers that commonly follow charms such as, "3 pr nr 2 a. 1 c" (i.e., three Pater Nosters, two Ave Marias, and one Credo) have been treated in the same fashion.

Notes

1. This kind of necromantic material tended to be collected in dedicated necromantic handbooks in the Middle Ages and continued in the sixteenth century, although they were more frequently mixed with other sorts of magic as we find here. That a different manuscript source was used from the rest of the book is suggested by the abrupt change in both ink and style of handwriting at the end of this section (fol. 10r). In addition, no further explicitly necromantic material appears after the switch to charms.

2. Lea Olsan has traced the copying of a corpus of twenty-three charms in the fourteenth and fifteenth century, ten of which are found in this collection. A close relative of Cambridge, University Library, Additional 9308, fols. 14v–86v was thus the source for at least a portion of the material in this section (fols. 10v–21r and 25v–26v) as well as the final section of the book (fols. 44r–45r). Items 12, 13, 14, 17, 20, 21, 26, 31, 32, and 35 are all textual relatives of charms Lea Olsan has edited and identified. See Olsan, "The Corpus of Charms in the Middle English Leechcraft Remedy Books," in *Charms, Charmers and Charming: International Research on Verbal Magic*, ed. Jonathan Roper (New York: Palgrave Macmillan, 2009), 214–37.

3. Eamon Duffy, *The Stripping of the Altars: Traditional Religion in England, C. 1400–C. 1580* (New Haven, Conn.: Yale University Press, 1992), 53–87.

4. Davies, *Cunning-Folk*, 83–84.

5. Roughly two-thirds of cunning folk were men, but I know of no examples of women participating in conjuring demons for treasure. See ibid., 68–69, 93–96.

6. Ibid., 68–72.

7. Lea Olsan, "The Marginality of Charms in Medieval England," in *The Power of Words: Studies on Charms and Charming in Europe*, ed. James Alexander Kapaló, Éva Pócs, and William Ryan (New York: CEU Press, 2013), 135–64.

8. Lea Olsan, "Latin Charms of Medieval England: Verbal Healing in a Christian Oral Tradition," *Oral Tradition* 7 (1992): 117–18; Olsan, "Charms and Prayers in Medieval Medical Theory and Practice," *Social History of Medicine* 16 (2003): 343–66.

9. Olsan, "Latin Charms of Medieval England," 118.

10. Olsan, "Charms in Medieval Memory," in *Charms and Charming in Europe*, ed. Jonathan Roper (New York: Palgrave, 2004), 59–87.

11. Olsan, "Latin Charms of Medieval England," 124–33.

12. On textual amulets see Don C. Skemer, *Binding Words: Textual Amulets in the Middle Ages* (University Park: Pennsylvania State University Press, 2006).

13. Oxford, Bodleian Library, Ashmole 1378.

14. Richard Kieckhefer divides the necromantic experiments in the Munich Handbook into illusionist, psychological, and divinatory experiments. See Kieckhefer, *Forbidden Rites*. For a survey of the various applications of ritual magic see also Klaassen, *Transformations of Magic*, 89–186.

15. See for example Juris Lidaka, "*The Book of Angels, Rings, Characters and Images of the Planets*: Attributed to Osbern Bokenham," in *Conjuring Spirits: Texts and Traditions of Medieval Ritual Magic*, ed. Claire Fanger (University Park: Pennsylvania State University Press, 1998), 51–53. For a survey of numerous cases of the use of wax images for various nefarious purposes see George Lyman Kittredge, *Witchcraft in Old and New England* (New York: Russell & Russell, 1956), 74–91.

16. See Gösta Hedegård, ed., *Liber iuratus Honorii: A Critical Edition of the Latin Version of the Sworn Book of Honorius* (Stockholm: Almovist & Wiksell International, 2002), 3, 9–15.

17. The *Ars notoria* took a somewhat more convincing approach by insisting that the operator seek permission in a dream to embark on rituals to receive intellectual gifts from the angels. On the ritual processes of the *Ars notoria* see Julien Véronèse, "Magic, Theurgy, and Spirituality in the Medieval Ritual of the *Ars Notoria*," in *Invoking Angels*, ed. Claire Fanger (University Park: Pennsylvania State University Press, 2012), 37–78.

18. Claire Fanger, "Virgin Territory: Purity and Divine Knowledge in Late Medieval Catoptromantic Texts," *Aries* 5, no. 2 (2005): 200–225. For the crystallomantic operations of Humphrey Gilbert in the 1560s see Klaassen, "Ritual Invocation and Early Modern Science."

19. This being said, auditory or visual dissociative experiences can be achieved using the techniques of ritual magic. See Frank Klaassen, "The Subjective Experience of Medieval Ritual Magic," *Magic, Ritual, and Witchcraft* 7, no. 1 (2012): 19–51.

20. For a general discussion of treasure hunting by magic see Johannes Dillinger, *Magical Treasure Hunting in Europe and North America: A History* (New York: Palgrave Macmillan, 2012). Dillinger is heavily focused on Germanic cases. For a survey of cases of treasure hunting in late medieval and early modern England see Kittredge, *Witchcraft in Old and New England*,

204–13. One of the oldest complete necromantic handbooks, Oxford, Bodleian Library, Rawlinson D. 252, is substantially concerned with treasure hunting. See Klaassen, *Transformations of Magic*, 134–55. One peculiar manuscript holds that the devil finds and tries to keep buried treasure for himself in the hopes of buying his salvation on the day of judgment. Oxford, Bodleian Library, eMus 238, fol. 1.

21. See Duffy, *Stripping of the Altars*, 266–98.

22. Christopher W. Marsh, *Popular Religion in Sixteenth-Century England: Holding Their Peace*, Social History in Perspective (New York: St. Martin's Press, 1998), 211–14. For a more thorough discussion of the relationship of this manuscript to Scot and of its relevance to the religious history in Elizabethan England see Frank Klaassen, "The Return of Stolen Goods: Reginald Scot, Religious Controversy, and a Late Sixteenth-Century Manuscript of Magic," *Magic, Ritual, and Witchcraft* 1, no. 2 (2006): 135–77.

23. Keith Vivian Thomas, *Religion and the Decline of Magic* (New York: Scribner, 1971).

24. Robert W. Scribner, "The Reformation, Popular Magic, and the 'Disenchantment of the World,'" *Journal of Interdisciplinary History* 23, no. 3 (1993): 475–94.

25. See Duffy, *Stripping of the Altars*, 266–98.

The Text

[1] **A proven experiment for making a male or female thief return to you in person if he should be in any place within the kingdom of England.**

First make two images of wax, that is, an image of a man and an image of a woman, and when they are done at the same time with both of them write in the front of the image "Yris" with this character ▽ and in the neck of the head "Sibilia" with this character ⌐⌐⌐ and in the top of the head "Azaria" with this character. o—⌐ ⌐o Then in the chest the name of the operator with these names Eleazar and Maligare, and this character ⊞ƒ₂ₐᵍ, and in the back opposite them this character ⌐ƒ₈. Then make fire from dried whitethorn or from a thorn that is called eglantyne. Then take the aforesaid images, one in your hand and the other in the hand of your associate, and say this prayer: [1v]

God, founder and revealer of every invisible thing, to whom no secrets lie hidden, humbly we entreat your majesty that you deign to send Alexander Tebbe and Helen Tebbe alias Dragis to us in the strength of their crimes, yielded before us, that we may deserve to come to the worthy fatherland.[1] Amen.

God, will you not revive us again that your people may rejoice in you?[2]

Let us pray.

Omnipotent and eternal God, founder and master of all things, disseminator

[1] **Experimentum probatum ad faciendum furem hominem vel mulierem revenire ad te in propria persona si sit in aliquo loco infra regnum Angliæ.**

In primis fac ymagines duas de cera, videlicet ymaginem hominis et ymaginem mulieris et quando factæ sunt simul scribe in fronte ymago Yris cum ista karactare ▽ et in collo capitis Sibilia: cum ista karactare ⌐⌐⌐ et in nodulo capitis scribe Azaria cum ista karactare o—⌐ ⌐o deinde in pectore nomen operantis cum istis nominibus: Eleazar Maligare cum ista caractes ⊞ƒ₂ₐᵍ et in dorso erga hac karactar ⌐ƒ₈ et tunc fac ignem de alba spina desiccata. Vel de spina quæ vocatur Eglantyne. Tunc accipe imagines predicte unam ymago in manu tua; et alteram in manu socij tui et dic istam orationem. [1v]

Deus omnium conditor: absconditorum et revelator cui nulla secreta latent; maiestatem tuam suppliciter exoramus vt Alexandrum Tebbe Elena Tebbe alias Dragis ad nos emittere digneris in robore suorum facinorum coram nobis concessis [read concessos] vt ad dignam patriam pervenire mereamur Per christum dominum nostrum. Amen.

Deus tu conversus vinificabis nos. Et plebs tua letabitur in te

Oremus.

Omnipotens sempiterne Deus omnium conditor et magister omnium rerum virtus

of the virtue of all things from whom no secret lies hidden,[3] we humbly entreat that, through the invocation of your holy names, you command your spirits Sabaoth,[4] Uriel, and Raguel to obey my injunctions that they make Alexander Tebbe and Helen Tebbe, alias Dragis, come back or turn back to me, confessing their crime, so that we might be able to complete prayers of thanksgiving in your church. [2r]

Then take the two images to the fire but certainly take care that the wax not liquefy and then take both in your hand and say as follows.

I conjure you Angels of God, Sabaoth, Uriel, and Raguel, by the great potency of God the Father and the Son and the Holy Spirit, and by these names of God, which I invoke in my support: I am Alpha and Omega and first and last and Agla, and by this name of God, Tetragrammaton, and by this name of our Lord Jesus Christ at which every knee of celestial, terrestrial, and infernal beings is bent[5] and by the delights of heaven in which you are, that in whatever country within the kingdom of England you compel Alexander Tebbe and Helen Tebbe to return to us by the virtue of these characters written in these images, and to return to us in all vigor, just as I fashion them in these images with this ring of thorn.[6]

And then prick the character with your needle. [2v]

And that you not rest neither day nor night sitting, going, sleeping, or waking until they come to us. And let their heart melt on their arrival just as this wax of

[read virtutis] propagator cui quem nullum latet secretum te suppliciter exoramus vt per inuocationem sanctorum nominum tuorum iubeas spiritus tuos Sabaoth Urielem et Ragnelem preceptis meis obedire vt faciant Alexandrum Tebbe Elena Tebbe alias Dragis ad me revenire vel revertere et facinus suum confitentem in Ecclesia tua gratiarum actiones valeamus adhorere peragere Per christum Dominum nostrum Amen. [2r]

Tunc teneas ymagines tuas ad ignem sed cave omnino ne liquescat cera et accipe ambas tunc in manus tuas et dic vt sequitur.

Coniuro vos Angeli Dei Sabaoth Uriel et Raguel per potentiam summam Dei patris et filij et spiritus sancti, et per ista nomina Dei, qua in auxilium meum invoco, Ego sum Alpha et ω et primus et novissimus et Agla, et per istud nomen Dei Tetragramaton, et per istud nomen Domini nostri Iesu Christi in quo omne genu cælestium terrestrium et infernorum flectitur, et per gaudia cæli in quibus vos estis vt in quacumque patria infra regnum Angliæ Agitetis Alexandrum Tebbe Elena Tebbe ad nos revenire per virtutem horum karacteres quæ in hijs ymaginibus scripta sunt et in omni robore ad nos revenire provt ego in his ymaginibus infingo cum hac armilla spinea.

Et tunc pinge karectarem cum Acute [read acu tuo]. [2v]

Et quod non cessemini die neque nocte sedendo evndo, dormiendo, vel vigilando quousque ad nos veniant. Et fluat cor eorum in adventu eorum sicut fluit hæc

the image melted from the face of the fire until they come to us and they confess their transgression.

Then keep both images without damage in a box in clean cloths because if they are damaged in any part, that part will be weakened accordingly on the persons. Know for certain that this experiment is true and approved and without any danger to soul or body since it is done by three angels, Sabaoth, Uriel, and Raguel.

End of this experiment. [3r]

cæra ymaginis a facie ignis quousque ad nos veniant et fatentur transgressionem.

Tunc custodias ymagines ambas in cista in mundis pannis absque lesura, quia si in aliquo ledantur ille secundo parsonis destruetur. Scias pro certo quod istud Experimentum est verum et approbatum et absque ullo periculo animæ aut corporis quia factum est per istos tres Angelos, Sabaoth, Urielem et Raguelem.

ffinis huius Experimenti [3r]

[2. Divination with a crystal]

Herin thow shall knowe as much as to mans nature doth belonge to knowe. But aske no evill thinge for yf you do thow shall lose an eye or thy wittes &c.

Graue Agla in a newe Christall vpon the backesyde in Ebrewe letters and let therbe sayde .9. masses over it .1. of the Trinitye 2. of our Ladye .3. of the holy Crosse .4. of the Angels .5 of the Evangelistes, 6 of S^{ct} Ihon Baptist, 7. of the holy ghost, 8. of all saintes, .9. of the 3 kinges and after everye masse lett Saint Ihons gospell be redde in Englyshe and sprinkle the Christall wth holy water, & set it in siluer or gilte woode & in the daye of ♀ or ♃ it must be prepared & finished in the .3. days and houlde the glasse betwene the sunne & him & saye as followeth. But aske no fylthy or vnlawfull thinges & be thow cleane & in cleane place, or els thy glasse must be newe consecrated. [3v]

1. O my lorde in whose presence are all, thinges wch be in heaven earth & sea & deapes, Blesse me I beseech thee y^t there maye appeare to me in this glasse by the holy name Agla & by the merites of S^{ct} Ihon Baptist & the Evangelistes howe N. or N.[8] doth. And yf yt shall be fortunate, then the white prickes or spottes doe appeare in this glasse assendinge, yf it shall be vnfortunate then the white spottes do appeare desendinge. And yf it shall be neyther fortunate or vnfortunate then that the whight prickes may remaine in the midst. But yf ye demaunde for any man, Beast or boake or any materiall thinges, yt shall appeare in the verye lykenesse y^t it is of, though it be in the midst of the sea. But yf it appeare not in the glasse wth the sayinge of the first praer, wch many times it doth. Then say the rest of the prayrs and most surelye thow shall haue thy desyre. But [4r] yf thow

wilt worke for treasure or science[9] yow must be cleane both in bodye and clothinge.

2. O my lord god in whose presence are all thinges, wch be in heauen, earth, sea & the deepe places I beseech thee y^t it maye appeare in this glasse to .N. or N. by the vertue of the holye name Agla & by the merites of the blessed virgen Marye thy glorious mother.

3. O my lord &c. by the merites of thy blessed passion y^t thow didest suffer for vs sinners & by all thy woundes & I beseech &c.[10]

4. O my lord god &c. By the merites of thy most blessed resurrection wherew^th all the companye of holye Angelles & all thy saintes did reioyce & were glad I beseech thee &c.

[5]. O my Lorde god &c. by the merites of Sct Longes[11] the knight wch did pearce thy holy syde wth a spare and by the merites & prayers of all thy sayntes I beseech thee &c.

Finis.[12] [4v]

[3. Ritual to exorcise demons guarding a treasure][13]

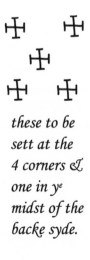

these to be sett at the 4 corners & one in y^e midst of the backe syde.

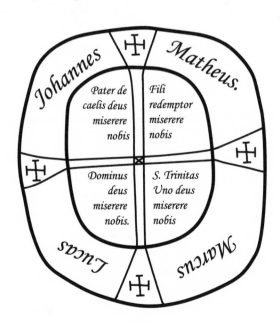

Jesus the Nazarene, King of the Jews, give us your grace. Amen. In my name they will cast out demons, speak in new tongues, pick up snakes, and if they drink anything deadly it will not harm them; they will lay their hands on the sick and they will be well. Halleluiah.[14]	Ihesus nazarenus Rex Iudeorum dona nobis gratiam tuam. Amen. In nomine meo Demonia eijcient, linguis loquentur novis, serpentes tollent, et si mortiferum quid biberint non eis nocebit. Super egros manus imponent et bene habebunt. Alleluia.

Deus in nomine tuo &c .54. Deus misereatur. &c .67.[15]

O Thow Spirit or Spirits [5r] wch keepe this grounde and treasure or earth, I coniure yow and charge yow by the mightye powre of god and by his strength, and by all the might powre and strength of the holy and blessed trinitye, That y^w or yowe depart from this treasure earth and ground. Depart oh thow spirit or spirites I charge yow and commaunde yow by all the power and strength of Allmightye god the father of heauen, and by the vertue & diuinitye of Iesus Christ our Lorde coequall wth the father & wth the holy ghost ye thyrde persone in Trinitye.[16]

Departe Oh thow spirit or spirites, I commaunde yow by the vertue strength & might of Iesus Christ the kinge of glorye, & by the vertue & loue of the holy ghost & by all the stronge mansion of Ihesus Christ kinge [5v] of all goodnes, & by ye vertue of the loue & mercye of Ihesus Christ ye onely sonne of the lyvinge God, & by the vertue of ye obedience of Iesus Christ when he was obedient to the death of the crosse, wch lyveth & rayneth wth god his father & the holye ghost in the perfecte Trinite. I coniure the, y^w spirit or spirites, by the fearefull powre of ye iudgement of him wch shall iudge all mankinde & all kinges & all Devylles & wicked spirites. I coniure y^e or yow by him to whom all knees doo bowe both in heauen, earth, & hell.

Depart oh y^w spirit or spirites from this place, grounde, & treasure, & y^t y^w or ye come not nighe vnto it by ye space of an hundreth myles vntyll we haue taken & obtayned our willes & pleasures by ye vertue of the holy ghost & predestination of God, in whose name I commaunde ye spirit or spirites y^t keepe this Treasure to depart from [6r] this place & grounde & not to come nighe vnto yt by ye space of on hundreth miles, neyther to vexe, trouble nor feare vs, vntyll we haue had our full minde & pleasure.

I coniure ye y^w spirit or spirites by the vertue of all heauens & celestiall creatures worshippinge ye omnipotent God. Depart Oh y^w spirit or spirites from this place

& ground through the vertue of allmightye god, & of all earthlye thinges both quicke & deade movable & vnmoueable worshippinge ye omnipotent God. Depart oh y^w spirit or spirites from this place through the vertue of the person of Iesus Christ & of the sweete face of Iesus Christ wch was smitten vpon & wth spottle deformed.[17] So be y^w or ye spirit or spirites smitten wth the fyre & paynes of hell, yf ye depart not by & by from this place & grounde & come not neare it by an hundreth miles, vntyll we [6v] haue obteyned our minds, through ye vertue & strength of ye Rope wch bounde ye armes of christ, wherw^th he was drawne & stretched vpon ye crosse. So be ye spirites or spirites drawen stretched & nayled wth the most strongest paynes of hell wth fyre cheines except ye depart by & by. Depart oh y^w spirit or spirites by ye great payne the w^ch, christ suffred in his feete when he was nayled vpon the crosse. So be y^w or ye spirit or spirites nayled & persed wth ye paines of hell fire except ye departe by & by. And yf ye depart not by & by ye fire of hell wch shall alwaye burne & never be quenched descend & fall downe vpon yow spirites & burne yow, So y^t ye shall never haue rest nor ease. And as ye spayre painfullye persed ye syde of Jesus christ, So be ye spirite or spirites painefullye pained so y^t yow from this day forth shall never haue rest nor ease. All thunders & lightininges wth all the fyers of hell fall downe vpon yow, ye sworde of death wth all the tormentes of [7r] all ye diuylles in hell descende downe vpon yow & remaine vpon yow for ever, except ye depart incontinent from this place & grounde & not to come nighe yt by an hundreth miles vntyll we haue taken our mindes & pleasures therin.

Depart Oh y^w spirit or spirites. I coniure yow & charge yow by ye vertue of the bloud of the sauiour of all mankynde & by the vertue of ye bloude & water y^t christ swette vpon ye mounte Olyvete before his bytter passion when he was in an Agonye, & ye Angell of ye lorde comforted him declaringe to him what a great misterye he should bringe to passe through his blessed death,[18] of ye wch misterie O ye wicked spirite or spirites y^t keep this treasure be noo partakers, but those, wch beleeue in his death. Depart from this place Oh ye wicked spirit or spirites I charge & commaunde yow by ye infinite word of God [7v] that y^w come not neere it by ye space of an hundreth miles for ye space of an hundreth dayes nexte followinge, nether to trouble vexe nor delude vs, neyther to drawe it awaye nor to chaunge yt into anye other manner of coloure, But to lette it remaine where it standeth w^thout craft, falsheade, guile, or dissimulation, neyther to drawe it deper nor lower into ye earth, but onlye to remaine in ye owne proper place.

I coniure ye spirite or spirites by ye wordes y^t christ spake in the tyme of his most blessed passion,[19] when he prayed for them y^t crucified him saying, Father repute not this vnto them, for they knowe not what they doe, And by these wordes wch he spake to his holy mother sayinge, woman behould thy sonne, & to his disciples, behould thy mother, & by y^t holy words I thirst, y^t is the health of mankinde,[20] & by these wordes, Eloy. Eloy. [8r] Eloy. lamazabthany, y^t is my god my god why hast thow forsaken me, & by these wordes, yt ys ended, And by these holy wordes, father into thy handes I commende my spirit.

Depart Oh ye spirit or spirites from this place & ground by & by w^thout any craft or guile or any manner of deceit. I coniure ye y^w spirite or spirites by ye vertue of Christes passion, & resurrection, and also by ye vertue of his holy Assention, And by ye fearefull comminge of him to ye Iudgement, where ye & all your fellowes shall receiue iust iudgement meete & accordinge to your offences, except ye depart from this place & ground.[21]

The vertue of the omnipotent god the father of all saintes in heauen excommunicate[22] yow and all his [8v] Angels excommunicate yow & cast yow into ye everlastinge fire & paines of hell where never shalbe comford nor hope, ease nor rest. And christ ye onelye begotten sonne of ye father[23] curse yow & bynde yow wth all ye paines aforesaide. The holy ghost wth all ye church of God excommunicate yow and curse yow from all hope and forgiuenes, ye holye Trinitye curse & excommunicate yow, wth all ye sorrowes paines and tormentes of hell fall downe vpon yow and remaine vpon yow vntyll ye last daye of dome, except ye depart immediatlye. All fires lighteninges & thunders curse yow all sorrowe & malediction fall downe vpon yow & remaine for ever Oh ye rebellinge Spirites except ye nowe departe & neyther hurt trouble nor vexe vs nor drawe nor convaye away ye treasure from vs, but suffer it to remaine here in this place y^t we may obtaine it w^thout any craft subtiltye [9r] or guile of yow or any of yow by vertue of all y^t is aforespoken or hereafter shalbe spoken. Amen.

I charge yow spirites I constraine yow & I commaunde yow y^t ye depart from this place & treasure & y^t ye come not nere yt by an hundreth miles for ye space of these 30 days next followinge. I coniure yow spirites by y^e .i. word y^t god spake in ye creation of the worlde[24] sayinge, lette there be lightes & so it was done, the 2. word he saide lett there be firmament betwene the waters and lett it devid the waters, & so it was done, ye 3 word y^t god saide lett ye waters vnder heaven gather themselues together into one place y^t ye drye lande maye appeare, & so it was done, the .4. worde was when he commaunded ye trees & the hearbes to springe, sayinge, lett ye earth bringe forth greene grasse & y^t beareth seade, & fruitfull [9v] trees everye one bearinge fruite in his kynd, & so it came to passe, ye 5 worde was when god made the sonne & the moone & ye starres sayinge, Let there be a light in ye firmament of heaven to devide ye day from the night y^t their maye be tokens signes dayes & yeares, & lett them be lightes in the firmament to shine vpon ye earth, & so yt was done. the .6. word was when he made ye fyshes & byrdes, sayinge, Lette ye waters bringe forth y^t move & haue lyffe, & fowles to flye vnder ye firmament of heauen, & so it came to passe. y^e .7. word was when god blessed them: sayinge growe & multiplye vpon the earth. the .8. worde was when god saide lett ye earth bringe forth lyvinge fowles everye one after his kinde: & so it was done. the .9. worde was when god made man sayinge, Lett vs make man in our symilitude after our liknes, y^t he maye haue rule over fyshes of the sea & fowles vnder heaven & over [10r] all cattell, & over all ye earth, & over all wormes y^t creepe vpon ye earth. y^e .10. word was when god sayd growe & multyplye yow & fulfyll ye earth, Subdue it & haue dominion over ye fyshes of the sea, & over ye fowles of ye ayre, & over all y^t creepe vpon ye earth. By ye vertue of all these wordes and of all names of god I coniure & compell yow[25] Oh ye spirites & straitlye commaunde yow to depart from this place & treasure, & neyther to convaye it, nor drawe it lower, nor to change it into any other colour or colors, but onelye to let it remayne in the owne proper substaunce as it was when it was first sette heere, & not to come neare it by an hundreth miles vntyll such tyme as we haue fulfylled our minds, willes & purposes. In ye name of god the father, and of god the sonne, and of god the holye ghost. Amen.

Marke this well y^t is written on ye other syde pertaining to this.[26] [10v]

He that doth discharge the grounde must be a Preist havinge a stoole[27] about his necke & holy water, and a bunch of ysope[28] to cast ye holy water on the grounde and turne his face into the east, and reade devoutlye this aboue writen 3 tymes.

Operis huius finis.[29]

[4. A charm for] Agewe.[30]

In the name of the Father and of the Son and of the Holy Spirit. Amen. But Peter was lying with a fever on a rock of marble and coming to him Jesus said to Peter, "Why are you lying here?" Peter responded, "Lord, I lie here from a bad fever." And Jesus said to him, "Rise and

In nomine patris et filij et spiritus sancti. Amen. Petrus autem iacebat febricitatus super petram marmoriam et perveniens illi Jesus ait petro, "Quid iaces hic?" Respondit Petrus, "Domine iaceo hic de mala febre." Et dicit [read dixit] ei Jesus, "Surge et dimitte illam." Et continuo

get rid of it." And immediately he arose
and got rid of it. And Peter said to the
Lord, "I beseech you that whoever carries upon himself [these] written
[words] that fevers not harm him, neither cold nor hot, daily, two-day, three-
day, four-day, five-day, six-day,
seven-day, eight-day, or nine day." [11r]
And Jesus said to him, "Let it be for you
just as you have sought in my name." Let
it be. Let it be. Let it be. Amen.

surrexit et dimisit eum [read eam]. Et dixit
Petrus, Domino. "Rogo te vt quicumque ei
portauerit super se scripta quod non
noceant ei febre [read febres] frigido
neque calide cotidiana, biduana triduana
quartana quintana sextana septana octana
aut nonana." [11r] Et aiit illi Jesus, "Fiat tibi
sicut petisti [read petistis] in nomine meo.
Fiat. Fiat. Fiat. Amen.

[5.] A prayer against theeues & wicked spirites

In the name of the father, et cetera.
Through Jesus the Nazarene, king of the
angels, through Mark, Matthew, Luke,
John, and through all virtues of the body
and blood of our Lord Jesus Christ,
through the power of the blessed Virgin
Mary and through the nine orders of
angels, through the twelve apostles,
through the 144,000 innocents who daily
sing a new song before the face of God,[31]
I conjure you demons, thieves, elves, and
falling sickness that you not have power
over this servant of god, N., nor over any
member of his body. Through Jesus
Christ, savior of the world who lives and
reigns through every age. Amen.

In nomine patris etc. Per Jesum Nazare-
num regem Angelorum per Marcum,
Matheum, Lucam, Johanem et per omnes
virtutes corporis et sanguinis dominum
nostrum [read domini nostris] Jesum
Christum per potestatem beatæ Mariæ
virginis et per nonum ordines Angelorum
per xii apostolos per centum quadraginta
quatuor millia innocentum qui quotidie
cantant canticum nouum ante conspec-
tum dei Coniuro vos demones latrones,
Elphos et morbum caducum vt non habe-
atis potestatem huic famulo die N. non
aliquo membro corporis suae perce [read
per] Jesum Christe Saluator mundi qui
vivis et regum [read regnas] per omnia
secula. Amen.

[6.] ffor to finde out a theefe[32]

Take the white of any hens eye and spuma argenti y^t is for to saye ye scum of
siluer y^t fleeth aboue, when it is meltinge[33] & wine & minge y^{em} together, and wth
y^t painte an eye on the wall on this mannerwise ⬭⊃⟶ and when thow hast
painted the eye on the wall say then this here following. [11v]

Glory to you, Lord God of our fathers.
We confess you, and we praise and bless
you. We pray to you Lord that you deign
to reveal the truth of this theft to us just

Gloria tibi domine Deus patrum nostrum.
Te confitemur teque laudamus atque beni-
dicimus. Precamur te domine vt veritatem
huius furti nobis manifestare digneris

as Achan to your servant Joshua.[34] And
just as you revealed the truth concerning
the two harlots to Solomon, you also
showed the two elders accusing Susanna
to be false, and you turned aside the
Apostle Mathias in the election by lot,[35]
in this way deign to reveal to us the
truth of this theft and to show your
omnipotence concerning what we seek,
who are blessed forever. Amen.

[insert sicut] Achor seruo tuo Iosuæ. Et
sicut Salamon verum de duabus meretrici-
bus reuelasti duos quoque falsos presbros
[read presbiteros] susannam criminantes
ostendisti et Matheum Apostolum in elec-
tione sorte declinasti, ita nobis huius furti
veritatem ostendere dignaris et manefe-
stare de quo nunc requirimus omnipoten-
tiam tuam qui es benedictus in secula
seculorum. Amen.

So then in the presence before them all y^t y^w hast in suspicion, and when he
comes y^t is gyltye, and y^f he looke on that eye y^t is painted on ye wall his right eye
will begynne to water. And yf yt be so that y^w aske him of y^t thinge y^t is done
awaye and he forsake it take then a broche[36] or a nayle of brasse & sett yt rightlye
to the eye y^t is painted on the wall before him & smite on the nayle wth a betell &
say thus, Rabbas seller Rabasasger, and constraine y^t false theefe for to yelde, and
bringe againe y^t he hath stolen, and he shall smite his hand vpon his eye and
gyue a great crye.

[7.] Another knowedg for to bringe out a theefe.

Take barlye cornes & washe y^{em} in water y^t is called aqua pensili [read pensilis].[37]
And do them out wth house vnder ye skye and also many men & wemen as [12r]
thow hast suspected to set ech on his name to his corne & as thow namest y^e
cornes names lett them fall into a vessel wth water & y^t corne y^t draweth toward
ye ground he y^t is named after is gylty &c.

[8.] ffor theues

Jesus passed through the middle of them
and went on his way.[38] Jasper brought
myrrh, Melchior frankincense, and
Balthazar gold.[39] Hold their jaws in a
bridle and bit, those who do not draw
near you.[40] May terror and dread fall
upon them; by the might of your arm,
let them become still as a stone until
your people pass by, that people of
whom you have taken possession.[41] Let
their eyes be darkened so they cannot
see. Let them not think evil things in
their hearts. And let their backs be bent

Iesus autem transiens per medium illorum
ibat. Jasper fert mirram thus melchior Bal-
sha Balthasar aurum. In camo et freno
constringe maxillas eorum qui non
approximat ad te. Irruat super eos formido
et pauor in magnitudine brachij tui, fiant
immobilis quasi lapis donec pertranseat
populus tuus domine iste populus quem
tu possedisti. Obscurantem [read
obscurentur] oculi eorum ne vidiant [read
videant] in corda eorum non cogitant
[read cogitent] mala, et dorsa eorum semper incurua. Domine Iesu Christe saluator

always.[42] Lord Jesus Christ, savior and good shepherd, lion, wolf, warrior of this world, let them keep, let them proclaim, let them see, let them preserve, you who govern all our things and our bodies and our homes. Three bodies with unequal merits hang from branches: Dismas and Jesmas, and in the middle, divine power. Dismas sought the highest, Jesmas descended to the lowest.[43] Say these verses that you not lose your things in theft. Kiriel, Christos, Kiries. Our father. And lead us not. But deliver us.[44] Lord, be to us a tower of strength from the face of the enemy.[45] + tetragrammaton + hely + helion + labanekl + etc. [12v]

et pastor bone leo lupus huius mundi preliator, custodiant predicant visitant [read visitent] servant [read servent] que gubernant cunctas res nostras et corpora nostra et domos nostras. Disperibus [read disparibus] meritis pendunt tria corpora ramis Dismas et Jesmas medio diuina potestas, Summa petit Dismas descendit ad infima Jesmas. Hos versus dicas ne furto tu tua perdas kiriel christos kiries. Pater noster. Et ne nos inducas. Sed libera nos. Esto nobis domine turris fortitudinis a facie inimici + tetragramaton + hely + helion + labanekl + &c. [12v]

[9.] For the feuer quartan[46]

Take iij leaues of sauge & wright on ye first lefe + Iħs natus est on ye second lefe Iħs crucifixus est in the .3. Iħs resurrexit et His deliberet ab hec malo[47] & say .3. aue .2. day as many & on y^e .3. day as many.[48]

In nomine patris et filij et spiritus sancti amen.[49] Almightye god father sonne & ye holy ghost as ye meekelye came to the virgine mary here on earth to take owre kynd as it was thine will to bringe vs out of thraldome,[50] so sende thy sweete grace through ye virtue of ye godhead that this maladye which that is here[51] vanishe awaye, as is come, y^t it neuer more ake nether smart ytch nether prich shoot swell nether worke then did your wound lord so ye were stonge to ye hart lord as I beleeue y^t it is so, soe send thy sweete grace that this maladye mought awaye goe also lord as ye be bate of all sorrowe & mischife as Mocyse gret[52] sowe & ye bodylye appearred to him in tokeninge & in lykenesse of fyer the great, soe lord father & sonne & holy spirit as I beleeue lord y^t it is south so send y^t sweet grace that this malidye may nowe & ever goe awaye amen for charitye. In nomine patris et filij et spiritu sancti Amen. et dic quinque pater noster aue et credo[53] [13r]

[10.] A prayer for a yearbe.[54]

In nomine patris et filij et spiritus sancti amen.

One three crosses of 3 deed bodyes honge three, the[55] certaine were theeus ye thirde christ left dismas & Gismas medio diuina potestas[56] Christ amidst y^{em}

was. Dysmas to heauen he went & Jesmas to hell was sent. christ y^t died on ye roode when thy mother by ye childe stoode, through the vertu of ye bloude, saue me & my good wthin & wthout and all the howse abought to my byddinge where they bene, what I byd y^{em} to doe, starke be their synnewes & their paines & their limbes & their armes almightye & here then sythe dreed darkenes & dowbt close y^{em} all about as in all wrought wth stone wth ye crampe in here tounge crampinge & crokinge fanite[57] in her footinge through ye might of ye Trinitye, saue my good & me In ye name of iesu ye signe then of Iesu, wth holy benedictitye all abowte as be wthin & wthout wthin this place all about In nomine patris & .3. pater noster 3. aues and one creede. [13v]

[11. Charm for aches][58]
In nomine patris et filij et spiritus sancti amen. Iesu on ye earth roode vpon an asse, as his sweet will was his asses bloude, & christ abode his asse looke downe right, & christ did saue light. he set fleshe to the fleshe & bloude to bloude & bone to bone. he blest him & bad him rise & gone in the name of ye father & of ye sonne & of ye holy ghost o god in persones three that this ach shall never more deare thee, by ye vertu of gods fleshe & his bloude in trinitye

dic 9 pr nr & 9 aiues & 3 creedes & bene convalescit.[59]

[12.] This is a good medicien for fevers[60]
Take a sauge leafe & wright theron x^c,[61] & lett ye seeke[62] eat ye first day & say a pater noster & aue & a creede, the second day on another lefe angelus nunciat[63] & lett ye sycke eat it in ye same manner, & ye 3 daye wright on the 3. leafe Johannes predicat[64] & let ye sicke eat it & say 3 pr nr & .3. aue & .3 creede & when he is hole charge him y^t he let a preist say 3 messes ye first of ye holye ghost Spiritus domini repleuit etc.[65] ye second day of saynt Mychael, & ye 3 of Sanct Johannes ye baptist & after when he names ye fevers take vp his hande and blesse him & saye i. pr. nr. i aue & a creed & he shall be whole [14r]

[13.] A prayer for the blody flyxe[66]

In the name of the Father and of the Son and of the Holy Spirit. + Amen. + Jesus stood before the river Jordan and put in his foot and said, "Stay, water. By God I conjure you." The soldier Longinus pierced the side of our Lord + Jesus Christ and blood and water immediately flowed out: blood of redemption and

In nomine patris et filij et spiritu sancti. + Amen. Stabat + Iesus contra flumen Iordanus et posuit pedem suum et dixit, "Sta aqua. Per deum te coniuro." Longinus miles latus domini nostri + Iesu christi lancea perforauit et continuo exiuit sanguis et aqua, sanguis redemptionis et aqua baptismatis. In nomine patris, restet

water of baptism. In the name of the Father, let the blood stand still. In the name of the Son let the blood stop. In the name of the Holy Spirit let not a drop of blood go out of this servant of God, N. Just as we believe that Holy Mary is the mother and truly gave birth to the infant Christ, so let the veins which are [full] with blood retain it, so let the blood stand still like the Jordan stood still when Christ had been baptized in it.[67] In the name of the Father, et cetera.

sanguis. In nomine filij, cesset sanguis. In nomine spiritus sancti, non exeat sanguis gutta ab hoc famulo dei N. Sic credimus quod sancta maria est mater et verum infantem genuit christum sic retineat venæ quæ [insert plene] sunt sanguine, sic restat sanguis sicut restat [read restabat] iordanis quum + christus in ea baptizatus fuit. In nomine patris &c.

[14.] For a man y^t may not sleepe for sicknes[68]

Take & wright these wordes on a lawrell leafe + thismall + Ismael + adiuro vos per Angelos vt soporetur iste homo N.[69] & ley it vnder his head y^t he wott[70] not therof & lett him eate lettuse & drinke popyseede wth ayle

[15.] A prayer against theeves

+ In Bethelem god was borne, betwene two beastes to rest he was layd. in y^t stead was nother theefe no man but ye holy trinitye. y^t ilke selfe god y^t ther was borne defend our bodyes & our catell from theeves & all maner of mischiefes & harmes where so we wende by londe or by water by night or by daye by tyde or by tyme. 5 pr nr 3 aue & i creed [14v]

[16.] Pro febribus

Take vi almaundes & wright on ye first + deus est pater ++. 2 christus sanctorum remedium +++ filius est veritas ++++ christus sanctorum remedium +++++ deus est pater ++++++ filius est veritas.[71] in nomine trinitatis dic v. pr nr 5. aue & i. crede

[17.] If thy freind lye sicke & y^w wouldest faine witt whether he shall lyve or dy of y^t sicknes[72]

Take v. croppes of veruaine in thy right hande hand & ley y^{em} on thy lefte hande & saye over him in ye worshippe of ye 5 woundes y^t Christ suffred on ye roode tree for to by manes soule out of thraldome y^t ye man y^t is sicke tell me the sooth through ye vertu of god & of godes word whether he shall lyue or dye of ye sicknes & blesse him .5. tymes & take y^{em} then in ye right hand againe & goe to thy friend & take his right hand in thine & aske him howe he fayres while those hearbes are betweene y^t he wott not & how he hopes of himselfe & he shall through the grace of god & of the verueyne tell ye thee sooth sickarlye[73] [15r]

[18. For] Axes, a good prayes

Iesus as y^w art kynge of blys & thy mother y^t mayden is the Iewes[74] say she non is, thow shyld[75] my body from ye axesse 3 in nomine patris et filii et spiritus sancti amen v. pr nr 5 aue & i. creede.

[19.] ffor ye tooth ache

Take 3. cropps of rosemarye & 3. cropps of verveine & chafed in thy hand & put it to ye sore tooth. et dic .5. pr nr in honore beata Appolonie et pro anima patris et matris euius.[76]

[20.] Pro febribus medicina probata[77]

Take an apple & cutt it in 3 peeces & on ye first part wright these wordes Iħs ageos dñs[78] & on y^e .2. part wright xp̄s otheos dñs .3. on ye 3 part wright resur-rexit a mortuis dñs[79] & gyue him to eat & he shall be holl by gods grace .3 pr nr 2 a. 1 c

[21.] For women y^t traueleth wth childe[80]

Wright these wordes in parchment & binde aboute her body + maria peperit xp̄m + Anna Mariam + Elizabeth Johannem + Cecilia Remigium + Sator + Arepo + tenet + Opera + rotas.[81]

[22.] Another

Give her to drinke deteyne & she shall haue a child wthout trauaile.

[23.] Good prayer for ye child y^t is dead in a womans wombe

when thow comst to ye howse where ye woman is in, stope thy right foot on ye threshould & make a signe of [15v] the + & say in nomine patris + et filij + et spiritus sancti + amen +

Anna gave birth to Samuel + Elizabeth the precursor + Mary the savior + And you woman bring forth what is in you + O infant whoever you are, whether a male infant or female, come forth. Christ calls you. Christ commands that you quickly come forth. Come for baptism.	Anna peperit Samuelem + Elizabeth precursorem + Maria saluatorem + Et tu mulier fac quod in te est. + O infans quicumque es, aut infans masculus aut fæmina, veni foras. Christus te vocat. Christus imperat vt cito exeas. Veni foras ad baptismum.

say thus thrice & 3 pr nr. 3 aiues & a creed & shee shall fare well by ye grace of god almightye

[24.] A good prayer for ye fallinge sicknesse[82]

+ In the name of the Father + and of the Son + and of the Holy Spirit. + Amen. Jasper brought gold + Melchior frankincense + Antropa[83] myrrh + whoever then + carries this charm with him + names of the kings + is freed from the falling sickness through devotion to the Lord. + Amen. + Mark. + Matthew. + Luke. + John. + Thus all male and female saints of god[84] + pray to god + for N. here, so that from this falling sickness + he might be saved and liberated. Amen. +

+ In nomine patris + et filij + et spiritus sancti. + Amen. Jasper fert aurum + thus Mechizar + Antropa Mirram. + Hæc quicumque tum + secum fert + nomina regum + soluitur a morbo domini pietate caduco. + Amen. + Marcus. + Matheus. + Lucas. + Johannes. + Sic omnes sancti et sanctae dei + orate deo + pro N. isto, vt a morbo isto caduco + possit saluari et liberari. Amen.

+And gyue it him written in a scroule of parchment, & let him sowe it in leather or in cloth & beare yt abowt his necke, & he shall fast Sc̄t Gregoryes fast, bread & water, & yf he may not drinke water let him gyve a peny for ye love of god & he shall amende soone.

[25.] Another.

Take a bee & drawe out her tounge & gyue the sick man to drinke yt in ale y^t he wott yt not & he shall be deliuered of y^t sicknesse forever by the grace of god. probatum.[85]

[26.] A prayer for a hawe in a mans eye[86]

In nomine patris + et filij + et spiritus sancti + amen + I coniure the hawe in the name of ye father + & ye sonne + & ye holy ghost + that from this tyme forwarde y^t thow never greeue more this eye of thys [16r] man N. our lord Iesu christ + yf yt be thy will drawe out this hawe and clense ye eye of N thy servaunt also verely & also sotherlye, as thow clenst ye eye of Toby + Agios + Agios + Agios + Sanctus + Sanctus + Sanctus + Christus vincit + Christus regnat + Christus imperat + xp̄s sine fine viuit et regnat[87] + in nomine patris et filij et spiritus sancti amen 3. pr nr 3 aue i c etc.

[27.] For toothache

Write around his jaw Rex + Pax + nax + Agla + In nomine domini nostri Iesu xp̄e filij dei viui N. And say three Pater Nosters and at whichever Pater Noster say Rex + pax + nax + Agla In the name of our lord Jesus Christ, son of the living God let N. be whole. We believe, Lord— sign the teeth [i.e., make a sign of the cross over the affected teeth]—you have visited your male or female servant, you who signed the five barley loaves and thence fed the five thousand men [and will free] you N. from this toothache just as you resuscitated Lazarus from the tomb—sign the mouth.[88] In the name of your Father. Say three Pater Nosters. "+ In the name of the Father I discovered you.+ In the name of the Son I sought you. Cross of Christ + Cross of Christ. + Cross of Christ. + Father and Son and Holy Spirit I deliver you, N." And say it 3 times. 3 p. n. 3 a. i c. In the name of the Father and of the Son and of the Holy Spirit. Amen. [16v]

Pro dolore dentium

Scribe sirca maxilla eius Rex + Pax + nax + Agla + In nomine domini nostri Iħu xp̄e filij dei viui N. Et dic ter pr nr et ad quili- bet pr nr dic, "Rex + pax + nax + Agla in nomine domini nostri Iesu christi filij dei viui sanus sit N. Credimus domine"— signa dentes—famulum tuum vel famu- lam tuam, qui signasti quinque panes hordiacios [read hordeaceos] et inde satis- fecisti quinque milia hominum, visitasti. [insert et liberabis] te N. ab hoc dolore dencium sicut resuscitatasti Lazarum de monumento. Et signa os. + In nomine patris tuum. Dic ter pater noster. + In nomine patris inveni te + in nomine filij quaesiui te. [insert+ Crux] christi + crux christi + crux christi + pater et filius et spiritus sanctus. Delebo [read delibero] te N." Et dic 3 tymes. 3 p. n. 3 a. i c. In nomine patris et filij et spiritus sancti amen. [16v]

[28.] Dolore dentium

Take virgins wax[89] & wright therin + ay + loy + Sadaloy + donicaloy + liberator dencium[90] & lay yt vnder his head & sleepe theron

[29.] Dolore dencium

Take & wright this + Re + Re + Re +[91]

The blessed Apollonia underwent a weighty martyrdom for God. Tyrants bound her and evil men broke her teeth and in that torment she prayed that whoever invoked her name would not feel a toothache.[92] Pray for us gentle Apollonia.[93] Let us pray. God, you who liberated good Apollonia from the hands

Beata Apalonia graue martirum pro dom- ino sustinuit. Tiranni eam ligauerunt et malos [read mali] dentes eius fregerunt et in illo tormento orauit vt quicumque nomen suum invocauerit, dolorem den- cium non sentiret. Ora pro nobis lenta [read lenis] Appollonia. Oremus Deus, qui bonam Appoloniam de manibus

of enemies and heard her prayer, who
heard the intercession of Saint Laurence,
that you completely expel from my teeth
this pain and may Saint Apollonia the
martyr by the virtue of Jesus Christ and
the intercession of Saint Laurence daily
defend me from danger to my teeth
within and without. Amen. Let all celestial [and] terrestrial things say, "+ In the
name of the Father and of the Son and of
the Holy Spirit. Amen."

inimicorum liberasti et eius orationem
exaudisti, te quis [read qui] intercessionem Sancti Laurencij [insert audisti], vt a
dentibus meis penitus dolorem expellas
et a periculo intus et exterius dencium ne
sancta Appolonia martiri per virtutem
Iesu christi et intercessionem sancti Lau-
rentcij cotidie me defendat amen dicant
omnia cælestia [insert et] terrestria + In
nomine patris et filij et spiritus sancti.
Amen.

[30.] ffor pricking of a thorne

In yᵉ worshipp of yᵉ crowninge of our Lord god kneele downe & say 5 pr nr. 5
aveys & a creede & wᵗʰ ye grace of god yt shall neuer dare[94] the more. [17r]

[31. Three Good Brethren Charm][95]

There wer 3 good brethren yᵗ went to yᵉ mount of oleuete good herbs for to seeke
for to heale their brethren woundes & all other wounds. their they mett wᵗʰ our
lord Iesu christ. whether be the sonne so yᵉ 3 good brethren,[96] we be comde lord
to yᵉ mount of Oleuete good herbes for to seeke for to heale our brethren wounds
& all other woundes. Turne ye againe ye 3. good brethren & take oyle of a olyfe
tre & the wolle of a blacke shippe & ley it to your brethrens woundes & to all
other woundes & yᵗ shall heale your brethrens woundes & other woundes
through yᵉ virtu of yᵉ baptisinge yᵗ our Lord was baptised & through yᵉ vertu of
yᵉ sweet milke yᵗ our Lord suckt on his mothers brestes. Giue grac yᵗ this wounde
fester not nor ake not nor boyle not no more then did the woundes of Iesu when
he was taken downe of yᵉ crosse. In nomine patris et filij et spiritus sancti amen
3 pr nr. 3 a i c.

[32. To staunch blood][97]

Iesus yᵗ was borne in Bethelem & baptised was in yᵉ water of fleui iordaine. yᵉ
child was good yᵉ water wᵗʰstood N. Be stand yᵉ bloud stand bloude staunch
bloud in yᵉ vertue of godes bloode. in nomine patris et filij etc. N. et dicas 3 pr nr
3 a. i c. [17v]

[33.] for the head ache

Take ground Iuy & polipodium on yᵉ wall & scrape then together wᵗʰ butter &
frye yᵉᵐ together & put yᵉᵐ in a bagge of lynnen & lay it on yᵉ head warme as he
may suffer & say thus

Who was crucified on the scaffold was offered for the people. Nail, blow, and lance. Crown, weeping, and thorn. Good Jesus Christ, in your five wounds sanctify [this remedy] for me in this difficulty in the power of Jesus. Amen. Anamazapta.[98]

Qui crucifixus in patibulo oblatus est pro populo. Flavis [read clavis] Fostes [read fustis] et lancia: corona flexus [read fletus] et spinia. y [read in] tua v vulnera piæ Iesu Christe [insert hoc remedium] sanctificare mihi mac [read in hac] angustia in virtute iesu. Amen. Anamazapta.

[34.] Pro morbo caduco[99]

Take & say in his eare anamazapta 3 times & turne away from him & he shalbe hole Or wright these wordes in a ringe, what metell so yt be, & beare yt vpon y^e & saye 3 p n 3 a i c.

[35.] for ye feuer[100]

Take 3. obleyes & wright on ye first pater est apha et ω & gyue ye sike to eate ye first daye, on ye second wright filius est vita & make 2. crosses & gyue ye sicke to eate on ye seconde day, & on ye 3 wright sp̄s sc̄tus est benedictum & make 3 crosses & kneele downe & say wth good devotion .5. pr nr & 5 a & a creeede & thow shalt be hole. [18r]

[36. Protective amulet][101]

Sainte Leo ye pope of Rome wrote y^es names to kinge Charbis [sic] of fraunce when he went to the battaile of rownliuale & say: what man y^t bareth these wordes vpon him y^t day shall he haue no dread of his enimies to be overcome in battaile, nor he shall never be burnd wth fyre, nor drowned wth water nor he shall never dye in strife & hatred nor he shall never dye soddaine death, nor ther shall never no wicked spirit hurt him, nor he shall never haue sicknesse nether ye axes, nor ye fevers, nor he shall never be falsly be damned before any iudge nor he shall never haue wrath of man or woman w^thout great guilte nor he shall never miscarye in no neede, nor he shall never haue no disease of thundringe nor of lightninge nor feare his trauelynge nor he shall never haue ye fallinge evill, nor he shall not dye thoughe he were hanged & y^t was proved by Tresilion ye iustice of Londuen[102] & yf a woman be in trauelinge of childe & shee beare these names vpon her the woman shall be deliuered, & ye child shall come to christendome & ye woman to purification through the virtue of these holy names of our Lord Iesu christ following on the other syde. [18v]

Ihs + xp̄s + messias + sother + Emanuel + Sabaoth + Adonay + vnitas + Trinitas + sapientia + via + vita + veritas + virtus + op̄s + h̄o + Vsion + Saluator + Caritas + Æternitas + Creator + redemtor + Requies + finis + vnigenitus + fons + spes

+ sacerdos + ymas + Otheos + origo + manus + splendor + lux + gracia + fons + mundus + imago + paracletus + columba + corona + Propheta + humilitas + fortissimus + altissimus + paciencia + athanatos + kyros + yskyros + et mediator + A + G + L + A + Tetragramaton + caput + Alpha + et omega + primogenitus + et nouissimus + panton Craton + et ysus + ego sum qui sum + agnus + ouis + vitulus + serpens + Aries + leos + vermis[103] + vnus pater + vnus filius + vnus sp̄s scts + Ely + Ely + Ely + lamazabathani + Iasper fert aurum + Thus Melchior, Antropa mirram + hæc quicumque tum secum fert nomina regum + Soluitur a morbo dn̄i pietate caduco[104] + Ananizapta + Ananizapta + Ananizapta + Iħs nazarenus rex Iudeorum filij dei miserere mei amen + Sana me et salua me et costodi me domine deus meus ab omni malo et ab omnibus infirmitatibus meis[105] amen + Michael + Gabriel + Raphael + Saraphiel + Sariel + [19r] Vriel + Tobiel + Barathiel + Reguel + Deus abrahami + Deus Isaacci + Deus Iacobi + Petrus + Paulus + Andreas + Jacobus + Philippus + Simon + Barnabas + Thomas + Iohannes + Tadeus + Marcus Matheus + Lucas + Johannes + vt me defendant ab omni malo et periculo et ab omnibus infirmitatibus meis amen.[106] 3 pr nr 3 avi i c et dicas. In principio erat verbum etc.[107]

[37.] A prayer for the toothach[108]

Take first v leaued grasse[109] & stampe yt and laye yt to the holer cheecke,[110] and say thus Abraham laye on sleepe. Ora pro nobis[111] vpon the mounte of olyvet ora pro nobis their came our lorde to, ora pro nobis, sleepe on Abraham he sayde him to, ora pro nobis, I ne wake no I ne sleepe, but on the toth ake I weepe. Arise Abraham & goe with me N. & shall it never dayre[112] thee nor never no man that these words can. & then say 3 p. nr. a 3 i c. [19v]

[38.] A prayer for yᵉ tothe ach[113]

What manner of ill yᵗ ever thow be on gods behalfe I coniure thee, wᵗʰ yᵉ blessed crosse + yᵗ Iesus was done on wᵗʰ force. I coniure yᵉ wᵗʰ nayles three yᵗ Iesus was nayld vpon a tree. I coniure yᵉᵉ wᵗʰ yᵉ crowne of thorne yᵗ on Iesus head was done for scorne, I coniure yᵉ wᵗʰ yᵉ blessed bloud that Iesus bledd vpon yᵉ roode. I con-iure yᵉ wᵗʰ woundes .5. yᵗ Iesus suffred in his lyfe. I coniure yᵉ wᵗʰ yᵉ holy spare, yᵗ Longis till his hart cane bare. I coniure yᵉ nevertheless wᵗʰ all the vertues of yᵉ messe. in yᵉ honour of our blessed Lady & sainct Buttolphe & sainct apolline & sainct Petronilla, say 5. pa. no. & 5 ave & one creede in the honour of god.

[39.] ffor the toth ache

Mel. Marchabeus.[114] Izache. hicsananie. hicsananie. hicsananie. 3 tymes weder-hylwe Christ helpe.[115]

[40.] An experiment for wounds[116]

Take a peece of leade & on y^t say this prayer, Lord Iesus christ y^t with thy precious bloude hath ransomed vs synfull men on ye crosse, sende thy blessing on this leade, y^t what soever sicknesses or woundes yt toucheth after this tyme, through the vertue of the holy passion y^t he may receiue health. Amen. In nomine patris et filij et spiritus [20r] sancti Amen. Then say 5 p. ñr .5 a & on creed & make of y^e lead a 4 cornered plate made after this forme, wth 5. crosses & at every crosse say a pr nr. in y^e worshipe of y^e 5. woundes of our lord Iesu Christ. Amen.

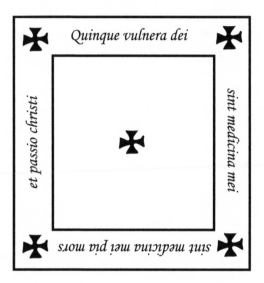

Then settinge y^e plate to y^e wound, or to the sore saye thus as verelye as y^e wounds of Iesu christ ranckled not, neyther roted neyther wormes ingender, neyther fester nor canker, nor no venomus matter, soe this wounde or sore neyther rancle nor roote nor fester, nor canker nor venomus matter maye yt greene, but christ Iesu through his might perfectlye to heale yt Amen

And then say this prayer followinge.

Almighty god everlasting health of all them that on thee haue beleeved, heare thow the prayer of thy servaunt, for whom we beseech thee to helpe of thy great mercye that when he is whole he maye gyve the laude and prayse in the holy church through Iesus christ our saviour and redeemer Amen. [20v]

[41.] A prayer against fayres[117] say as folloeth

N. thou are sticken wth ye fayres. I praye god & ye blessed Lady blesse thee againe & againe 9 times & be present health vnto thee for sweet saint charitye. say soe 3 times together & name the partye then make a + let yt be for yow or on the partye, & say 3 times more then make another crosse +[118] say In nomine patris etc. then say y[e] lorde Iesu blesse thee N. & be present health vnto thee & defend thee from all pinchinges gripinges strikinges & from all evill tounges Lord Iesu + 3 tymes + for thy precious bloude, & soe in y[e] honour & worshipp of thee o god & for the health of thee will I saye 9 p̄r nr. & one creede & then say by god healpe he shalbe well presentlye +

[42.] A prayer for a pricke wth a sword, dager, or thorne

I blesse thee in y[e] name of God y[e] father, god y[e] sonne, & god y[e] holye ghost. Sweet Iesus christ y[t] was pricked wth a pointe, wth bonitas.[119] I thee annoint for Iesus christes sake, that thow doe never wheale nor ake. In nomine patris et filij et spiritus sancti Amen, with 3 pa. 3. a. & one cr.

[43.] A prayer for the stytche[120]

Abraham lay & slept vnder mount olivet, Iesus came by & sayd sleepest or wakest Abraham. I sleepe not Lorde nor I wake not I am soe pricked wth a stake. rise vp Abraham & followe me there shall never stake hurt the more nor non y[t] cann saye these wordes in gods name amen. [21r]

[44.] A prayer for bleedinge[121]

O lorde Iesus christ y[t] was in Bethlem borne & baptized in y[e] water of flem iordayne, the water was wilde & woode & through the vertue of this childe y[e] water stoode. In y[e] name of the father, y[e] sonne, the holy ghost stinted maye this bloode be. say this nine tymes over

[45.] A prayer against swellinge[122]

Sweet Iesus on y[e] earth was found, he was beaten, he was bound, he was pricked, he was stonde, yet he never sweld nor bled, nor by y[e] grace of him noe more shall this. yt is to be sayd 9 times

[46.] A prayer against wormes

In y[e] hower of our lord benedicitye our Lord met wth Rabbay saying Peters brother where hast thow bene, at Rabby, at the band of 9 wormes, turne againe Rabbay & slaye these wormes everye one from 9. to .8. from 8. to .7. from .7. to .6. from 6. to 5. from 5 to 4 from 4 to 3 from 3 to 2 from 2 to i, from i to non & say it 9. tymes over.

[47.] ffor staunchinge of bloude

Repeat these 3 verses followinge 3 times over by hart wth name of y[e] party to whom yow shall saye.

Stay blood in the vein,	Sta sanguis in vena, sicut christus stetit in
Just as Christ stayed in his pain.	sua pena. Sta sanguis in te sicut christus
Stay blood in yourself,	stetit in se. Sta sanguis infixus, sicut chris-
Just as Christ stayed in himself.	tus stetit crucifixus
Stay blood fastened inside,	
Just as Christ stayed crucified.	
or other wise	
The blood remains inside yourself	sanguis manet in te, sicut christus fecit in
Just as Christ did in himself	se. Sanguis manet in tua vena, sicut chris-
Let the blood remain in your vein	tus in sua pena. Sanguis manet in te fixus
Just as Christ was in his pains.	sicut christus quando fuit crucifixus. [21v]
Blood remain fixed inside	
Just as Christ was crucified. [21v]	

[48. Agnus dei amulet][123]

These vertues vnder these verses written by pope Vrbane ye first to ye emperour of ye Græcians are conteined in a priapt or tablet to be continuallye worne about one called Agnus Dei, wch is a lyttle cake, havinge the picture of a lambe car-rienge of a flagg on ye one syde; & christes heade on ye other syde, & is hollow: so as ye gospell of St Ihon; written in fine paper is placed in the concauitye therof: & yt is thus compounded or made, even as they themselves report

Balsamus et munda cera, cum chrismatis vnda conficiunt agnum, quod munus do tibi magnum, fonte velut natum, per mystica sanctificatum: Fulgura desur-sum depellit, et omne malignum, Peccatum frangit, vt christi sanguis, et angit, Prægnans seruatur, simul et partus liberatur Dona refert dignis, virtutem destruit ignis, Portatus munde de fluctibus eripit undæ.[124]

Balme, virgine wax, & holy water, an Agnus Dei make: A gyft that wch non can be greater, I send y^e for to take ffrom founteine cleare the same hath issue, in secret sanctifide. Gainst lightning yt hath soveraigne vertue & thunder cracks beside. Ech haynous synne it weares & wasteth, Even as christs precious bloude. And wemen whiles their travell lasteth, It saues yt is so good. It doth bestow great gyftes & graces on such as well deserue: And borne about in noisome places, ffrom perill doth preserue. The force of fyer, whose heate destroyet. It breakes and bringeth downe. And he or shee that [22r] this inioyeth, no water shall them drowne.

[49.] A prayer against shott or a wastcote of proofe[125]

Before ye comminge vp of these Agnus Deis, a holy garment called a wastcote for necessitye was much vsed of our forefathers, as a holy relike, etc. As giuen by the pope, or some such archconiuror, who promised thereby all manner of imutabilitye[126] to the wearer therof; in somuch as he could not be hurt wth any shott or other violence. And otherwise, that woman y^t would weare yt should haue quicke deliveraunce: the composition therof was as followeth.[127]

On Christmas daye at night, a thrid must be sponne of flax by a lyttle virgine girle, in the name of ye deuill: & yt must be by her woven and also wrought wth ye needle. In ye brest or forepart therof must be made wth needle worke two heades; on ye head at the right syde must be a hat, and a longe beard; ye left head must haue on a crowne, & y^t must be soe horrible, y^t it maye ressemble Belzebub, & on each syde of ye wastcote must be made a crosse.

[50. Protective amulet of Pope Leo][128]

The epistle of S. Savior[129] wch Pope Leo sent to king Charles sayinge y^t whosoever carrieth ye same about him, or in what day soe ever he shall read yt, or shall see yt, he shall not be killed wth any iron toole nor be burned wth fyre nor be drowned wth water, neither any evill man or other creature maye hurt him, & yt is as followeth [22v][130]

The crosse of Christ is a wonderfull defense + the crosse of Christ be always wth me + ye crosse is it wch I doe alwayes worship + ye crosse of christ is true health + ye crosse of christ doth lose ye bands of death + the crosse of christ is ye truth & the waye + I take my iournye vpon ye crosse of ye lorde + ye crosse of christ beateth downe every evill + ye crosse of christ giueth all good thinges + the crosse of Christ taketh awaye paines everlastinge + ye crosse of christ saue me + O crosse of christ be vpon me, before me, & behinde me + because ye ancient enimie cannot abide the sight of thee + ye crosse of Christ saue me, keepe me, governe me, & direct me + Thomas[131] bearing this note of thy diuyne maiestye + Alpha + Omega + first + and last + middest + and end + beginninge + & first begotten + wisedome + vertue +

[51.] A cha prayer wch must never be sayde, but caried about one, against theeues[132]

I doe goe & I doe come vnto yow wth ye loue of god, wth ye humilitye of christ, wth ye holynes of our blessed ladye, wth ye fayth of Abraham, wth ye iustice of Isaac, wth ye vertue of David wth ye might of Peter wth ye constancye of Paule, wth ye worde of god, wth ye authority of Gregorye, wth ye prayer of Clement, wth ye floud of Jordan p p p c g e g a q q est p t i k a b g l k 2 a x t g t x a m g 2 4 2 i que p x c g k q a 9 9 p e q q r.[133] Oh onely [23r] father + oh onlye lord + And Iesus + passing through the middest of them[134] + went + In the name of the father + and of the sonne + & of the holy ghost + Amen.

[52. Amulet of Joseph of Arimathea][135]

Ioseph of Arimathea did find this writinge vpon ye woundes of the syde of Iesus christ written wth gods finger when ye bodye was taken awaye from ye crosse. Whosoever shall carrye this writtinge about him, shall not dye an evill death, yf he beleeue in christ, & in all perplexityes he shall soone be deliuered, neyther let him feare any daunger at all. Fons + Alpha et omega + figa + figalis + Sabbaoth + Emmanuel + Adonay + O + Nerah + Elay + Ihe + Rentone + Neger + Sahe + Pangeton + Commen + a + g + l + a + Matheus + Marcus + Lucas + Johannes + + + titulum[136] triumphalis + Iesus nasarenus rex Iudeorum + ecce dominicae crucis signum + fugite partes adversæ, vicit leo de tribu Iudæ, radix, Dauid,[137] aleluijah, Kyrieeleeson, Christe eleeson, pater nr. aue maria, et ne nos, et veniat super nos salutare tuum: Oremus, &c.[138]

[53. Lay indulgence][139]

W^ch shall say 5. p. n. 5 a & one creed pitiouslye behouldinge these armes of christ passion[140] ar graunted 30 two thowsand seven hundreth fiftye fyve yeares of pardon. [23v]

[54.] A defensiue prayer[141]

May the sign of the cross defend me from evils present, past, and future, interior and exterior. Let this holy mixture of the body and blood of our Lord Jesus Christ become for me, and for all taking it, health of mind and body, and a salvific preparation for the life that must be earned and gained.

Signum sanctæ crucis defendat me a malis præsentibus, præteritis, et futuris interioribus et exterioribus. Haec sacrosanta conmixtio corporis et sanguinis domini nostri Iesu christi fiat michi, omnibusque sumentibus, salus mentis et corporis, et ad vitam promerendam, et capessendam, praeparatio sautaris.

[55.] A prayer of ye holy crosse[142]

Nulla salus est in domo, nisi cruce munit homo superliminaria. Neque sentit gladium, Nec amisit filiu [sic], Quisquis egit talia.

No health w^thin the howse doth dwell, Except a man doth crosse him well, at everye doore or frame, He never feeleth the swords pointe, Nor of his sonne shall loose a ioint, that doth performe the same.

Furthermore as followeth:

Ista suos fortiores, semper facit et victores morbos sanat et languores, Reprimit dæmonia, Dat captiuis libertatem, Vitæ confert novitatem, Ad antiquam dignitatem, Crux reduxit omnia. O Crux lignum triumphale, mundi vera salus vale, Inter ligna nullum tale, Fronde, flore, germine Medicina christiana, Salua sanos, ægros sana, Quod non valet vis humana, Fit in tuo nomine &c.

It makes hir souldiers excellent, And crowned y^em wth victorye, Restores the lame & impotent, And healeth euerye maladye. The diuels, of hell yt conquereth, Releaseth from imprisonment, Newnesse of life yt offereth, It hath all at comaundement. O crosse of wood incomparable, To all ye world most holsome: No woode is halfe so honorable, In branch, in bud, or blossome. O medicine wch christ did ordaine, The sounde saue everye hower, The sicke & sore make whole againe, By vertue of thy power. And y^t wch mans vnablenesse hath never comprehended, Graunt by ye name of holynesse, It may be fullye ended, &c. [24r]

[56.] This prayer is taken out of ye primer[143]

Omnipotens + Dominus + Christo + Messias + Iesus + Sother + Emanuel + Sabaoth + Adonay + vnigenitus + maiestas + Paraclytus + Saluator noster + Agios + Iskiros + Agios + Adanatos + Gasper + melchior + et Bathasar + Matheus + Marcus + Lucas + Iohannes + hel + heloim + Otheos + Agla + Tetragrammaton + Iehoua + ya + Saday + Homonsion + Esereheye + Saluator + Alpha + et Omega + Primogenitus + Principium + et finis + via + vertitas + vita + virtus + Sapientia + Mediator + Agnus + Ovis + Leo + Os + verbum + Imago + Lux + Gloria + Sol + Splendor + Panis + fons + Ianua + Sponsus + Pastor + Sacerdos + Propheta + Sanctus + Omnipotens + Misericors + Deus + immortalis + Rex pacificus + Oriens + Charitas + mons + Aeternus + Creator + Redemptor + vitis + Substantia + Bonitas + Summum bonum + Spes + Fides + honor + spiritus + flos + filius + primus + et novissimus + Christus vincit + Christus regnat + christus imperat[144] + Trinitas + Dietas + Vnitas + Bonitas + atque maiestas +

We adore you and call upon your name, Lord, blessed God in eternity. Visit us with your salvation[145] and guide me in the way of peace. Be mindful of me, Christ, king of glory, and hear me in your strength, and free me from every tribulation,[146] from ill will, from perplexity, and from the dangers, of all my enemies visible and invisible; let these

Te adoramus atque invocamus, domine, nomen tuum, benedictus deus in æternum. Visita nos in salutari tuo et in via pacis me derige. Memor esto mei Christi [read Christe] rex gloriæ, et in virtute tua exaudi me, et libera me ab omnibus tribulationibus, malicia, angustij [read angustia], et periculis omnium inimicorum meorum visibilium et invisibilium; vt ista

names protect me from every adversity; let them fully free me from plague and infirmity of body and soul. And let these names of the kings (Gasper etc.) stand by with succor. And let the twelve apostles, that is Peter et cetera, and the four evangelists, that is Matthew et cetera, stand by me in all my needs and defend me and free me from all dangers both of body and soul, and from all evils past, present, and future. The Lion of the tribe of Juda, the Root of David, has prevailed.[147] Kerielyson Christe elyson Kerielyson + [24v]

nomina me protegent ab omni adversitate; plaga, et infirmitate corporis et animæ plene liberent. Et assistent in auxilium ista nomina regum Gasper + &c. Et duodecim Apostoli, videlicet Petrus &c. et 4 Evangelistes et videlicet mathæus &c. mihi assistent in omnibus necessitatibus meis ac me defendant et liberent ab omnibus periculis et corporis et animæ, et omnibus malis præteritis, præsentibus et futuris. Vicit Leo de tribu ~~David radix Iesse~~[148] Iuda radix David Aleliuha, Kerielyson Christe elyson Kerielyson + [24v]

[57.] A prayer to make taciturnitie in tortures[149]

Imparibus meritis tria pendent corpora ramis, Dismas et Gestas, in medio est diuina potestas, Dismas damnatur, Gestas ad astra leuatur:

Three bodyes on a bough doo hang, for merites of inequalytye Dismas et Gestas, in the midst the power of diuinytye. Dismas is damned, but Gestas lyfted vp aboue the starres on hye.

[58.] And also:[150]

My heart pours forth good words,[151] always the truth I will speak to the king.

Eructauit cor meum verbum bonum, veritatem umquam dicam regi

*Otherwise: As the milke of our Ladye was lussious to our Lord Iesus Christ; so let this torture or rope be pleasant to mine armes & members.

Otherwise: But Jesus passing through the midst of them went his way.[152]

Otherwise: Iesus autem transiens per medium illorum ibat

*Otherwise: Yow shall not breake a bone of him.

[59.] Counter prayers against these & all other wichcrafts, in yᵉ sayinge also whereof witches are vexed &c.[153]

My heart pours forth good words, I will speak all my works to the king.[154]

Eructauit cor meum verbum bonum dicam cuncta opera mea regi

*Otherwise: O Lord, open my lips and my mouth will declare the truth.[155]

*Otherwise: Domine labia mea aperies et os meum annunciabit veritatem

*Otherwise: Destroy the arm of the wicked criminal and the wicked tongue will be overturned.[156]

*Otherwise: Contere brachia iniqui rei et lingua maligna subuertetur

[60.] To put out the theefes eye[157]

Read yᵉ seuen psalmes wᵗʰ yᵉ letanye & then must be sayde a horrible prayer to Christ & god the father wᵗʰ a curse against the theefe. Then in the midst of the steppe of your foote, on yᵉ ground where yow stande, make a cricle lyke an eye, & write ther aboute certeine barbarous names, & driue wᵗʰ a coopers hammer or ades into the midst therof a brasen nayle consecrated saying Iustus es Domine et iusta iudica tua.[158] Then the theefe shall be bewrayed by his crynge out. [25r]

[61.] Another waye to finde out a theefe.[159]

Sticke a payre of sheeres in yᵉ rinde of a syve, & let two persons sett the topp of ech of their forefingers vpon yᵉ vpper part of yᵉ sheers howldinge yᵗ wᵗʰ the syve vp from yᵉ ground steddilye, & aske Peter & Paule whether A B or C hath stolne the thinge lost & at the nomination of the guiltye person, the syve will turne rounde.

[62.] To spoyle a theefe a witch or any other enimye & to be deliuered from yᵉ evill[160]

Vpon yᵉ Sabboth daye, before sunrisinge, cutt a hazell wand, saying: I cutt yᵉ o bough of this summers growth in the name of him whom I meane to beate or mayme. Then couer the table & saye + In nomine patris + et filij + et spiritus sancti + ter. And strickinge theron saye as followeth (english, it he that can) Crochs myroch esenaroth + betu + baroch + ass + maaroth + & then saye: holy trinitye punish him yᵗ hath this michiefe, & take yt awaye by thy great iustice, Eson + Elion + Emaris + Ales + Age. & strike the carpet with your wande.

[63.] for the crampe[161]

Bero, berco, bercoro, these three wordes must be saide three times when the crampe come vpon man or or woman, or as it is in another booke Bero, Baro, Bartora. [25v]

[64.] A horse that is forspoken

The forespoken commeth when yᵗ an vnhappye creature nameth yᵉ beast & byddeth not god saue him, & then yᵉ horse eyen will water, & he will morne. take

therfore & make a crosse in his forehead ye length of an almond & bowe[162] a pennye to S Loye[163] & then put yt wthin thy shynne & crosse him & say .3 p. n. in ye worshippe of the trinitye, & when the horse is hole take out the pennye, & offer to S. Loye then take a nayle & put yt through even betweene ye grystle nose & the bone & there will come out the quantytye of a pynt of watry bloud y^t was congeled there when he was soe forspoken, & then stoppe his eares a daye & night after wth black woll & then vnstoppe them againe, & let him bloude on both syds, & on both, vaynes under the eye & he shalbe holle

[65.] The night mare[164]
ffor ye night mare take a flynt stoune y^t hath an hole through on his owne growinge, & hange yt over the horse, & then wright thus in a byll as foloweth here. Saynt George our Ladyes knight, he walked both day & night, tyll y^t he had her, founde: he her beate & he her bounde, tyll trulye her troth, shee to him plyght, y^t shee should not come wthin the night wthin 7 roodes of a longe spare, there as S Gorges name is named thrise. And let this scripture be hanged abovte his mane. [26r]

[66.] ffor to staunch bloude[165]
To staunch bloude, first make a crosse there as he bleedeth wth this blessinge. In nomine patris et filij et spiritus sancti Amen. As verelye as god was borne in Bethelem & baptysed was in fleui Iordaine, as verelye as the floude stoode, rest thow bloude. In nomine patris &c. And say .5 p. n. in the worshipe of ye 5 woundes & also 5 Aves. [44r. Intervening folios blank.]

[67.] Pro animalibus[166]
Wright as hereafter in parchment + Iasper + melcher + Balthaser + Christofer-rus and y^t writing wth a great warell nedle, drawe it through ye right eare of ye beastes,[167] & then say in ye worshype of god & 3 kinges of Colyn[168] & sainct Christofer, orate pro nobis[169] wth this prayer ensewinge to sainct Christopher.

Whoever gazes upon the face of Saint Christopher assuredly that day shall be oppressed by no illness. In nomine patris, et filij, et spiritus sancti. Amen. Jesus you are witness where Christopher is called. Violence, hunger, or evil plague holds no sway here, and no human nor any beasts undergo graver things; he surrenders them without delay, in the hour of death. Martyr Christopher, for

Christoferi faciem sancti quicumque tuetur illo nempe die nullo languore gravetur. In nomine patris, et filij, et spiritus sancti. Amen. Tu Iesus es testis vbi christoferus nominator: vis, fames aut pestis mala ibi non dominatur, nec homo nec pecora quevis subiuntur graviora; hæc dedit absque mora existens mortis in hora. Martyr christofere, pro saluatoris honore ipsos mitte fore dignos dietatis amore; pro

the honor of the savior, send these people to become worthy of the love of the deity. For the people of Christ, confer salvation, the good thing you sought by dying; and take away heaviness of mind. Make the examination of the judge mild in all respects. Amen.

Pray for us blessed martyr Christopher, that we be made worthy of the promises of Christ.

Let us pray.

Vouchsafe merciful God, that we who make commemoration of Christopher, your blessed martyr, by his merits and prayers, be free from sudden death by pestilence and hunger, and from fear. May these animals have health through you Jesus Christ, savior of the world, whom he himself [i.e., Christopher] deserved to carry in his arms, our lord Jesus Christ. Amen. Iesus + maria + Johanes + christoferus + Jasper + melchior + balthasar + "In that time Angel Gabriel was sent [44v] to the virgin, etc."[170] and after that "In the beginning was the word, et cetera."[171]

Take holy water in this manner: "In the name of the Father and of the Son and of the Holy Spirit Amen. Lord Jesus Christ omnipotent God, bless this creature of water[172] just as you blessed the water, bitterness converted into sweetness, and the water drawn from the rock, and just as you blessed the water of the River Jordan, by which accordingly you desired to be baptized, and just as you blessed the water at the wedding feast of Cana in Galilee, which you turned into wine, and just as that same water was blessed

populo christi bona res quod moriendo petisti, confer salutem, et mentis tolle gravanem [read gravamen], Iudicis exanem [read examen] fac notis in [read mite sit] omnibus Amen.

Ora pro nobis beate martyr Christophere, ut d / i / p / x /

Oremus.

Concede quis misericors deus, vt qui beati Christoferi martyris tui commemorationem agimus, meritis et precibus vt a morte subitania [read subitanea] peste ac fame, et a timore [insert liberemur]. Animalia ista habeant sanitatem per te Iesu christe salvator mundi, quem ipse meruit portare in brachijs dominum nostrum Iesum christum, Amen. Iĥs + maria + Johanes + christoferus + Jasper + melchior + balthasar + In illo tempore missus est Angelus Gabriel [44v] vsque ad finem [read virginem] etc'. et postea 'in principio erat verbum etc.

Accipe aqua benedictam in hunc modum in nomine patris et filij et spiritus sancti Amen. Domine Jesu christe omnipotens deus benedic hanc creaturam aquæ sicut [insert benedixisti] aquam amaritudinem, in dulcedinem conversam, et aquam de silice productam, et sicut benedixisti aquam fluminis Jordani ita qua voluisti baptizari et sicut benedixisti aquam ad nuptias Canæ galaliæ, quam in vinum convertisti, et sicut ipsa aqua fuit benedicta, quæ manavit de latere tuo in die passionis tuæ, ita tu deus omnipotens

which flowed from your side on the day of your passion, accordingly you, God omnipotent father deign to bless and sanctify this creature of water by your holy name that the health of all your cattle or beasts may come about for all the faithful pouring it forth to the honor of you, o Jesus savior of the world.[173] In nomine patris et filij et spiritus sancti. Amen. Pater noster. Ave maria.

pater benedicere, et sanctificare digneris hanc creaturam aquæ, nomine sancto tuo vt fiat sanitas omnium pecorum vel bestiarum tuorum cunctis fidelibus ipsam fundentibus ad honorem tui Jesu salvator mundi. In nomine patris et filij et spiritus sancti. Amen. pater noster Ave maria

Note that this ought to be said three times and in the end a Credo should be said, and in whatever way you want it may be poured out in this water over holy water, which will have been blessed by a priest on the Lord's day according to the measure of one vial and let it be given to animals when any one of them is ill. They will not have illness, but soon in time will be delivered as has been proven. As often this word of blessing is said, sign over the water in the manner of a cross with your hand. In nomine patris et filij et spiritus sancti. Amen.

notandum est quod hæc debent dici ter, et in vltimo dicatur credo, et qualibet vice infundatur in ista aqua super benedictam aquam, quæ fuerit benedicta a sacerdote in die dominico pro mensuram vnius filiole [read fiole], et detur animalibus cum aliquis eorum sic [read sit] infirmus. Non habebunt infirmitatem, sed breve infra tempus deliberabuntur vt probatum est. Quotiens hoc verbum benedixisti [read benedictionis] dicatur signa aquam in modum crucis cum manu tua, In nomine patris et filij et spiritus sancti. Amen.

[68.] For sick pigs

In nomine patris etc. Lord God Christ Father and Son and Holy Spiritbless this creature of barley in the name of the Father et cetera that it be a wholesome remedy, and aid to human kind and livestock through the invocation of your most holy name that the pigs who will eat of it may remain sound and healthy, and may thrive and grow old by your name through our lord Jesus Christ your son, who with you et cetera. Whence I conjure you, barley, by the Father and the Son and the Holy Spirit, by Mark, Matthew, Luke, and John, and by the twelve prophets of God, and by the twelve apostles, and by the forty-four

Pro porcis infirmis

In nomine patris etc. Domine Deus christus pater et filius et spiritus sanctus benedic istam creaturam ordei in nomine patris etc. vt sit salutare remedium, et auxilium humano generi et pecori per invocationem sanctissimi nominis tui vt porci qui ex eo gustaverint sani et salui permaneat, et in nomine tuo [45r] valeant et senescant per dominum nostrum Iesum christum filium tuum qui tecum etc. Unde coniuro te ordeum per patrem et filium et spiritum sanctum per martium matheum, Lucam et Johannem et per dei duodecim prophetas, et per duodecim Apostoles, et per centum quadraginta quatuor milia innocentum martyrum vt illa animalia

thousand innocent martyrs, that these animals which eat of you may suffer nothing bad, neither from this infirmity, nor from a future one of this kind nor from one taken away. Saint James sat sadly on the marble stone. Then came Jesus and asked him, "Why do you sit and why are you sad?" And he said, "Lord, tell me, what should I make for my animals which you have given to me and it [the disease?] has borne away from my throat." The Lord said, "Take barley that I have prepared for your work, and give it to your animals that they may receive good health." Amen. Then say 3 pater noster et 3 Ave ma. et vno credo

quæ de te manducant nullum malum habeant nec de hac infirmitate, nec de futura de talis [read tali], nec de Elate [read elata]. Sanctus iacobus sedebat tristis super petra marmoriam [read marmoream] tunc venit Iesus et ait illi, quare sedes et es tristis, et dixit, domine iube me que faciam animalibus meis que mihi donasti tulitque de gutture meo. Ait dominus, accipe ordeum quod preparavi ad opus tuum, et da animalibus tuis vt ipsi accipiant sanitatem. Amen. Tunc dic 3 pater noster et 3 Aue ma. et vno credo.

And it should be noted that whenever someone says this, "N. ought to pour out holy water," then he says a Pater Noster making a cross with two fingers and his thumb. Then he piles up the barley, and in the end should be said a Pater Noster and Ave and Credo. Often proven, but it is necessary for this to be recited three times. [45v]

Et notandum est quod quotiescumque Aliquis dixerit istam, N. debeat infundere aquam benedictam, tum dixerit pater noster faciendo crucem cum duobus digitis et police suo. Deinde cumelat [read cumulet] sursum ordium, et in vltimo dicatur pater noster et Ave, et credo. Sæpe probatum fuerit sed oportet tribus vicibus recitari. [45v]

[69. Three Biters Charm] for yᵉ woman[174]

Bitters + Bitters + Bitters + three the hart doth thinke + the eye doth see + In the name of God the father + God the sonne + and God ye holy Ghost blesse thee + Amen + Catton.

[70. Three Biters Charm] ffor the man

Bitter + Bitters + Bitters + Three + the black bitter hath bitten the + In the name of God the father + God the sonne + God the holy Ghost blesse thee + Amen + Catton

[And in margin:] Then nyppe thrice in thre severall places.

[71. For bloating]

Elicampanam for yᵉ winde collicke to be drunke with ale or wine

Notes

1. It seems likely the implication is "heaven" or "celestial fatherland."

2. Psalm 85:6. Also used in the Ordinary of the Latin Mass. Francis Procter and Christopher Wordsworth, eds., *Breviarium ad usum insignis ecclesiae Sarum*, 3 vols. (Cambridge, U.K.: Alma Mater Academia, 1879–86), 2:53, 153, 239.

3. This seems to derive from the liturgy (either the Sarum or Bangor usage) that read, "Deus cui omne cor patet, et omnis voluntas loquitur, et quem nullum latet secretum." Francis Henry Dickinson, *Missale ad usum insignis et præclaræ ecclesiæ Sarum*, 4 vols. (Burntisland: E prelo de Pitsligo, 1861), 2:579. Possibly there was a copying error here with the scribe picking up the "cui" and then skipping to "nulum latet."

4. This is generally not an angel name but rather a conventional divine name.

5. A common liturgical formula based on Philippians 2:10–11.

6. The text has either "cum armilla sputa" (with a ring of spit) or "cum armilla spnea" (with a ring of thorn) but is not clear. The latter makes marginally more sense.

7. Conjectural. The first sigil is ambiguous and could also be ☿ or ♄. As is stands this would be mean Friday or Thursday.

8. This stands for "nomen," meaning the operator is to insert the relevant name here.

9. That is, perform magic to find treasure or to acquire knowledge.

10. The scribe intends the reader to repeat the first words of the previous prayer "O my lord God in whose presence are all thinges, wch be in heaven, earth, sea and the deepe places . . . ," to continue with "by the merites of . . ." as written in this line, and to conclude with "I beseech thee y^t it maye appeare in this glasse to N. or N . . ." Just so with the subsequent lines.

11. In apocryphal literature Longinus is a name given to the centurion who pierced Jesus's side with a spear during the crucifixion. Gospel of Nicodemus 16:7. In later traditions he is treated as a saint.

12. = The end.

13. How the scribe intended material on this page to be used is unclear. The instructions to put crosses in the corners and on the back suggests that the figure was intended as a talisman or lamina rather than a magic circle, although the text contains no clear indication how such an item is to be made or used. At the same time, the entire circular figure forms the initial *O* in the text that follows (i.e., "O thou spirit . . .") The text in the circular figure refers to the four evangelists—Matthew, Mark, Luke, and John—and then clockwise from the top right the text reads, "Son, redeemer of the world, have mercy upon us / Holy trinity, one God, have mercy upon us / Lord God, have mercy upon us / Father, God of Heaven, have mercy upon us." These phrases were drawn from and based on the Litany: "Pater de caelis Deus, miserere nobis. Fili redemptor mundi Deus, miserere nobis. Spiritus sancte Deus, miserere nobis. Sancta Trinitas unus Deus, miserere nobis." Procter and Wordsworth, eds., *Breviarium ad usum insignis ecclesiae Sarum*, 2:250. In addition to basic mistakes in Latin like "uno" for "unus" and otiose macrons on "dominus" and "trinitas," the line concerning the Holy Spirit has been replaced with "Dominus deus."

14. The scribe quotes Mark 16:16. It is not clear if this passage was intended to be part of the above figure or read out loud.

15. These two phrases are psalm incipits, suggesting the reader should recite them from memory and in Latin. Despite being in Latin, the psalm numbers that follow them employ the Protestant numbering system. The scribe's sympathy for the Latin of the "old religion" evidently did not drive him to a Catholic Bible, where they would be Psalms 53 and 66.

16. The passage alludes to the complex theology of the Trinity articulated in particular in the Athanasian Creed, employed by both the Catholic and Anglican churches.

17. Mark 14:65. The subsequent passage loosely follows the typical invocation of the instruments of the passion.

18. Luke 22:43 says only that the angel comforted Jesus on the Mount of Olives.

19. This is a common formula in conjurations and occurs in other conjuring manuals, such as London, British Library, Sloane 3846, fol. 69r; London, Wellcome Library, Wellcome 110, fols.

14v–16r; and London, British Library, Additional 36674, fol. 71r. A similar formula appears below using the ten words spoken during creation (fols. 9r–10r). Reginald Scot discusses this in *Discoverie of Witchcraft*, bk. 2, chap. 8 and bk. 15, chap. 24. The invocation draws on the accounts of the passion from all four gospels. Jesus intercedes on behalf of his executioners in Luke 23:34. He addresses his mother and disciples and cries "I thirst" in John 19:26–28. The call "Eli, Eli, lama sabachthani?" echoes Psalms 22:1 and occurs in Matthew 27:46 and Mark 15:34. In John 19:30 Jesus says "It is finished" and in Luke 23:46 "Into your hands I commit my spirit."

20. A common interpretation of Jesus's words was that he thirsted for the salvation of all human souls.

21. In theological terms this is a peculiar claim, since it is generally understood that the devil and his minions were damned irrevocably at the time of the fall. The threat that demons should suffer greater punishments due to disobeying the good Christian conjurer is nonetheless quite common in necromantic manuals.

22. Excommunication means removal from the community of the faithful; in Catholic terms it means being barred from the sacraments. Once again this is an odd threat to make against a creature already outside the Church and not under any circumstances having access to the sacraments. Nonetheless, invocations of demons commonly take the form of curses and it is in this sense that the term should probably be understood.

23. John 3:16.

24. This passage draws on the first creation account in Genesis 1. Like the formula found above that uses the words Jesus spoke during the passion (fols. 7v–8r), this formula is also attested in other manuscripts. See for example British Library, Additional 36674, fol. 43r.

25. The creation myth of God speaking the world into existence is the foundational demonstration of the power of divine words. Here the incantation links these unknown divine words spoken by God with the known divine names used here and elsewhere in magic operations or charms.

26. That is, what is written on the next page (fol. 10v).

27. Stole, a liturgical garment.

28. In the Old Testament hyssop (an herb in the mint family) is used for purification rites. See for example Numbers 19. This began with its use for marking the doors in Exodus 12:22–23. In Christian settings, Psalm 51 was employed in both Catholic and Lutheran liturgies in "Asperges," a ritual in which the congregation is sprinkled with holy water: "Asparges me hysopo et mundabor" (Ps. 50:9 Vulg.), translated as 'Thou shalt purge me with hyssop, and I shall be clean' (Ps. 51:9). Hyssop commonly appears as an element in medieval ritual magic practices. See for example the Boxgrove Manual, item 2.

29. = The end of this work.

30. An almost identical charm in London, British Library, Sloane 121, fol. 163r, is discussed by Olsan in "Latin Charms of Medieval England," 132. Olsan compares this charm to others that employ a dialogue with Jesus. The charm echoes, but does not accurately recount, the cure of Peter's mother-in-law of a fever in Matthew 8:14. It also echoes Jesus's suggestion that one will receive what one asks for in his name in John 14:13–14 and 16:23–24. Like items 37 and 42 below, it also follows the common "encounter charm" pattern described by Ferdinand Orht and Lea Olsan. See Olsan, "Three Good Brothers Charm."

31. A common medieval explanation for the 144,000 taken from the tribes of Israel in the final days (Rev. 7:4) is that they are the male children slaughtered by Herod (Matt. 2:16–18). These biblical passages were rehearsed in Elizabethan liturgy for Innocents Day. See William Keatinge Clay, ed., *Liturgical Services: Liturgies and Occasional Forms of Prayer Set Forth in the Reign of Queen Elizabeth* (Cambridge, U.K.: Cambridge University Press, 1847), 84–85.

32. A common operation for thieves conventionally known as the Eye of Abraham. Another version of the same charm appears in item 61. Other manuscript examples include London, British Library, Additional 34111, fol. 75r, Sloane 3846, fols. 41r and 83r–v, and Sloane 3542, fol. 19r. See Stephen Stallcup, "The 'Eye of Abraham' Charm for Thieves: Versions in Middle and Early Modern English," *Magic, Ritual, and Witchcraft* 10, no. 1 (2015): 23–40.

33. Also known as litharge, this is lead oxide, a by-product of the silver smelting process that had been used since antiquity for various medical and cosmetic purposes. See Mary Oikonoma-kou et al., "Litharge from Laurion: A Medical and Metallurgical Commodity from South Attika," *L'antiquité classique* 68 (1999): 299–308.

34. The text has "Achor seruo tuo iosuæ," which makes no sense. Joshua has a servant named Achan, punished in Achor; perhaps the two names are confused here.

35. This passage recalls several biblical stories in which the truth was revealed. For the theft of Achan and his punishment in Achor, see Joshua 7:16–26. Solomon discovers the true mother of an infant in 1 Kings 3:16–28. For the story of Susanna, a book regarded as apocryphal by Protestants, see Susanna 1. Mathias was chosen by lot to replace Judas as the twelfth apostle in Acts 1. The text has "declinasti" (turned aside). It is possible that this is a mistranscription of "declarasti" (made manifest).

36. A general term for a pointed implement.

37. The meaning of this is unclear. It roughly translates as hanging or pendant water. It is not impossible that this is a euphemism for urine or a man's urine.

38. Luke 4:30.

39. This is a reference to the biblical account of Jasper, Melchior, and Balthasar, the three wise men who visited Jesus shortly after his birth in Matthew 2:1–12.

40. Partial quote from Psalm 31:9 Vulg. that does not entirely make sense without the pre-ceding phrase "Nolite fieri sicut equus et mulus, quibus non est intellectus. In camo et freno maxillas eorum constringe, qui non approximant ad te" ("Do not be like a horse or a mule, without understanding, whose temper must be curbed with bit and bridle, else it will not stay near you"; Ps. 32:9).

41. Direct quote from Exodus 15:16.

42. A direct quote from Psalm 68:24 Vulg.—"Obscurentur oculi eorum, ne videant, et dor-sum eorum semper incurve" (Let their eyes be darkened that they see not; and their back bend thou down always)—which has been bisected by a short additional phrase.

43. A Latin version of the common Dismas and Gismas charm that appears in English below in item 10 and in another Latin version in item 57. Other related examples of this Latin formula occur in Oxford, Bodleian Library, Ashmole 1378, pp. 62 and 77. In the account of the crucifixion in Luke 23:39–43, Jesus is crucified between two thieves (*latrones*). According to later traditions, their names were Dismas and Gismas (Gesmas). Unsurprisingly, their names are commonly invoked in charms for stolen goods or theft. See for example Oxford, Bodleian Library, Rawlinson D. 252, fol. 121r. See also London, British Library, Additional 36674, p. 89.

44. This appears to have been drawn from a responsory form of the Lord's Prayer. Full stops are the standard way to represent ellipses in this circumstance. See Francis Procter, *A History of the Book of Common Prayer* (New York: Macmillan, 1907), 188.

45. Psalms 61:3 (Ps. 60:4 Vulg.).

46. A quartan fever is a fever that relapses every four days, common in certain types of malaria.

47. The three Latin phrases are "Jesus was born," "Jesus was crucified," and "Jesus rose and may Jesus deliver from this illness."

48. That is, say three Ave Marias on three successive days.

49. = In the name of the Father and of the Son and of the Holy Spirit.

50. The manuscript has "as it was zo ile will to bringe vs out of thraldome."

51. The manuscript has "which is here not." This seems like a simple error, although it is conceivable that it refers to the dormant stage of the illness.

52. = Moses lamented, called out.

53. This charm departs from the usual pattern and asks for five Pater Nosters, Ave Marias, and Creeds (or perhaps the intention is only one Creed, which is usual).

54. The intent could be that this should be a prayer to be recited while picking an herb. However, given that the charm seems to be for protecting one's house and goods, it seems more likely this is a mistranscription of herber (from herberwe), meaning home. See *DIMEV* 4259;

Douglas Gray, "Notes on Some Middle English Charms," in *Chaucer and Middle English Studies in Honour of Rossell Hope Robbins*, ed. Beryl Rowland (London: Allen and Unwin, 1974), 100. Cf. items 8 and 57.

55. Possibly this was is a mistranscription of "two," which makes better sense, referring to the thieves.

56. The fragment is drawn from the Latin version of this charm meaning "in the middle, the divine power."

57. = vanity?

58. On this charm see Jonathan Roper, *English Verbal Charms* (Helsinki: Suomalainen Tie-deakatemia, 2005), 96–99.

59. Literally, "he/she rightly gets better," possibly a mistranscription of "convalescet," "he will get better."

60. For a close relative of this charm, see Olsan, "Corpus of Charms in the Middle English Leechcraft Remedy Books," 224.

61. It is unclear if the charm intends one to write "Christus" or the abbreviation.

62. = sick [person].

63. = the angel announces.

64. = John preached [i.e., Saint John the Baptist].

65. "The spirit of the lord has refilled." This refers to a passage in Wisdom or the Wisdom of Solomon (1:7), which was considered apocryphal by Protestants but was an antiphon in common liturgical use prior to the Reformation.

66. For a close relative of this charm, see Olsan, "Corpus of Charms in the Middle English Leechcraft Remedy Books," 218. Charms for bleeding that invoke the story of Longinus, the soldier who pierced Jesus's side with a spear during the crucifixion, are common. See Olsan, "Latin Charms of Medieval England," 130. At no point in the New Testament does Jesus bid the Jordan River stand still.

67. For the Jordan stopping (although not when commanded by Christ), see Joshua 3:13–16. For this common story of Jesus stopping the river see items 32, 44, and 66.

68. For a close relative of this charm, see Olsan, "Corpus of Charms in the Middle English Leechcraft Remedy Books," 219. Writing on leaves and drinking water or wine in which they have been infused occurs in other magical contexts. See Véronèse, "Magic, Theurgy, and Spirituality in the Medieval Ritual of the *Ars Notoria*," 44.

69. = I adjure you by the angels that this man, N., should sleep.

70. = know.

71. The almonds would thus contain (translating the Latin) "1. + God is father, 2. ++ Christ, balm of the saints, 3. +++ the son is truth, 4. ++++ Christ balm of the saints, 5. +++++ God is father, and 6. ++++++ the son is truth."

72. For a close relative of this charm, see Olsan, "Corpus of Charms in the Middle English Leechcraft Remedy Books," 219.

73. = assuredly tell you the truth.

74. The reading is conjectural. The last three letters are not clear.

75. The MS has "styld."

76. = and say five Pater Nosters in honor of blessed Apolonia and for the souls of her father and mother [assuming "eius"]. See Olsan, "Latin Charms of Medieval England," 130. Among the tortures inflicted on Saint Apollonia during her martyrdom was having all of her teeth pulled. She is therefore called on in cures for toothaches.

77. = an approved medicine for fevers. For a relative of this charm see Olsan, "Corpus of Charms in the Middle English Leechcraft Remedy Books," 220–21.

78. = Christus Agios Dominus. The first and last words are "Christ" and "Lord." The middle one should be "Agios," a mistranscription of the standard Greek word meaning saint or sacred. It initiates a Greek formula employed sometimes in the Latin liturgy, "Agios O Theos" (Ἅγιος ὁ Θεός), meaning "Holy God," which is picked up in the next part of the charm.

79. = resurrected from the dead, Lord.

80. For a relative of this charm see Olsan, "Latin Charms of Medieval England," 219. This charm, as with the one that may be found at the end of this folio, follows the common practice of invoking Anne, Elizabeth, and Mary for childbirth. See ibid., 130.

81. The Latin elements are "Mary gave birth to Christ + Anna to Mary + Elizabeth to John + Cecilia to Remigius." Cecilia is evidently a mistranscription of Cilinia, traditionally the mother of Saint Remegius. See "Genovefa (423–502)," in Jo Ann McNamara, John E. Halborg, and E. Gordon Whatley, *Sainted Women of the Dark Ages* (Durham, N.C.: Duke University Press, 1992), 28.

The last formula is a palindrome usually written in a square as follows.

S	A	T	O	R
A	R	E	P	O
T	E	N	E	T
O	P	E	R	A
R	O	T	A	S

The meaning of the text is not clear, but it became one of the most long-lived magic squares, comparable in longevity to "abracadabra" (also a palindrome and typically written in a triangle form). Although its first appearance, prior to 79 CE in Pompei, suggests it might not be Christian, that the letters can be construed as an anagram for paternoster in the shape of a cross plus *a* and *o* for alpha and omega standing on the arms may account for its tremendous popularity and survival. See J. Gwyn Griffiths, "'Arepo' in the Magic 'Sator' Square," *Classical Review*, n.s., 21, no. 1 (1971): 6–8. It became common in childbirth charms. See for example Olsan, "Marginality of Charms in Medieval England," 143–44. For the long view see Richard-Ernst Bader, "Sator Arepo: Magie in der Volksmedizin," *Medizin-Historisches Journal* 22 (1987): 115–34.

82. For a useful discussion of this charm and its history see Katelyn Mesler, "The Three Magi and Other Christian Motifs in Medieval Hebrew Medical Incantations: A Study in the Limits of Faithful Translation," in *Latin into Hebrew: Texts and Studies. Volume I: Studies*, ed. Resianne Fontaine and Gad Freudenthal (Leiden: Brill, 2013), 164–66. A similar prayer may be found in Scot's *Discoverie of Witchcraft*, 231–32.

83. This should be Balthazar. The alternate name used here is unusual.

84. This phrase derives from the Litany of the Saints and was perhaps originally drawn from a primer or book of hours. See for example Stephen W. Lawley, ed., *Breviarium Ad Usum Insignis Ecclesie Eboracensis*, 2 vols. (Edinburgh: Surtees Society, 1880–82), 1:934. The York usage quoted here sometimes includes both *sancti* and *sanctae*, which the Salisbury usage does not.

85. The term "probatum" is frequently added to "secrets" or magic operations. It has less the sense of having been experimentally evaluated (although it includes that sense) than having been examined and deemed fit or perhaps approved. For use in medical contexts, see Claire Jones, "Formula and Formulation: 'Efficacy Phrases' in Medieval English Medical Manuscripts," *Neuphilologische Mitteilungen* 99, no. 2 (1998): 199–209; Francisco Alonso-Almeida and Mercedes Cabrera-Abreu, "The Formulation of Promise in Medieval English Medical Recipes: A Relevance-Theoretic Approach," *Neophilologus* 86, no. 1 (2002): 137–54.

86. A "hawe" refers to some sort of growth in the eye. For a close relative of this charm see Olsan, "Corpus of Charms in the Middle English Leechcraft Remedy Books," 217–18.

87. = Christ conquers + Christ reigns + Christ commands + Christ lives and reigns without end.

88. This passage refers to the miracle of the loaves and fishes in John 6:1–5 and to the raising of Lazarus in John 11:38–44. The translation is somewhat conjectural.

89. Typically "virgin wax" simply meant wax that had not been used before. It remains unclear whether the scribe understood this to be something else, such as a substance owned by a virgin or somehow associated with virgins.

90. = liberator or savior of teeth.

91. It is not clear if the following prayer is also to be written or simply recited.

92. As above, Apollonia is invoked for a toothache. See Olsan, "Latin Charms of Medieval England," 130.

93. The Latin has "slow" Apollonia, which seems an unlikely intent. I have suggested reading this as *lenis*, but *sancta* (saint) is also conceivable.

94. = dure [i.e., trouble].

95. This common charm is discussed at length in Olsan, "Three Good Brothers Charm." For a Latin relative of this charm see Olsan, "Corpus of Charms in the Middle English Leechcraft Remedy Books," 221. See also Ilona Tuomi, "Parchment, Praxis and Performance of Charms in Early Medieval Ireland," *Incantatio* 3 (2013): 60–85.

96. The section of the charm is awkwardly abbreviated. In the conventional medieval version Jesus asks the brethren where they are going; they respond (as here) that they are looking for herbs to heal their brethren's wounds. Here the intent seems to be similar: "'Whither?' [was said] by the Son. So the Three Good Brethren [said] . . ."

97. For a close relative of this charm see Olsan, "Corpus of Charms in the Middle English Leechcraft Remedy Books," 219. This text follows the form of the Latin charm to staunch blood (see above, item 13) by citing Jesus standing in the Jordan River. As Olsan suggests, the simple description of the "core element" (i.e., Jesus in the river) may have been enough to invoke the narrative expressed fully in the Latin version and its affective and/or magical power. "Latin Charms of Medieval England," 130.

98. The reading is very much conjectural after "spinia" (thorny). See Peter Jones and Lea Olsan, "Middleham Jewel: Ritual, Power, and Devotion," *Viator* 31 (2000): 249–90; Don C. Skemer, *Binding Words: Textual Amulets in the Middle Ages* (University Park: Pennsylvania State University Press, 2006), passim, for *ananyzapta* (sometimes *ananizapta* or *anazapta*). The word "ananyzapta" occurs as an element in other amulets and prayers. For amulets, see item 36 below; for prayers see Eamon Duffy, *Marking the Hours: English People and Their Prayers, 1240–1570* (New Haven, Conn.: Yale University Press, 2006), 94. It also occurs in conjunction with the three kings' names on the Coventry Ring. British Museum, "Coventry Ring," AF.897, http://www.britishmuseum.org/.

99. = For falling sickness [i.e., epilepsy].

100. For another version of this charm see Olsan, "Corpus of Charms in the Middle English Leechcraft Remedy Books," 217.

101. The charm refers to the battle between Pope Leo III and Charlemagne at Roncevaux or Roncesvalles in 778, mythologized in the *Chanson de Roland*. For other versions of this charm see London, British Library, Sloane 121, fols. 183v–184r; and Scot, *Discoverie of Witchcraft*, 232–33.

102. The reference to Tresilian is curious. Robert Tresilian was executed for treason in 1388. Thomas Favent's politically motivated account of the execution has Tresilian boldly declaring on the scaffold that he could not be harmed due to items he carried on his person. He was stripped and several amulets were removed from him before he was successfully hanged. This hardly seems a "proof" of the power of anything he might have had on his body. Thomas Favent, *Historia siue narracio de modo et forma mirabilis parliamenti apud Westmonasterium anno domini millesimo CCCLXXXVI regni vero regis Ricardi secundi post conquestum anno decimo, per Thomam Fauent clericum indicata*, Camden Miscellany 14, Camden 3rd ser. 37 (London: Offices of the Royal Historical Society, 1926), 17–18. Partially translated in Thomas Bayly Howell, Thomas Jones Howell, William Cobbett, and David Jardine, eds., *Cobbett's Complete Collection of State Trials and Proceedings for High Treason and Other Crimes and Misdemeanors from the Earliest Period to the Present Time*, 33 vols. (London: R. Bagshaw, 1809), 1:115–19. Nonetheless a long history of associating this textual amulet with Tresilian's execution is attested in the devotional miscellany of the monk John Northwood. See London, British Library, Additional 37787, fols. 175v–176r. Don Skemer regards the reference to Tresilian as an addition to the charm by Northwood rather than simply an element in the charm he copied. This is credible inasmuch as the execution was contemporary. Northwood wrote his book between 1386 and 1410. See Skemer, *Binding Words*, 193–99. Although Tresilian appears in a late-Elizabethan play titled *Thomas of Woodcock*, no mention of the magical talismans he was reputed to have used is made in it.

103. Many of the names in this list and often sections in the same order (e.g., *agnus, ouis, vitulus, serpens, aries, leos,* and *vermis*) appear in the "Alma chorus domini," a portion of the liturgy which provides a list of divine names. See Dickinson, *Missale ad usum insignis et praecl-arae ecclesiae Sarum,* 1:439–40 (Feria quinta post Pentacosten). Cf. lists of divine names in Boxgrove Manual, items 12 and 13.

104. = whoever then carries the names of these kings with him + will be free from the falling sickness by the mercy of the Lord. The scribe or a previous scribe has incorporated a charm for epilepsy into this list of divine names, seemingly unaware of the Latin meaning. At least, if he did understand it, the scribe of this manuscript copied out the Latin as he found it. The same words appear in item 24 above. The use of similar sentence fragments from other charms in the remainder of this passage suggests the same.

105. = Heal me and save me and care for me, lord my God, from every evil and from all of my infirmities.

106. = that they defend from every evil and danger, and from all of my infirmities. Amen. This is a grammatical fragment. It is possible that a main verb such as "I invoke" was understood prior to the list of saints' and angels' names (i.e., "I invoke Michael, Gabriel . . . that they . . .").

107. = In the beginning was the word, et cetera. The intention is evidently that one is to recite the first chapter of the Gospel of John from memory. The passage was commonly used in exorcisms and also appeared in magic practice. See for example Oxford, Bodleian Library, Rawlinson D. 252, fol. 35v.

108. The same encounter charm pattern is found in item 43.

109. = cinquefoil.

110. Presumably this means to lay it to the hollow inside the cheek against the teeth.

111. = pray for us.

112. = dure [i.e., trouble].

113. Cf. *DIMEV* 2153, which shares some common lines.

114. = Maccabeus.

115. *Hicsananie* is evidently a corruption of *hic sanare* (heal this). The meaning or source of *wederhylwe* is obscure.

116. A relative of this text may be found in Cambridge, University Library, D.5.76, fol. 67v. The text of figure 2 reads, "Let the five wounds of God / be medicines to me. / As medicines to me let the dutiful death / and passion of Christ be." This is a common prayer. See for example Sloane 3160 quoted in Tony Hunt, *Popular Medicine in Thirteenth-Century England: Introduction and Texts* (Cambridge, U.K.: D. S. Brewer, 1990), 98.

117. = fairies.

118. A marginal note has "9 times wth 3 +."

119. = goodness.

120. This text employs the "encounter charm" pattern, as does item 37.

121. *DIMEV* 1018 lists sixteen versions of this charm. Cf. items 13, 32, and 66.

122. Roper, *English Verbal Charms,* 104–9.

123. Items 48–62 were copied from Scot, *Discoverie of Witchcraft* (1584), 230–31. All subsequent references are to this edition.

124. The scribe has copied the translation of this passage provided in the *Discoverie* below. As a result, here and below I have not provided an additional translation of the Latin.

125. Scot, *Discoverie of Witchcraft,* 231.

126. Scot has "immunitie."

127. Scot has "in this order following."

128. Scot, *Discoverie of Witchcraft,* 232–33.

129. The intent here is probably "the epistle of the holy savior."

130. The final five words were added by the scribe.

131. This is not the name of the scribe of the Antiphoner Notebook, since it also appears in Scot. Presumably it reflects an earlier version of the amulet in which the scribe wrote in his own name.

132. This section in Scot is titled "A popish priapt or charme, which must neuer be said, but carried about one, against theeues." Scot, *Discoverie of Witchcraft*, 233. The scribe began to write "charm" but evidently decided that he preferred not to use Scot's word and wrote "prayer" instead.

133. Strings of letters such as appear here may simply be understood as magical words, but in some cases they originate as abbreviations of prayers. For an example of prayers abbreviated in this fashion see London, British Library, Sloane 3849, fol. 40r. For a short formula abbreviated in this way see item 67 below. The scribe's transcription from Scot is perfect except for the fourth-to-last letter, which is an *o* rather than an *e*. The scribe also adds "Amen" to the end of this item. In Scot this is followed by a charm for epilepsy and a protective amulet of Pope Leo (*Discoverie of Witchcraft*, 231–33). He has already copied other versions of both of these (items 36 and 24 respectively) and so skips over them here.

134. Luke 4:30.

135. Scot, *Discoverie of Witchcraft*, 233–34.

136. Scot has "titulus."

137. "Titulus triumphalis" is a common phrase used to refer to the letters affixed to the cross above Jesus, INRI (i.e., *Iesus Nazarenus Rex Iudaeorum* or Jesus the Nazarene King of the Jews). John 19:19–20, cf. Luke 23:38. The phrases that follow are "Behold the sign of the lord's cross. + Flee you hostile powers. The Lion that comes from the tribe of Juda, from the stock of David conquered." The first phrase occurs elsewhere in charms. See Stephen A. Mitchell, *Witchcraft and Magic in the Nordic Middle Ages*, Middle Ages Series (Philadelphia: University of Pennsylvania Press, 2011), 227. The second one echoes Revelation 5:5.

138. For another version of this charm related to the Scot version, see Christopher Wordsworth, ed., *Horae Eboracenses: The Prymer or Hours of the Blessed Virgin Mary According to the Use of the Illustrious Church of York*, Publications of the Surtees Society 132 (Durham, U.K.: Andrews & Co., 1920), 80. See also László Sándor Chardonnens and Rosanne Hebing, "Two Charms in a Late Medieval English Manuscript at Nijmegen University Library," *Review of English Studies* 62, no. 245 (2011): 181–92; Lawley, *Breviarium Ad Usum Insignis Ecclesie Eboracensis*, 1:889.

139. The passage in Scot reads, "I find in a Primer intituled The houres of our Lady, after the vse of the church of Yorke, printed anno 1516. a charme with this titling in red letters; To all them that afore this image of pity devoutly shall say five *Pater nosters*, five *Aues*, and one *Credo*, pitiouslie beholding these armes of Christs passion, are granted thirtie two thousand seuen hundred fiftie fiue yeares of pardon. It is to be thought that this pardon was granted in the time of pope *Boniface* the ninth; for *Platina* saith that the pardons were sold so cheape, that the apostolicall authority grew into contempt." *Discoverie of Witchcraft*, 234.

140. Illustrations of the instruments of the passion are typically included in written charms, although not in this manuscript or in Scot. See Mary Agnes Edsall, "*Arma Christi* Rolls or Textual Amulets? The Narrow Roll Format Manuscripts of 'O Vernicle,'" *Magic, Ritual, and Witchcraft* 9, no. 2 (2014): 178–209.

141. Here the scribe has combined what Scot calls "A papistical charm" and "A charm found in the canon of the masse" in a single new charm. He also discards Scot's translations. *Discoverie of Witchcraft*, 234.

142. The scribe has adjusted Scot's wording of the title from "charm" to "prayer." From that point on, this item duplicates Scot except for minor spelling variations and the fact that Scot lays it out in verse form. Ibid., 235.

143. Scot only provides the first four divine names in this section, noting that there are thirty-four missing. Scot continues with "Ista nomina me protegant . . ." The scribe has filled in the list that follows from some other source, including some of the following phrases (i.e., from "Iesus" to " . . . et invisibilium / . . . and invisible"). He connected the added material to Scot's text with "vt," making the Latin somewhat clumsy. The original intent was simply a connected series of statements rather than purpose clauses. The scribe also added the concluding phrase "vicit Leo de tribu Iuda radix David." Ibid., 236. Cf. Wordsworth, *Horae Eboracenses*, 126.

144. = Christ conquers + Christ reigns + Christ commands.

145. Psalms 106:4 (105:4 Vulg.).

146. Although it does not quote the Bible precisely, this passage evokes the language of the Latin Psalms with phrases like "memor esto" and "exaudi me."

147. Revelation 5:5.

148. This copying error suggests that the scribe had some familiarity with church Latin, the phrase "radix iesse" (i.e., the stem or root of Jesse) being a commonly cited biblical verse and a key linking of Jesus to the messianic prophesy of Isaiah. See Isaiah 11:1 and Romans 15:12. The biblical passage explicitly linking Jesus to David through Jesse may be found in Luke 3:23–38.

149. Scot, *Discoverie of Witchcraft*, 259. The Dismas and Gismas formula also appears in items 8 and 10.

150. Ibid., 259. The scribe has reproduced the asterisks used as dividers in Scot. Scot provides no translation.

151. Psalms 45:1 (44:1 Vulg.). The scribe follows Scot and duplicating his marginal reference to Psalm 44.

152. Luke 4:30.

153. Scot, *Discoverie of Witchcraft*, 260.

154. Psalms 45:1 (44:1 Vulg.).

155. Psalms 51:15 (50:17 Vulg.).

156. Psalms 10:15 (9:36 Vulg.).

157. Scot, *Discoverie of Witchcraft*, 262. Cf. above, item 6.

158. = You are just Lord, and just are your judgements [assuming "iudicia"].

159. Scot, *Discoverie of Witchcraft*, 262–63. The scribe has not transcribed a considerable section in which Scot rejects this widespread practice as "verie bable" and attempts to debunk it. The practice employs a pair of shears that are made of a single piece of metal. These are clamped around the wooden band forming the outside of the sieve (i.e., the rind). Two people then suspend the two items from the upper part of the shears with their fingers so that the sieve can rotate. The practice is the poor man's version of the common key and psalter method also for detecting thieves. Both employ the ideomotor phenomenon, the mechanism behind the modern ouija board.

160. Ibid., 269–70.

161. This section is not taken from Scot's *Discoverie of Witchcraft* and was written by a later hand, the same one that writes on folio 45v.

162. = vow.

163. Saint Eligius, or in French Éloi, is among other things the patron saint of horses and horsemen.

164. *DIMEV* 4601. An almost identical charm (although evidently not the source of this passage) may be found in Thomas Blundeville, *The Fower Chiefyst Offices Belongyng to Horsemanshippe. . . .* (London: By VVyllyam Seres dwellyng at the west ende of Paules churche, at the signe of the Hedgehogge, [1566]), 17–18. Blundeville explains that nightmares (in the classic sense of a bad dream) affect both humans and horses. He says of this passage, "A fonde folishe charme, which bicause it may perhappes make you gentle reader to laugh, as well as it did me, for recreation sake I will here rehearse it." It may be of interest that this passage also includes some anti-Catholic sentiment as we find in Scot. After recounting the charm he concludes, "With suche proper charmes as this is, the false Fryers in tymes paste were wonte to charme the money out of playne folkes purses." A slightly different version of this charm is listed as a cure for an incubus in Scot, *Discoverie of Witchcraft*, 87. See also Kittredge, *Witchcraft in Old and New England*, 220.

165. Cf. items 13, 32, and 44.

166. This entire item was at some stage adapted from liturgical sources and has deep roots in medieval devotion. The text is closely related to the commemoration of Saint Christopher in the *Burnet Psalter* (fol. 23r–v) and *Horae Eboracenses*, although it is ordered differently and contains many transcription errors. The operation with holy water that follows the prayers is certainly an addition. See Michael Arnott et al., "The Burnet Psalter," University of Aberdeen

Special Collections, http://www.abdn.ac.uk/. See also Wordsworth, *Horae Eboracenses*, 132–33. The line "ut d / i / p / x /" is an abbreviation for "ut digni efficiamur promissionibus Christi," a formula employed in masses commemorating particular saints (e.g., on a particular saint's day). Terence Bailey, *The Processions of Sarum and the Western Church*, Studies and Texts (Toronto: Pontifical Institute Publications, 1971), 49–50. It was also used as a response in the liturgy for the "suffrages of the saints." Suffrages are addressed to saints as models of Christian behavior and follow a standard formula, including an antiphon (addressing the saint), a versicle and a response (as above), followed by a collect or prayer addressed to God. The text reflects this structure of these two usages, including the word "oremus" (let us pray), which typically introduces the collect. The opening Latin sentence appears in the *Burnet Psalter* (fol. 23r) but is also a common inscription found under statues of Christopher. See Robert Favreau, *Etudes d'épigraphie médiévale: Recueil d'articles de Robert Favreau*, vol. 2 (Limoges: Presses Universitaires de Limoges, 1995), 79.

167. That is, sew it to the animal's ear.

168. The skulls of the three wise men who visited Jesus's nativity were said to be housed in the cathedral at Cologne in Germany. As a result, even in England, the wise men were commonly known as the "Three Kings of Colyn" and chapels by that name may be found in in Bristol and Kingston.

169. = pray for us.

170. Luke 1:26. The passage alludes to the annunciation, that is, when Gabriel was sent to tell Mary that she would conceive and become mother of the Son of God. Since this is supposed to be citing a biblical passage, the scribe has evidently mistranscribed "virginem" as "finem." The translation depends on a conjectural insertion.

171. John 1. The prologue to the Gospel of John was regularly recited in masses in England before the Reformation. It is also commonly associated with exorcisms.

172. This is a common formula used in liturgical exorcism, such as in the exorcism for salt. "Exorciso te creatura salis . . . (I exorcize you creature of salt . . .)," in *Manuale ad usum percelebris ecclesie sarisburensis*, ed. A. Jeffries Collins (London: Henry Bradshaw Society, 1960), 1.

173. This passage makes a number of allusions to water in the Bible. Moses drew water from the rock in Numbers 20:9–11 and made bitter water sweet in Exodus 15:23–25; Jesus was baptized in the River Jordan in Mark 1:9–11 and Matthew 15:13–17; Christ changes the water into wine in John 2:1–11; and at the crucifixion water flowed from a wound in Jesus's side in John 19:34.

174. Items 69–71 were written by a later hand, the same one that wrote the last item on folio 25r.

Introduction

Sometime in the late sixteenth century Owen Lording, the Protestant parish priest of Boxgrove, Sussex, commissioned a scribe to produce a copy of this manuscript. The scribe was less than accomplished and produced an artless manuscript in which the ink regularly bled through the paper and was sometimes splattered or smeared, making it difficult to read. Lording may well have been unhappy with the final product, and a conflict over whether he should pay for the manuscript might explain the somewhat officious note affixed to the first folio. This cites the local notary, George Stent, as a witness to the contract and gives the date Friday, February 13, 1600, 7 p.m. The original does not survive and the author is unknown, but since the author evidently employed the 1578 edition of Agrippa's *De occulta philosophia* it was more than likely written in the last decades of the century.[1] It was probably originally written in English, since there is no evidence that it was translated and it seems unlikely that the parish priest would have had the resources to engage a translator as well. The original author, who was probably not the scribe, drew on a variety of sources typical of sixteenth-century magicians: manuscripts and printed books, Renaissance magic and medieval magic. Like his forebears in the traditions of ritual magic he sought to discover and construct a true, good, and coherent practice of magic from sources that were not systematically unified. Also like them, the magic he made was an idiosyncratic synthesis.

The volume epitomizes the world of learned magic in Elizabethan England for a variety of reasons. In its pages we can see a well-versed enthusiast of medieval learned magic using the new materials on magic available in print. But it was not simply a process of reading and interpreting Henry Cornelius Agrippa, the most influential of the Renaissance magi, on whose *De occulta philosophia* he certainly drew. The writer was also clearly immersed in the older traditions of ritual magic and, because medieval sources were far less circumspect about providing specific how-to instructions, he employed them as the basis for his rituals. Very much like other contemporary magicians he read Agrippa's encyclopedic and esoteric writings through the lens of practical works on magic, in this case two of the major works of medieval invocation magic—the *Thesaurus spirituum* and *Liber consecrationum*—as well as the *Liber quartus de occulta philosophia* pseudonymously attributed to Agrippa (hereafter *Liber quartus*) and the *Heptameron* pseudonymously attributed to Peter of Abano.[2] All the printed sources, and probably all the manuscript ones as well, were written in Latin and none of the printed works was released in translation until the mid-seventeenth century. So by writing in English the author made learned magic available to a wider reading audience, the priest of Boxgrove among them.

The Operations and Their Sources

There are two interrelated levels of magic discussed in the text. The lamens or amulets described in the first ten folios invoke the power of various planetary spirits, good and bad, for a variety of purposes, including provoking or confirming love, currying the favor of superiors, gaining material wealth, protection from harm or witchcraft, and curing diseases. The author provides considerable lists of materials to be employed in making these as well as the ideal times for their creation and the names and figures to be engraved or written on them. Although much more complex than many of the forms of astrological magic that had been circulating in Europe since the twelfth century, they assume a similar set of principles. To greater and lesser degrees all things in the world contain occult properties imbued in them at the time of their creation by the heavens. Similarly numbers, symbols, and words can connect with, transmit, or focus these powers. When a magician constructed amulets in the proper way, a powerful symphony of occult influences was focused in one artifact: the magic talisman or, as our author would have it, lamen. In turn, the user could employ its effects for various purposes.

Unsurprisingly, this part of the system was in part built from the intellectual resources of the first two books of Henry Cornelius Agrippa's encyclopedic *De occulta philosophia*. The first of these concerned "elemental magic," that is, sources of magical power specific to the material world such as metals, herbs, or stones. The second concerned "celestial magic," by which Agrippa meant a slightly higher form of magic relating to the abstractions of mathematics, words, and symbols as well as the celestial creatures and influences to which these symbols were intrinsically linked. So, in addition to a good deal of other information, Agrippa is also the proximate source for the magic squares featured in the center of the lamens. Deriving from ancient sources, the sum of all the horizontal and vertical rows is the same within any of these squares. This kind of mathematical harmony was regarded as particularly powerful and is typical of this level of magic in Agrippa, which sought similar mathematical structures or harmonies in various places.[3] This material from Agrippa was used in combination with materials drawn from two more practically oriented printed works of magic: the pseudonymous *Liber quartus de occulta philosophia* and *Heptameron*, attributed respectively to Agrippa and Peter of Abano.

Although the author makes clear that these lamens may be used in the invocation of spirits, and this is anticipated by his lengthy descriptions in the first section of how spirits look when they manifest themselves, he only takes invocations up in a concrete way in the remaining twenty-seven folios. He begins with instructions on making pentacles or lamens to call spirits (different from those already described), including four sample images (item 10). This is followed by a miscellany of other important information (i.e., spirit names, sample circles, and lists of divine names). A considerable portion of the volume is then dedicated to instructions for consecrating the equipment employed in conjuring, such as suffumigations (i.e., substances to be burned like incense), water, oil, fire, swords, and magic books. In fact, typical of ritual magic manuals, a full third of the volume is dedicated solely to prayers for consecration (fols. 16v–25v). Following this, the scribe gives instructions on actual operations, beginning with the ways the operator must prepare himself and then moving on to the actual magic operations themselves, as well as how they should be conducted and concluded. The final pages of the book are taken up with a systematically organized set of magic figures for invoking spirits.

A considerable amount of time would be consumed in the preparation and execution of this magic. To begin with, despite the scribe's efforts to synthesize a variety of sources with different systems into something manageable, it would take some time to figure out what had to be done and in what order. Special materials had to be procured and assembled, of which some could simply be collected on a British roadside but others would have had to be purchased specially, perhaps from an apothecary. The lamens and other equipment could be made only at propitious times, considering both the disposition of the heavens and also the days of the week and planetary hours, and this might involve a period of waiting as well. More crucially one might have to wait up to two weeks for a waxing moon. Other equipment also had to be purchased and specially prepared, such as a ring or sword engraved with words of power. Once complete, all the equipment had to be consecrated, which certainly also would have taken a week or more to accomplish. In particular, the book containing one's incantations had to be consecrated over a nine-day period, during which a cycle of nine prayers had to be said three times a day by an operator who was both fasting and observing sexual abstinence. The other equipment also had to be consecrated and sprinkled with holy water, although no additional specific instructions accompany the long prayers of consecration provided for many of these items. All of this had to take place in a specially prepared room. The operator also had to engage in at least three days of quasi-ascetic practices (fasting, sexual abstinence, etc.) in advance of any operation, assuring that he had purified himself appropriately. He then had to be properly groomed and wearing clean and sweet-smelling clothing. Keep in mind, to this point, not a word of conjuration has been uttered nor a single conjuring circle prepared.

All the limitations on the time one could operate had to be observed again when one wished to conjure a spirit. More crucially, if cloudy or disturbed atmospheric conditions prevailed or arose during the operation all would have to be abandoned for the next propitious time, and one can only imagine how difficult this might have been in the notoriously unstable British weather conditions. Nothing of one's operation should be revealed to anyone but compatriots worthy of sharing the secret. These compatriots could help one prepare, carrying clothing, equipment, and stools to the site of conjuring, but they, too, needed to be of good character and have prepared themselves in a fashion similar to the master. The actual conjuring operation involved drawing a circle with consecrated chalk somewhere between nine and seventeen feet in diameter. Each of the conjurations would have to be said twenty-eight times, seven times in each cardinal direction and, although the text is not specific, presumably this would apply to each stage of the operation. Since the text does not provide explicit examples, one would have to employ another text for these and they would typically involve a prayer for assistance, a call to a specific spirit, the binding of that spirit, a charge in which a specific demand was made of it, and then a license, allowing it to depart but usually demanding a peaceful return to the operator when required. Each of these stages typically involves relatively lengthy prayers or invocations of the kind seen in the consecration of the book. If success was not achieved, the author counsels, one should try again, mentioning that sometimes it might take months. Finally, the license to release or send an evil spirit back to its appropriate place had to be said even if the spirit had not appeared because it might be lurking somewhere nearby to harm the operator when he leaves the circle.

The consecrations and instructions on conjuring are drawn largely from Latin printed editions of the *Liber quartus* and the *Elementa magica* and from manuscript sources including the *Thesaurus spirituum* and *Liber consecrationum*. Aspects of the text suggest other manuscript sources as well. For example, the author draws divine names from some unnamed manuscript. Some aspects of the instructions, such as the concerns raised about recalcitrant spirits hiding after an operation to surprise the magician, do not appear in the texts mentioned, although they may be elaborations original to the author of this text as well. For more detail on the specific sources used in various sections of the manuscript, refer to the chart in the appendixes and the notes throughout the edition.

Notable Features: Secrecy, Nature, and Experience

The author emphasizes the importance of secrecy, and specifically secrecy within a devoted brotherhood of male compatriots. This common knot of ideas typical of late medieval ritual magic texts was in equal measure reality, male fantasy, and advertisement. By the seventeenth century, in part no doubt due to the vernacularization process, female practitioners increasingly employed aspects of the learned magic tradition.[4] But prior to this time, evidence suggests that learned magic was almost uniformly the preserve of men who had some level of university training and tended to conceive of themselves in clerical terms, if they did not in fact hold official clerical offices—in short, men like Owen Lording. Rules for practice in medieval ritual magic clearly exclude women, and the goals of the magic suggest an almost exclusively male audience. For example, the reasonably common operations for having sex with the woman of your choice or sometimes even a female spirit, or tales of swashbuckling magicians consorting with emperors, having sex with beautiful women, and flying about on magic horses, seem to be at once masculine fantasies and advertisements for the practice of magic. They certainly do not suggest that the authors or readers were women. Even the theoretically universal *Ars notoria* that offered the slightly more gender-neutral object of angel-infused learning was clearly intended for those attending university, which is to say, men.[5]

The quality of secrecy or exclusivity has enduring associations with magic and dovetails powerfully with this fantasy of learned masculinity.[6] The common requirement that magic secrets not be divulged to the unworthy no doubt served to intensify its perceived value and numinous qualities. But as we can see in this text, the secrets were understood to be held not by a single person, but a group. The instructions assume that a coterie of honorable, learned, and bold associates will assist the master in his operations. This took the realities of the clerical and learned worlds, which were still exclusively homosocial when this text was written and copied, and transformed them into fantasies of danger, adventure, and power. The use of "cipher" in this text to describe magical figures illustrates this mythology in a fascinating way. The term derives from an Arabic root that gives us the word "zero" and meant precisely that in medieval use. But by the 1560s it was being used in English in its modern sense to mean a code that disguises meaning from all but a select few. It was in this sense of occult (i.e., hidden) knowledge that the author of the Boxgrove Manual used it, although the association with mathematics and the world of arcane learning was, no doubt, part of its poetic sense as well.

The relationship of the system articulated here to the natural world is typical of medieval and Renaissance ritual magic. In principle, the lower levels of Agrippa's system, which is to say natural and celestial magic, could be used independently, although Agrippa warned against this.[7] For example, the lamens in the first section could be employed in ways that do not involve actually summoning spirits. Further, the structures of the natural world are conceived of as physical manifestations of spiritual realities (e.g., planetary spirits are ontologically connected with the physical planets) and so access to the spiritual is framed to some extent by the natural world. But, as in the case of Agrippa, the Boxgrove Manual clearly sets up these lower levels of magic as supports for the higher invocation magic that constitutes most of the volume. These operations follow medieval ritual magic in their use of consecrations, prayers, and invocations rife with scriptural allusions, in conjunction with rites and preparations typical of religious practice, such as fasting and sexual abstinence. They also clearly focus on seeking direct engagement with spiritual creatures, good and bad.

Illustrating the desire to create an explicitly Christian magic, the author follows the *Liber quartus* in promoting an image almost entirely lacking celestial and natural elements as the most powerful of all. The instructions for the lamen involving the apocalyptic Christ occupy a small portion of the text (item 23), but it is featured on the opening page of the volume, suggesting that the scribe, and potentially the author himself, regarded it as not just as particularly powerful but actually as central to, or definitive of, the performance of magic. In other words, like Agrippa, the system was understood as a thorough integration of natural and celestial elements into magic of a religious and Christian nature with a clear emphasis on seeking direct experience of the numinous. If the scribe's mundane goals such as love magic were not as mystical and promethean as Agrippa's, his emphasis on scripture, religious rite, and experience of the numinous reflect both the sensibilities of the great Renaissance magi and medieval ritual magic texts.

But if this kind of magic was all about the experience, were not all the practitioners ultimately disappointed when (as one might reasonably assume) it did not work? One can easily imagine how a prayer and accompanying ritual such as we see in the Antiphonary Notebook might make one feel better at a time of crisis or even somehow contribute to the cure of an illness. But the Boxgrove Manual proposes direct visual experience of spirits. Although the idea that someone might have a subjectively convincing experience of conjuring a spirit is certainly harder to imagine, all the evidence indicates that it could produce such an experience for at least a portion of those who tried it. No direct study of the neuropsychological effects of premodern ritual magic has ever been undertaken, but modern studies of other traditions suggest that sexual abstinence, fasting, isolation, repetitive prayers and rituals, and other such actions can bring about, or make one more disposed to, visual and auditory dissociative experiences. In addition, Tanya Luhrmann has demonstrated that the techniques of visualization employed by modern charismatic Christians and pagans can provoke startling and subjectively convincing experiences in a significant portion of the population. As is common in ritual magic, the Boxgrove Manual requires fasting, sexual abstinence, and periods of isolation. More crucially, it includes long prayers full of highly visual and tactile stories meant to be said in a spirit of devotion and emotional engagement, something that probably worked very much like modern guided visualization exercises. All this suggests that the author, Owen Lording, and a significant portion of other practitioners might well have experienced the phenomena it describes (or something like them).[8] Precisely what they saw and whether it was in any sense real or true is another question.

Historical and Intellectual Context

The blend of medieval and Renaissance sources in the Boxgrove Manual is typical of this period. The author probably assumed the framing cosmological structure of Agrippa's *De occulta philosophia* since he drew materials from the first two books, particularly the correspondences between natural and celestial elements. At the same time he does not use Agrippa's terminology, so the issue remains unclear. Certainly the scribe had to go elsewhere to get practical information about how to actually perform the magic. Like other classic texts of Renaissance magic, such as Ficino's *De vita coelitus comparanda*, Agrippa's work was not a particularly useful practical manual. It provided a good deal of information in encyclopedic form and said many inspiring things about high magic, but Agrippa was circumspect about telling his readers precisely how to do it. Unsurprisingly, pseudonymous printed works attributed to Agrippa and others appeared soon after the publication of the *De occulta philosophia*, evidently responding to a popular hunger for such information. The author employed these as well as the texts on which they were largely based: late medieval manuscripts of ritual magic that had been circulating in manuscript sometimes for centuries. Interestingly, the author does not feel it is necessary to provide explicit instructions on the actual invocation of spirits, despite the fact that this is the principal goal of the operations, presumably because this was easily available in other manuscripts. Rather, he regards his synthesis of the arcane material in the printed sources with manuscript traditions to be his central task. This habit of employing Agrippa to supplement older traditions is typical of many sixteenth-century enthusiasts of magic who cited him more often than any other contemporary writer.

The author follows the older traditions in one other crucial way. Ritual magic works tended to be quite unstable and were subject to constant rewriting, extraction, reformulation, and synthesis. In part this derived from the textually chaotic nature of the tradition and the often-fragmentary nature of the manuscripts available to individual scribes that literally forced them to synthesize their own sort of magic. But an explicit culture of rewriting also surrounded ritual magic, a culture that did not end with the birth of the printed magic book. The texts tended to represent great historical mages as divinely guided editors, often inspired by God, angels, or other spiritual agents, who had come to understand the arcane texts of magic they discovered through long practice and engagement, and rewrote them for subsequent generations of worthy mages. This mythology encouraged scribes already dealing with chaotic and often contradictory sources to imagine themselves to be like these great mages, and to rewrite or synthesize entirely new works. Whether the author of the Boxgrove Manual had such a grandiose self-conception is not clear, but when he set about to make his magic book he certainly produced an original synthesis of a diverse variety of sources the same way earlier writers in the tradition had done.

The author also evinces the changing world in which he lived. As we have seen he drew heavily on the growing library of printed books on magic, and by transferring information from these Latin books and other Latin manuscript sources into an English book of magic he was also part of a larger process in which learned magic was re-created in the vernacular and popularized. In fact, he not only translated material into English but also synthesized a new set of practical instructions. In this way, whether he intended it or not, he was acting as what William Eamon calls a "cultural broker," one who repackaged learned material for a nonexpert, lay, or non-Latinate audience.[9] It is thus significant that the surviving version is not an autograph but a copy of the original text made at someone's request. There was clearly a market for such texts, and this market was just as active half a century later when numerous vernacular translations of medieval and renaissance magic texts were published in London.[10]

The most ubiquitous (if quite subtle) changes in magic texts in this period resulted from the Reformation. The heavy emphasis on rites made enthusiasts of ritual magic particularly sensitive to theological changes. Many of the trappings of Catholic practice have been removed from this text (e.g., Ave Marias, invocations of the saints, martyrs, and virgins).[11] The Protestant numbering of the Psalms is also observed (e.g., fol. 25v), and while most medieval conjurations regularly refer to biblical stories, the references to scripture are particularly heavy in the Boxgrove Manual, perhaps reflecting Agrippa's emphasis on the Bible and his humanist or crypto-Protestant sensibilities. At the same time, it needs to be emphasized that not every scribe adapted older magic practices in this way. The compiler of the Antiphoner Notebook, for example, responded to the Reformation by seeking out the old religion, arguably in a more intensified form.

Other subtle changes may be detected in this volume as well. Many late medieval treatises on ritual magic, such as the important source for this work, the *Thesaurus spirituum*, required the services of a priest to assist in a variety of preparatory rituals like saying particular masses over magical equipment. Such texts also required specific masses to be used in preparation, such as the mass of Saint Cyprian.[12] Despite copying his rules of operation from the *Thesaurus spirituum*, the author does not require that a priest be involved in any way nor does he preserve the requirement of specific masses. In part this may have been motivated by Protestant de-emphasis on the role of the priest as a singular kind of spiritual mediator. In part it was also driven by changes in the liturgy and the fact that in Reformed areas one simply could not have the old masses said over one's equipment because the liturgy had changed. But the transition was not simply from Catholic to Protestant or to some neutral ground in between. Rather this situation appears to have given rise to a process of privatization. For example, the use of holy water continued in Anglican traditions, and one could have easily enough absconded with a bottle of it from a church. Nonetheless, the author moves the production of holy water and other kinds of consecrations from the church or altar to the magician's home, in which the place of operation includes not only space for the circle, but a kind of altar with an altar cloth (item 20). This may also be a function of popularization. The late medieval learned and clerical practitioners would have had much more direct access to priests and churches and may well have been able to perform the rituals themselves. The demand that a priest complete these tasks would also have been a way of reaffirming the sacramental monopoly held by the very people who typically wrote and transmitted medieval learned magic.

The Manuscript

Shelfmark: London, British Library, Harley 2267.

Date: According to a note pasted on folio 1r, completed by February 13, 1600. This is consistent with the hand.

Size/Material: Quarto. Paper. The manuscript has been rebound and the leaves mounted separately.

Scripts: The scribe was less than accomplished and produced an artless volume with numerous problems, including smudged letters, ink spills, and splatters. Ink used for emphasis and images (now brown and perhaps once red) regularly bleeds through the paper, obscuring the text on the other side of the leaf.

Citations of Sources

The author of the Boxgrove Manual drew heavily on numerous sources. To reduce the density and repetitiveness of the citations, particularly in items 2–8, and to provide an overview of how the book was assembled, these have been summarized in the appendixes.

I cite Vittoria Perrone Compagni's critical edition of Agrippa's *De occulta philosophia*, but for ease of reference to early printed versions of the *De occulta philosophia* and the English translation I include book and chapter references as well. Where it was critical to establishing questions of textual transmission I also include references to the 1578 edition published in Basel by Thomas Guarin, which the author of the Boxgrove Manual employed.

There is no modern scholarly edition of the *Heptameron* or *Liber quartus de occulta philosophia*. Consequently, I cite the 1578 edition. Given the lack of chapter headings in these two texts, I have also provided references to the relevant page numbers in the 1655 English translation by Turner.

Editorial Principles

This is a semi-diplomatic edition. Most abbreviations (excepting yᵉ and &) have been silently expanded. For readability and clarity "&c." has been rendered "etc." and "vz." as "viz." Where other minor corrections have been made for readability (such as the removal of duplicated words), such emendations have been indicated in the notes. Original capitalization has been retained. Original punctuation also has generally been maintained, although the scribe's full stops (slashes) have been rendered as periods and occasional additional punctuation has been added for clarity.

Most of the Hebrew names of God, demons, and angels derived from Henry Cornelius Agrippa. There seems little question that the scribe did not know the language, although it is possible that the author of the text did (assuming they were distinct people). The letters have been rendered optimistically, assuming the correct spellings as represented in Agrippa. More dramatic errors or alternate spellings not due to malformed letters have been preserved and the correct words identified in the apparatus. Latin phrases have been translated in the notes upon their first occurrence.

Notes

1. The scribe drew on Basel 1578 (VD 16 ZV 263). This edition contains not only the *De occulta philosophia* but also the pseudonymous *Liber quartus de occulta philosophia* and *Heptameron*, which were also important sources. The Boxgrove Manual shares numerous unusual spellings of angel and demon names peculiar to this edition. See the notes for items 4, 5, 7, 10, and 27 below. Some but not all of these irregularities are reflected in an earlier edition from Basel (ca. 1550) (VD 16 ZV 265). Finally, some errors in the texts cannot be attributed to any known edition and appear to be genuine copying errors, such as in the notes for items 2 and 27 below.

2. The *Thesaurus spirituum* is not yet available in a modern edition. I have employed principally London, Wellcome Library, Wellcome 110, fols. 57r–89v; and Sloane 3854, fols. 3r–45v; the former also includes an English epitome of the text (Wellcome 110, scattered through fols. 1–56v). Two versions of the *Liber consecrationum* appear in Kieckhefer, *Forbidden Rites*, 256–86.

3. The letters of the Hebrew alphabet can also be used to represent numbers. As a result, practitioners of kabbalah, the Jewish mystical and magical tradition, and their Christian enthusiasts could seek out meanings not only in letters of words but also in their numbers. For examples of kabbalistic and other numerological lore relevant to magic see *DOP*, 2:3–23 (253–321) and 3:25 (472–81). On magic squares and the complex mathematics that underlie the way they were used see K. A. Nowotny, "The Construction of Certain Seals and Characters in the Work of Agrippa of Nettesheim," *Journal of the Warburg and Courtauld Institutes* 12 (1949): 46–57.

4. While magic books were uncommon elements in the witch trials, toward the end of the seventeenth century female cunning folk both employed written sources and also fashioned themselves as more powerful by owning magic books. On the witch trials see Davies, *Cunning-Folk*, 70. On female cunning folk owning magic books, see ibid., 81–84.

5. Richard Kieckhefer first proposed the notion that learned magic was the preserve of a "clerical underworld" in *Magic in the Middle Ages*, Cambridge Medieval Textbooks (Cambridge, U.K.: Cambridge University Press, 1989), 153–56. For an exploration of the masculinity, learning, and ritual magic see Klaassen, "Learning and Masculinity in Manuscripts of Ritual Magic."

6. Jean-Patrice Boudet and Julien Véronèse, "Le secret dans la magie rituelle médiévale," *Micrologus* 14 (2006): 101–50. On secrecy in general see T. M. Luhrmann, "The Magic of Secrecy," *Ethos* 2 (1989): 131–65.

7. *DOP*, 3:1 (402–3).

8. T. M. Luhrmann, *Persuasions of the Witch's Craft: Ritual Magic in Contemporary England* (Cambridge, Mass.: Harvard University Press, 1989); Luhrmann, "The Art of Hearing God: Absorption, Dissociation, and Contemporary American Spirituality," *Spiritus: A Journal of Christian Spirituality* 5, no. 2 (2005): 133–57; Luhrmann, *When God Talks Back: Understanding the American Evangelical Relationship with God* (New York: Alfred A. Knopf, 2012). For an exploration of the possible neuropsychological mechanisms of premodern examples, see Klaassen, "Subjective Experience of Medieval Ritual Magic."

9. Eamon, *Science and the Secrets of Nature*, 85.

10. Among numerous works on magic published in London at this time are Henry Corne-lius Agrippa, *Three Books of Occult Philosophy*, trans. John French (London: Printed by R. W. for Gregory Moul, 1651); and *Ars notoria: The Notory Art of Solomon, Shewing the Cabalistical Key of Magical Operations. . .* , trans. Robert Turner (London: J. Cotrell, 1657).

11. Although it remains that Mary is mentioned from time to time and even as an intercessor ("& by yᵉ merytes & intercessyons of our blessed virgyn Mary"; fol. 24r) as well.

12. On the *Thesaurus spirituum* see the note for item 25 below. The *Sworn Book of Honorius* also required similar engagement with conventional religious practice, such as regular attendance at mass and also the weaving of its rituals into specific masses for the benefit of the operator.

The Text

Golde hill in ~~hampshone~~ Sussex.
Owin Lordinge of Boxgroue
disiringe it. February 13, 1600
at the howre of 7 a clocke
the afternone beinge friday
George Stent present.[1] [1v]

[1. Pentacle of the Apocalyptic Christ][2]

I am α et ω + The first and ye laste which is which was and which is to cum, I am
ye fyrst & the laste, beinge deade & am alyve, vnto ye ende of ye worlde. I haue y^e
keyes of death & of hell commaund, commaunde thy vertue oh Lorde confyrme
this oh Lorde, yat thow hast wrought in vs, let them be as dust, scattered with the
wynd, & y^e angell of y^e Lord dryuynge them, Let their weye be slyppery & darke,
& y^e Angell of y^e Lord folowinge them[3]

[2r]

What things ar attributed to the planets.[4]

[2. The Moon][5]

☽ hath of hearbes hysoppe, Rosemary and yᵉ herbe Selenotropion, which turneth toward yᵉ ☽ as marygolldes doth towardes yᵉ Sunne, Of place desartes, mountaynes, Rockes, waters, Seas, highe weyes, Of coloures, whighte, Reddyshe, purpe or greane, Of metalls sylver for house & exaltation . ♋ . ♈ . The quarter in the elemente North, or South. The seale of yᵉ ☽ 𝒴 The angell of the Moone, Gabryel, The intelligence of ☽ or hir goode angell Malachebetharsisim hed Beruahschehakim. The character of hir intelligence & The numbre of hir intelligence, 2321.[6] The caracter of hir Intelligence ⫶⫶[7] The devine names of God anwseringe hir intelligence elim . אלים . 81 & hod . חד .9 . The character of hir euyle angell ⟨ᴧ The name of hir euyle Angell Hasmoday. Now doth ffolowe the table of the Moone as apearethe hearafter Character lune. · ⚹ · ◇· [2v]

This is passing[8]

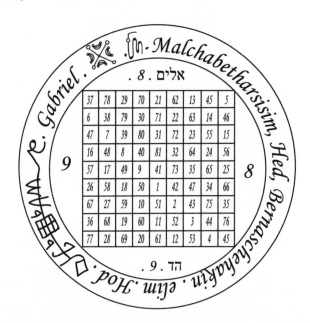

This table or image of ☽ made in Sylver when ☽ is in ♋ or ♉, in yᵉ daye & hower of ☽. and after consecratyon, anoynted & sprykeld with holy oyle & water and fumed with consecrated lignum aloes, & wrapped uppe in hyssop & Rosemary gathered in yᵉ day & hower of ☽ being in ♋ or ♉ & at a good aspecte with ♃, ♀, or ☉, and when yᵉ hearbes ar gathered, & at the gatheringe thy face towarde yᵉ South or weste, yᵉ hearbes also consectrated oyled & perfumed & with fyne lynen or lanne wrapped uppe together & consecrated in [3r] a desarte, wood, or coppes, & thear hydde or buryed for half a daye doth helpe yᵉ to yᵉ havynge of Gabriel or yᵉ intelligence of ☽ callinge his intelligence in A Sercle & hauyinge this table of ☽ or pentacle in thy hande, or lyinge by the, And being caryed abought yᵉ maketh the bearar welbeloued wythe goode lucke in trauayle, prosperinge in riches & health of body & taketh awey envye, and other hurtefull thinges

The eyery sprites on Mundaye doe cause Southwest wyndes, theare nature is to cary things from place to place, To tell of thinges paste. Theyre famylyar aperance is A greate large phlegmmatyke body, like thicke cloudes swelled face, redd and watery Eyes, bald heade, their motyon is lyke waues of yᵉ sea, The signe of their apparance is a greate shower by yᵉ Sercle, Theare particuler forme is A kynge or Archar rydinge vpon A bucke, A lytle boye, a woman huntynge, with bowe and arowes in hir hande, A cowe, a dooe a Goose, A greane or Sylver garmente or A Shafte

The suffumigacyon is Lignum aloes. [3v]

[3. Mercury]⁹

☿ hath of elementes, water & permyxte humores, of metalles, Stannum,¹⁰ of hearbes mercurierum,¹¹ & fynefynger, called pentaphylon¹² Of beastes dogges, of byrdes the Pye. Also syluer is a attrybuted to the planet ☿ Of places, scooles, shoppes, towns Of coloures, Whighte, reddyshe, purple or greane colour. Of Metalles Stanum. Of spices, ffrankynsence, clowes, synamon, cassia lignea, maces, baye-beryes, Masticke.¹³ for howse & exaltation¹⁴ ♊ . ♍ . The Quarter in yᵉ Elaments The Quarter in the fyrmament, South or Weste. The seale of ☿ is thus made ⌐☿⊕▭✕¹⁵ The Angell of yᵉ ☿ . Raphael The Intelligence of Mercury or mercuryes good Angel Tiriel . טיריאל . 260 . yᵉ caracter of his intelligence . ♫. The devyne names of Godde annswerynge his intellygence are these . Asboga . 8 . אזבגה . Din . דין . Doni . דני . The character of ☿ euyll angell ⌐ and ys called Taphtartharath . mercuries character in quadrato or thus videlicet ▦ a ✛ crosse [4r]

And now followth yᵉ table of ☿ with figures in A Square. As apeareth ouer¹⁶ & besydes yᵉ circumference conteynynge his caracteres & seale, with yᵉ deuyne names of god aunsweringe his Angell

8	58	59	5	4	62	36	1
49	15	14	52	53	11	10	56
41	23	22	44	45	19	18	48
32	34	35	29	28	38	39	25
40	26	27	37	36	30	31	33
17	47	46	20	21	43	42	24
9	55	54	12	13	51	50	16
64	2	3	61	60	6	7	57

This table of .☿. made in Syluer or elles in parchment, with his apropryed coloures,[17] in the daye & hower of ♀ & ☿ beigne in ♓ or ♍ gatheringe at yat hower merierum or Synkefoyle[18] with the face into yᵉ south or west, then consecrated, & wounde in A fyne lawne, & sprynkled with holy water Oyled & fumed with fankensence doth healpe yᵉ bearar to yᵉ intelligence of ☿ called Tyriel, being called in A [4v] Sercle, & houlden in thy hande, or layde by the And being caryed aboughte, yt dothe make yᵉ fortunate, in yat you goest Aboughte yt bringeth gaynes, & taketh aweye pouertye yt causeth dyuynacyon & knowledge of seacreate thinges in sleape. The spirites of yᵉ Eyere one wedynsdaye, giue South wyndes, to tell of thynges presente and to cum To gyue vyctory in warre, & to please Iudges & greate mean, To gyve healthe or syknes. Their famylyar aperaunce is A meane body, fayer, coulde & moyste well spoken, armed lyke A Souldeyer of shynynge coloure, his motion is lyke a syluer cloude, his signe of cumynge is to brynge sweate to yᵉ caller or Inuocante. There particuler forme is a kynge rydynge vpon A Bear, A fayer younge man A woman with A dystaff, A dogge, A Beare, A garment of dyueres coloures, A wande or a staff. The fumigacyon is Masticke.

[4. Venus][19]
♀ hath of Elementes, Eyar, & water of humores, flegme mixed with blud, yᵉ seade & genytores,[20] of taste sweate & unctious, & delectable, Of Mettalles, syluer & brasse, of hearbes, verueyne, vyoletes, valeryan, Thyme Also hamber muske, coryander, Aples, pears, reysons, of beastes, conyes, sheape, calues, [5r] Bulles, Of byrdes, yᵉ crowe, doue, sparowe. Of places, Meades, Gardens, bedchambers

& pleasante grene places. Of coloures whight, reddyshe, purple or greane. Also muske, hamber [i.e., amber], lignum aloes, redde sorell, Roses, Vyoletes, Safron, Of birdes the sparow & doue Of metall Syluer

For howse and exaltation ♉ . ♎ . ♓ . The quarter of yᵉ Elament, Southe. The character of Venus 🜊 or thus 8. The seal of ♀ is thus made, ♉ ⌇ Venus angell is called Anael. The good angell or intelligence of ♀ is called Hagiel אגיאל.[21] The caracter of hir intelligence ⩒ The deuyne name of God that answerethe hir intelligence אהא.[22] The character of hir euyle Angell is thys ⅋[23] yᵉ name of hir euill Angell ys called . kedemel . Venus table in cyphars, Ouer & besydes the circumference wherein ar hir seales characteres and Intelligence. with hir good angell Behoulde ♀ Table doth follow in yᵉ next syde vt pr[24] [5v]

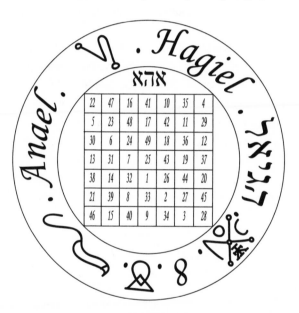

♀ Table, grauen in syluer, or draune in parchment, in yᵉ daye & hower of venus etc. vt dicitur.[25] Maketh peace, & dothe appease discorde, & getteth yᵉ loue of wemen, dyssolueth wychcrafte & ingendreth loue betwyn man and woman, & doth cause his cattell to increase, And beinge borne aboughte yow gyueth lucke in Iurneyes. The Spirites of yᵉ Eyer on ffrydaye are subiecte to Southwest[26] wyndes, & to prouoke meane & wemen to Loue, and to make their Enemyes their frendes by thuse[27] of ♀. also to make maryages & to allure meane to yᵉ loue of wemen [6r] To take aweye or gyue sycknes. Ther famylyar aperance is A goodly bodye of meane stature, A louynge & pleasant countenance, aperell whighte or greane gylte aboue, theare motyon is lyke a brighte starre, The signe of there aperance is to seame yat maydes shalbe playinge by yᵉ sercle, prouokeinge the Invocante to playe[28] There particuler forme is a kynge with a scepter, rydinge vpon a camell, a fayer mayde or elles A nakyd mayde, A Goate, A Camell, A dove, A whighte or greane garment, ffloweres, or ye hearbe Sanyn.

The fumigacyon of venus is costus[29]

[5. The Sun][30]

☉ hath of Elementes fyer, of humoures, pure blude, of taste sharpe & sweate, of mettalles, goulde, of herbes marygouldes, pyony, celydon, veruene myntes, zeodar, safron, balme, merierum, libanotis, aromaticus calamus, Baye, & Iue tree, clowes, synamon, peper, frankynsence, yelow colour. Of places, all lyght brighte & shy-nynge places, as goodely howses, churches, pulpytes. Of coloures, Goulde or yelow Safron colour. for howse ♌. The Quarter in the Elament, The Easte parte

The characters of the sunne is this . ⊠. or thus . Ɛ . [6v] The seale of the sonne . ⟊⟊⟊. Michael. the Angell of ye Sonne The Intelligence or goode angell of ye Sonne is called Nachiel נכיאל.[31] The character of his intelligence ↗ The deuyne names of God answereinge his Intelligence . he . הא . 6 . vav . ו . Eloh . 6 אלה. The name his Euill Angell is Sorath. סירת . The character of his euill Intelligence is this . ⌃ .

The table of ye Sonne in a quadrate in cyphars over & beside ye Sercumference with ye deuyne names of God, hir signacles Seales & charactes.

6	32	3	34	35	1
7	11	27	28	8	30
19	14	16	15	23	24
18	10	22	21	17	13
25	29	10	9	26	12
36	5	33	4	2	31

[7r]

This Table of the sonne made of goulde Or in parchment in yellow or goulden colour, in ye daye & hower of the Sunne The Sunne beinge in ♈ or ♌ and all thinges performed with consecratyons etc. The Spirits of ye Eyer one Sunysdaye doe cause Northen wyndes, To procure ffauour & loue, To take awaye or giue dysseases. There aperance is A thycke Sanguyne body, with goulden colour sprenkeled with bludde, & doe cause rumblinge in ye Elament & to procure sweate to the Inuocante. Theire particular forme is A kynge hauynge A Sceptre, & Rydinge vpon A Lyon, A Crouned kynge or A Queane, wythe Scepter, a Byrde, A Lyon, a cocke, A yelow or goulden vesture, a sceptre, A Tayle.

The fumygatyon of ye Sonne is redde Saunder and nota this table of ye Sonne in figures & caryed aboughte them, make ye bearar Amyable, gloryous, stronge in all his workes, & geueth ye fauour of princes and kynges, exaltinge him to promocyon, maketh him obteyne what they will [7v]

[6. Mars][32]

♂ . hath . of Element fyer, of humor choler, of taste such as ar amari,[33] sharpe & burnynge, Of metall, Stannum[34] coper & Goulde, But his right or trewe metall indeade is Brasse or coper, for Stannum & Goulde aperteyne to ♃. Of hearbes prickinge & burnynge thinges as, nettles Thistles, spearworte, Onyons, bearsefutt, Garlyke, Laurelle, Scamony. Of Places Backehowses, fornaces, fyer houses, Bakehowses & buchars Shoppes Of coloures, redde or purple. The place in the ffyrmament Easte or Northe for howse & Exaltacyon. ♈ . ♏ . ♑ . The Quarter in y^e Element, Easte nothest or Easte & Northe. The character of ♂ . 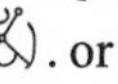 . or thus .  . the Angell of mars Samael. And his character is .  . The intelligence or hys goode angell is called . Graphiel . גראפיאל . his caracter is this  The deuine names of God that do annsweare this intelligence . Adonay. אדני . he . ה . His euyll angell ys called Barzabel. The character of Barzabell is thus . .

The table of ♂ in cyphars in a Square with a Sercumference viz. [8r]

This Table or ringe of ♂ grauen in a sworde, die & hora ♂,[35] Mars beinge in ♈, ♍, or ♑. Or made in a table of Brasse or Lamyna, geueth Vyctory ouer hys Enemyes. The Spirites of yᵉ Eyer on Tuysdaye ar Subiecte to sothern wyndes, & their nature is to make stryfe & contentyon & to gyue syknes or health. Theire ffamylyar forme is a longe cholericke body a fylthy looke, a broune colour, with hartes hornes, & gryphyns clawes, they they rore lyke madde bulles. Their motion is lyke burnyge fyer, & at their cumynge they brynge Thundringe & lyghtenynge by yᵉ Sercle. his particular form is A Kynge rydinge vpon A wolf, an armed man, a woman with a buckler, a gooate, a horse, a harte, a redde garment or wall. [8v]

The fummigacyon of ♂ is pepper.

[7. Jupiter][36]

♃ hath of Elementes, Fyer, of humoures Bludde, of savor sweate. Of metalles Stannum, Coper & goulde of hearbes Basyll, myntes, mace, Spyke, of treas, Oke, beache, Pople, Aple & peare treas, Oyle, reysons, lyquerice, Sugar, Almundes, walnutes, Rhabrbe, myrabolans, pyony rootes, manna, of beastes yᵉ sheape of ffoules hennes. All neate & fyne places Of coloures, All greane & myxed coloures. Of places in yᵉ fyrmament Easte or Northeaste / of spices lignum aloes / for howse & Exaltacyon . ♐. ♓. ♋ .

The seale of ♃ is . ⚹ ♌ ⅃. The character of Iupyter is thus made ⊠ or thus . ✕ . The Angell of ♃ answeringe his seale is called . Sachiel . & the Intellygence of ♃ or his goode spirite is called . Iophiel . יהפיאל . The character of his intelligence

. ⚏ . The deuyne names of God yat Doe answeare his Intelligence [9r] Abba, 4
. אבא . El. אל . 16 . The character of his intelligence or goode angell is wrytten
afore, The character of his Euyll intelligence is this ⟋ and the name of his
intelligence is called hismael . השמאל[37] . this hysmaell is called the Euill Angell
of Iupiter.

The Table of ♃ in cyphars, with his seales, charater & names of Godde viz.

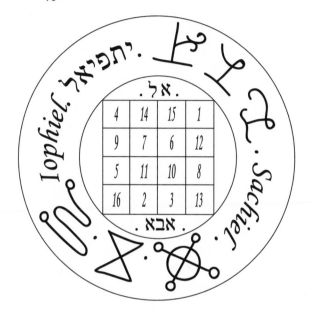

This Table of ♃ with his figures in a square made in coper or goulde, ♃ beinge in
♐, ♓, or ♋, die et hora ♃[38] or made in parchment with his apropryed coloures,
or a lamen made in Syluer, doth ouercum his Enemyes, & wychcrafte, & helpith
to dygnytye, & fauor of noble persons. Yf [9v] yt be borne aboughte yow. The
spirites of yᵉ Eyer one Thursdaye cause southe wyndes, To procure yᵉ loue of
wemen, To make meane merye to pacyfye contencyons, To take aweye or gyve
Sycknes Ther ffamylyar aperance is with a sanguyne choleryke Bodye of meane
stature and horrible motyon, mylde countenaunce and fayer speache, iron
colour, they cause coruscatyon & thunder by yᵉ Sercle, & meane apeare which ar
deuoured of Lyons.

Ther particular forme is A kynge rydinge vpon A harte with a naked sworde, a
mytred man in A longe garemente, a mayde with A croune of Bayes, a bull, a
harte, a peacoke, an Azure garemente.

The ffumygacyon for Thursdaye[39] is Safron

[8. Saturn]

♄ . hath of Elementes yᵉ Earthe. of humores malancoly. Sapor acetosus,[40] Of mettalles, Leade, Of hearbes Rewe and Affodil. of places such as ar darke Pyttes, Pooles, Solytary places, desartes Selles, caues, of colours such as ar blacke for howse & exaltacyon ♑ ♒ ♎. The place of yᵉ fyrmament, Easte or southeaste. The character of [10r] Saturne . ✳ . or thus . Ɔ . The seale of ♄ is made thus viz. ⊟ Ɉɹ Ɔ. The Angell of the daye is called Cassiel. The Intelligence of ♄ or his good Angell is called . Agiel . אגיאל . 49 . The names of God answering this intelligence ab . 3 . אב . hod . 9 . הד. Iah 15 . יה. Tetragrammaton . 45 The character of his Intelligence or goode Angell called Agiell is thus made . ✎ . The figure of his euile angell called zazel . זאזל . 45

The table of ♄ in a quadrate of cyphars in whose sercumference is his characteres, seales & yᵉ deuyne names of God as apeareth. ♄ euill intelligence is thus made ↘[41]

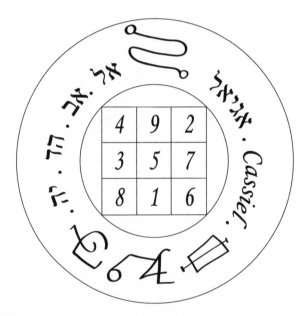

This Table or rynge of ♄ made in leade when ♄ is in ♑, ♒, or ♎. die et hora ♄ and all thinges done & consecrated vt ante dicitur.[42] Geueth good successe in busynes. The Eyery spirites on Saturdaye ar subiect to South wyndes, Their nature is to sowe dyscorde, hatred, euyle thoughtes. To kyll or mayme any person. His famylyar aperance is for yᵉ moste parte A longe & slender body, angry countenance, hauynge 4 faces one behynde yᵉ heade, an other before & eyther

noses bylled lyke a Gryphyn, & in eyther knee a face, all which faces ar of blacke
& shynynge cholour. Ther motyon is Agytacion of wynde, with A lytle movynge
of ye Earth. Their signe of cumynge is Earth whyter then snowe. Theire particular aperance is a beardyd kynge, rydinge vpon A dragon, an owle, a black garmente, A sycle.

The fumigacion is . brimston .

Finis de characteribus Sigillis et tabulis bonorum et malorum angelorum.[43] [11r]

[9. On binding people or things]

And no[44] many thinges may be done by bynding & with wordes, as thus, to
cause Loue or hate, secundly yat A thef shall not steale, ye dogges not barke etc.[45]
Also by touchinge with oytements as to procure loue or hate, syknes or health
Also by collyres or oyntement for the Eyes, yat by ye radyacion of ye Eyes Loue
or hatred is procured.[46] Or by kyssinge haueinge things in ye mouth.[47] Also by
characteres, herbes, Images, Seales, with Adiuracyons, consecratyons, etc. And
to procure loue vse sweate for hatred, euill sower.[48] Also for Loue take ye goode
intelligence of ♀ called Hagiel whose character is this . ⅄ . hir table is seyde afore.
ffor hatrted take hir Euill Angell Kedemyell[49] whose character is this. ⸗.[50] And
thus of all other intelligences take ye euyll Angell of ye planet and doe as is seyd
mutatis mutandis etc.[51] [11v]

[10.] To make lamens or pentacles To call good Spirites

In A newe mone,[52] in ye day and hower of the planet. & being in house or Exal-
tacon in a peace of plate 4 square, or in coloures apropryed to ye planet, & wrytten in parchment. Example: to call ♀ intelligence called Hagiel whose caracter is
this ⅄, hir table in cyphars is placed in ye mydes of the heptagonn.[53] & at y^e
hower of makynge Let ♀ be in ♉, ♎, or ♓ with ye deuyne names of god annswer-
ing hir intelligence, written aboughte, & 4 pentagoni[54] in ye 4 quarters & yf yow
will yow maye wright Anaell ye Angell yat ruleth on fryday, & also puttinge in
Anaelles seale which is this ♉ ∽ & ♀ other characteres which ar thus made
⅍ or thus . 8 . But ♀ table in cyphars with her intelligence which is called אגיאל
videlicet hagiel with the deuyne names of God is suffycyent. And yf yow call but
onely one as ye intelligence of ♀ called hagiel, yet must yow haue 4 pentagoni in
eche corner of ye square one, & looke soe many sprites as yow call so many
pentagony yow must make [12r]

Behould this Lamina or Table To call hagiell [venus] intellygence, for love & for
confyrmation therof, to make yt stronger I will call the kinge of ye Eyer

varcan(1)[55] & his ministeres amabiel(2), aba(3), Abalidoth(4), Flaef(5), and yᵉ Angelles of yᵉ Eyer anael(6) rachiel(7) Sachiel(8) & yf I will adde all the reste videlicet

Setchiel (9)	porna (14)	Turiel (20)	peniel (26)	Talui (32)
Chedisutamel	Sachiel (15)	Coniel (21)	penael (27)	Caracasa (33)
(10)	Chermiel (16)	Babiel (22)	penat (28)	core (34)
Corat (11)	Samael (17)	Cadiel (23)	Raphael (29)	amatiel (35)
Tamael (12)	Santamel (18)	Maltiel (24)	Raniel (30)	comissores (36)
Tenaciel (13)	famiel (19)	hufaltriel (25)	Doremiel (31)	spugliguel (37)
				amaday (38)
				abraym (39)
				agusita (40)
East	South	west	North	for yᵉ spring

Yf I call all these then I must haue 41 pentagoni for soe many spirits ther ar for [venus] orbe & yᵉ springe tyme. But I will call but onely these viz. Venus intelligence called hagiell the kinge [12v] varcan(2) his mynysteres, amabiel(3), Aba(4) Abalidoth(5). Flaef(6). the angelles of yᵉ Eyer Anael(7) Rachael(8) Sachiel(9) Soe yᵉ sum is 9 & therfor I must haue 9 pentagoni.

Behould this lamina for yᵉ angell of ♀ called Hagiel אגיאל.

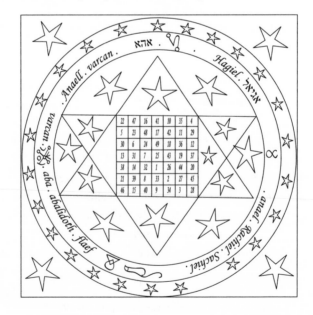

The fyrste Table .1.[56] [13r]

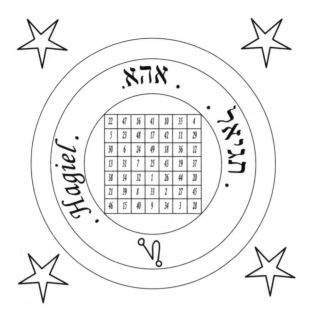

This lamen also is for haguell ♀ angell, to procure loue

The Secunde table for haguell [13v]

A Good pentacle or hexagonum of defence[57]

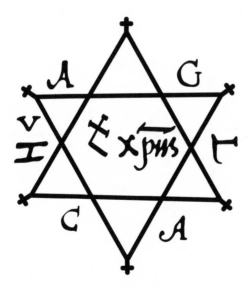

Make it dies et hora . ☿ . ☽ crescente,[58] in virgin parchement, or kyddes skyn
Then consecrate yt anoynt & perfume yt etc. Sed sit ☿ in ♍ aut ♊[59]

An other table to call hagiell Venus Angell / lamina 2a / The thirde Table [14r]

Or thus to call Hagiel Venus Agnell Tabula Tertia

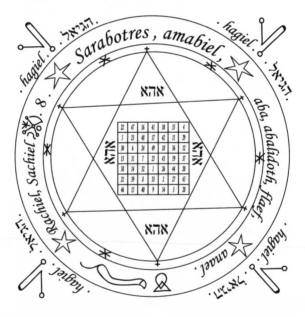

The 4th table of hagiell Venus Intelligence. take yat which shall lyke yᵉ beste But nota ♀ must be in ♉ . ♎ or . ♓ . ☽ crescente die et hora ♀, made in Sylver or vergyn partment consecrated, sprynkled annoynted & perfumed [14v]

[11.] The names of euil Spirites per cornelium[60] called Infernall

Astaroth, A false Accusar, Abbadon, A sower of dyscorde, Amaymon A Kynge of yᵉ South. Belyall, A deceyuer, with cardes & dyce & all maner of Games, one full of of Iniquytye Belzebub, a manyfeste Lyar demon or diabolus A proude & false deceyuer Egyn the kynge of yᵉ northe, Mererym, A trubler of yᵉ Eyer Mammon A temptor Oriens yᵉ kynge of yᵉ Easte paymon the kynge of the West, Python A false, Lyar, Sathan a false deceyuer, by illusyons, iudglynge[61] & intoxicatynge. nota Oriens, Paymon, Egyn & Amaymon, ar kynges of the fower quarters and Azael, Azazel, Mahazell & Samael ar fower kynges of yᵉ Eyar hurtynge yᵉ elementes [15r]

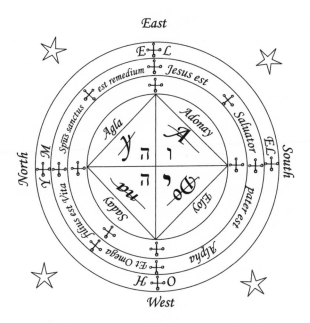

A Goode common Sircle to call Baron or any other one particuler Spirit[62] [15v]

[12.] The deuyne names of God per Libros manuscriptos videlicet[63]

Anereneton, Athanathos, Aries, Agyos, Elzephares, Elyoram, Egeryon, Eryona, craton, lapis, mediator, mons, Angelus, Gloria, Lux, Onotheon, Otheos, Ozanna, Mediator, Primus, Principium, petra, Pastor, Propheta, Primogenitus, Panthon, Panis, Splendor, Sother, Sapientia, Sol, Salus, Sponsus, Sacerdos, Stimulamathon, Serpens, ffons, Leo, vitis, vitulus, vermis, verbum, vitis, yskyros, Amorule, Taneha, Latysten, Rabur, Tancha, Escha, Aladia, Baralanensis, baldacheiensis, Panmarchie, et apologie sedes, Tetragrammaton, יהוה Iehovah.[64] [16r]

[13.] The deuyne names of God per Cornelium Agrippum.[65]

Adonay, Anaphexiton, Agla, Abyn, Asamie, Asaraye, Achym, Amyoram, Aty, Azia, Abraye, Achadan, Archmia, Alnaym, Anycke, Ay, Aye(3), Athanathos, Alpha et Omega, Anathay, Amen, Berysay, Bathat, Cados(3), Cantine, Calbat, El אל., Eloha, Elohym, Elohe, Eheye, Elyon, Esch, Escerchie, Emanuell, Eye(3), Eya, Elybra, Eschereye, hagyos, helyoren, he(3), hy(2), ha(2), hyn, hatym, heye(3), heya, hod, hu(3), Iod, Iah(2), Ioth, Ihesuh, יהשוה, Iskyros, Iaym, Ianycke, Ia(2), Ie, Ima, Ieya, Minosell, Marinata, messyas, Na, On, Otheos, Pha, primeumaton, paracletus, Rabur, Sabaoth, Saday, שדי, Sanctus, Benedictus, Ipse, Saraye, Sar, Sabbac, Saclay, Tetragramaton, Va(4), V, Ye, Ya(3). Orystyon [16v]

[14.] The consecratinge of the ffumygacyons[66]

O God of Abraham, god of Isaacke & God of Iacob, blesse this creature of Spices,[67] yat yt maye haue strengthe & vertue by his odoure, so as no phantazie or Enemy maye enter therein, by the vertue of our Lord Ihesus Chryste, who Lyueth & Reigneth, now & for euer worlde withought ende Amen. Then sprenkle yt with holy water.

[15.] The Consecrayon of the water[68]

O heauenly ffather which haste placed the ffyrmament in ye mydes of ye water & dyddeste in ye terrestryall paradice ordeyne A holy fountayne of water, from whence proceadeth fower Ryvars, which passeth through ye hoole worlde, And euen as thow dyddest make ye waters ye instrumentes of thy Iustyce, to destroye ye Gyantes, At ye Generall fludde of Noe, & for the destructyon of Pharaos hoste in ye redde [17r] Sea, & broughtest thy people Izraell through ye mydes therof on ye drye Sande, As also thorough ye flude Iordan, And as thow dyddest myraculousely, in ye desarte, bringe water oughte of ye rock And also as you broughteste water oughte of ye Iawebone of A Mylhorse Toothe, at ye prayars of Sampson, And as you haste apoynted ye water to be ye Instrument of thy mercye to ye forgyvenes of our Tymes, And for yat our sauyour Ihesus Chryste was baptized in ye fludde Iordan,[69] & thereby dyde clense & sanctyfye all wateres, who is a lyuynge fountayne, ye well of lyef and ye fludde of mercye. ffor these and all other thy myracles doone by water, O Lord + sanctyfye & + blesse this water that in thy holy name + Iehouah + Tetragramaton + , & Saday + [70] yt maye sanctyfye all thinges yat ar sprenkled therwith be yt place, Sercle, Instrument, experiment, fummygacion, booke or Sercle etc. And may haue power to abolyshe all euyll sprites & illusyons, & to make ye sprites called to be obedyent to the Exorcysor though Iesu Chryste our Lord Amen. In nomine patris et + fillij + & spiritus sancti, + Amen. fiat, fiat, fiat.[71] [17v]

[16.] The consecratyon of the Oyle[72]

O eternal ffather which in Exodus dyddeste apoynte ye Oyle of vnctyon & dyddest cause ye prophet to Anoynte dauyd kynge, O Lorde Ihesus Chryste whose name soundeth in Englyshe anoynted[73] And as in ye Reuelacyon of St Iohn there is mencyon made of two Olyue treas styllynge oughte holy oyle into hotte burnynge lampes afore ye face of God,[74] Sanctyfye & blesse Oh Lord this oyle, yat yt may haue power to subdue euyll sprites to make them obedient to the Exorcysor, and also to sanctyfye & make holy, the thinge or thinges touched therewith thoroughe Iesus Chryste our Lorde who lyueth & reyneth now & for euer world withouhte end, And Oh heauenly father, almightye, euerlastynge & of infynyte power, which by thy worde haste created & made all thynges, & which with thy right hande dydest rule the infernall Empyre, & dyddest cause Oyle to be consecrated, Therefore oh Lord in ye vertue of our Lord Iesus Chryste, & his precyous bludde shedynge & his humylytie, which dyd take humane forme of his mother ye blessed virgyn Mary, & which was obedynet to the [18r] Oh heauenly father euen to the deathe for me myserable Synnar, & all mankynde, I most humbly beseache the vouchesafe to vysytte this oyle by the holy Angelles, & to sanctyfye + blesse & cosecrate yt, that by ye vertue therof I may knowe thy omnipotente power, & sea thy inuisible sprites, & compell them & fulfyll my desyre, & shewe me all thynges yat I desyre, & yat by vertue of thys Oyle I maye bynde them all throughe our Lorde Iesus Chryste which lyueth now & for ever Amen.

Oh Lord Ihesus Chryste ye goode sheparde, of thy omnypotente maiestie & goodnes, vouchsafe to caste thy holy Eyes vpon this Oyle, & to + consecrate + blesse & + sanctyfye this Oyle by ye vertue of thy holy name & Iehovah יהוה + Tetragrammaton, + Agla + Sabaoth, Saday + Adonay + Eloy + & by ye vertue of ye blessed vyrgyn mary thy mother, & which of thyne humylytie dyddest leaue thy fatheres seate in heauen, & dyddest dwell withe thy mother as an Infante, vouchsafe I beseache y^e to blesse this Oyle yat I maye see & bynde these spirites [18v] which you haste created, & yat I maye speake with them when soeuer I will, through Ihesus Chryste our Lord Amen.

[17.] The consecratyon of the ffyar[75]

I exorcyse ye you creature of fyre[76] by hym which made all thynges that weare made, yat forthwith you mayste caste awaye all phantazies or Illusyons, whearby, you mayest not hurte in anye thynge[77] And oh sweate sauyour Ihesus Chryste which hast created ye fyar to be ye Instrument of thy iustyce, to the punyshment of wycked synnars, & for ye Iudgment of ye vnyuersall world as also you which dyddest appeare to moyses in A bushe of fflamynge fyre, & you which dyddest goe afore ye Chyldren of Izraell in a fyry pyllar, And you which dyddest apointe inextinguable fyar to be preserued in ye Tabernacle, of wytnesse, and beinge oughte dyddest miraculously kyndle yt agaeyne & dydest preserue yt pryuely vnder the water vnquenchalbe, ffor these & and all other thy [19r] Myracles wroughte by fyar,[78] and also for yat you arte a consumynge fyer, and in thy holy bybble called splendor die, lux dei, Lumen dei,[79] Blesse oh Lorde this creature of fyre, yat yt may be sanctyfyed and blessed to the prayse of thy holy name, & yat yt maye not be hurtfull to the bearar therof, or ye sears therof, through our Lord Ihesus Chryste which lyueth & reignethe world without ende.[80] This fyar must be put into A newe earthen pott

[18.] Consecratio Gladii[81]

O heauenly father, which of thy dyuyne maiestie dyddest sende a sworde to Iudas Machabeus, to cutte of ye enemyes from ye people of Izraell & in an other place in thy holy scripture dyddest saye, take vnto yow two edged Swordes & as our sauyor Iesus Chryste sayde to his disciples sell your coates & bye swordes, And as ye prophete dauyde sayde, he sauwe [19v] A bluddy Angell makeinge vppe his Sworde And for yat in Scripture thy holy power and name ys called the Sword of God, the rodde of God, the staff of God, the reuenge of God, and as all creatures terrestriall Celestiall & infernall doe quake & reuerence thy holy name, which is A Sword & consummynge fyre,[82] Graunte oh Lorde, yat this sworde beinge consecrated in thy holy name, And in ye name of ye father ye sunne & ye holy ghoste, and by thy infallyble name + Tetragramaton + Saday + Agla + & Iehouahe, yat all spirites, terrestriall, & infernall may quake & Obeye at ye sight therof to ye exorcysor beinge commanded & coniured in thy holy name, Graunte oh heauenly ffather thys vertue to this sworde, for Iesus Chrystes sake who Lyueth & Reigneth now & euerrmore worlde withought ende Amen.

Y^e sword should haue a sigall wrytten on one syde & + on + on thother syde & going to ye place saye litanias[83]

[19.] Consecratio libri siue pergameni[84]
[Prayer 1][85]

Oh Lord heauenly father which dyddest delyuer vnto moyses vpon ye Mounte Synay, ye tenne commandmentes [20r] in ye two tables of Stone, to the sanctyfy-inge of the Law ye prophetes & ye Scryptures delyuered by the holy ghoste, & doeste call ye holy Bybble thy Testament, The booke of God, The booke of Lief, ye knowlege of God, ye wysdum of God:[86] So Sanctyfye Oh Lord thys booke (yf yt be thy holy will & pleasure) yat yt maye forcybely bynd all sprites being called by thy dyuyne names, & peaceabely to appeare in a fayer forme withought hurtynge me or any Lyuynge Creature, & tellinge me ye truthe of all yat I shall demaunde, withoughte fraude or decepte, thorough Ihesus Chryste owre Lorde Amen. Oh inuysyble god, oh inestimable God, oh unchangeable God, oh incorruptible God, oh most holy God, oh moste highe god, oh moste gloryous god, oh moste mightye God ye God of all solace & mercy (& although vnworthy & full of iniquytye decepte and malyce) moste humbly desyrynge thy mercy beseachinge ye yat you wylte not look vpon all my innumerable synnes, but as you arte acustomed to haue mercy vpon Synnars and to heare ye prayer of ye humble & lowly so vouchsafe to heare me thy Seruaunte though vnworthy, cryinge vnto the for these Experimentes or Bondes in this booke [20v] To call Sprites by thy holy names thearin wrytten, yat yt may obteyne & haue the vertue yat yt ought to haue, to bynde moste mightely aereall & infernall Sprites, by this concecrated booke, will they nil they[87] & maye obey, me or any other Exorcysor to cum together, & ageyne to deperte and disperse them when he will, by thy moste holy name, which is wrytten with fowar Lettres[88] + On + Alpha, et Omega, the fyrst & ye laste, + El + Elohe + Eloy + Elehu + Sother + Emanuel + Sabaoth + Adonay + ya + ya + ye + ye + That thys booke with the bondes, therin, and these Experimentes for Sprites, Consecrations & inuocatyons, may haue force according to my desyre by thy Almightye powar you which syttest in ye most highest, To whome be prayse glory & honour world withought ende Amean. Ower ffather which arte in heauen etc.[89]

[Prayer 2][90]

O God ye maker of ye vnyuersall world, which haste extended the heauens aboue ye cloudes, & haste made the Earth in his stabylytie aboue ye water & haste geuen ye Sea his boundes which he can not passe, And haste placed ye sonne & mone & ye starres in ye fyrmament, All which thow dyddest by thy dyuyne wysdum, which also in ye syxte daye dyddest make man, accordinge to thy Image, & dydeste breathe into hym, ye holy Ghoste the spyryte of lyef, whome for hys dysobedyence you dyddest caste [21r] Ought of paradyse,[91] And you which dydeste destroye man in ye water at ye fludde & dyddest saue Nohe & all yat weare with hym in the Arke,[92] and you which dyddest appeare to Abraham in the Trynytie or thyrde person vnder the tree of Mambre,[93] And which dyddeste apeare to Moyses in ye mydest of A Bushe & spake vnto hym in a flame of ffyar, And you which dydest delyuer thy people oughte of ye captyuytie of Egypte & leddest them thorough ye redde Sea, And which gaueste thy lawe to Moyses in ye Mounte Synay, And you which madeste water cum oughte of ye Rock, And you

which dyddeste saue danyell from yᵉ Lyons mouth, And you which dydest delyuer yᵉ thre Chyldren, Sydrach, Misache & Abdenago from yᵉ fyery ffornace &
you which dyddest delyuer Susanne from fals accusatyon for yat she trusted in
the, And you which dyddest delyuer Ionas yᵉ prophete beinge thre dayes and
thre nightes in the whalles belly,⁹⁴ by these & many other myracles which thow
hast done, mercyfully heare yᵉ prayer of my thy vnworthy Seruaunte, And gyue
to thys booke (Experimentes and Inuocatyons) vertue & power ouer all euyll
Spirites, to congregate them, to loose, [21v] bynde curse & caste them into yᵉ
pytte of Hell, yf they doe not obeye my Commandment & me the Exorcysor, the
Lorde permyttyng yt which is holy and blessed who reigneth worlde withoughte
ende Amen. Our ffather etc.

[Prayer 3]⁹⁵

O most Gloryous Adonay, by whom all thynges weare made & created, moste
mercyfully heare my prayres, yat this booke & Instrument maye haue vertu to
bynde euyll spirites & meakely obeye yᵉ exorcisor me or any other, will they nyll
they, & fulfyll my commaundmentes, Thow which syttest in yᵉ most highest
commaundinge yt, you onely which keapeste all thynges to whome be all glory,
honoure and power worlde withoughte ende Amen Ower ffather etc.

[Prayer 4]⁹⁶

Oh most holy & most iuste Adonay. The fountayne of all godlynes, yᵉ kynge of
kynges & lorde of Lordes, which syttest in thy dyuyne maiestie & seest all thynges in hell, rulest all thynges, & conteynynge all thynges as yt weare in A hand-
full, & which by thy vertue doest moderate all thynges, which madest man
accordynge to thy Image of yᵉ moulde of yᵉ Earth, yat you mightest be praysed
vpon yᵉ Earthe as you arte in heauen, & yat all yᵉ Earth shoulde worshippe the,
and synge vnto the, And I though vnwrothy, will saye a psalme in honour of thy
name,⁹⁷ O you moste higheste Thearfor moste heauenlye [22r] ffather I appeale
to thy maiestie And with humble deuotyon meakely desyre the yat by yᵉ vertue
& gyfte of thy grace these prayers, consecratyons, coniuracyons Inuocatyons,
bandes of sprites, and experimentes which ar conteyned in thys Booke, may be
consecrated, that they may obteyne vertue & effecte, wherunto they ar apoynted,
& may perfectly gyue power to the exorcysor ouer euyll sprites that when they
shallbe called by him of these Experimentes, yat forthewyth they maye cum
from all places & may gyue trewe answeare, quickely & infallyblye, He grauntynge
yt to whome belongeth all honour & poure, whiche also reigneth worlde
witoughte ende amen. Our ffather which arte in heauen Etc.

[Prayer 5][98]

O Adonay Neloth, O Adonay. Anloth, Deolam, Natath, Adonay by whome all thynges weare created made & sanctyfyed, I call for thy mercy and thy infallyble power, by these moste holy names folowynge, yat you wouldest vouchsaf to gyue vnto me (thoughe thy vnworthy Seruaunt) the helpe of thy grace ouer these prayeres, Coniuracions, Consecratyons, Inuocatyons, bandes, for sprites, & Experimentes signed with thy moste holy names, yat is to saye + On El + Elohe + Coyha , heye, Elzephares, [22v] + Occinomos, + Onerteon + Stymulamathon + hely + Elyon + Eleoram + Messyas + Sother + Emanuel + Sabaoth + panton + craton + primus + principium + primogenitus + sapientia + virtus + Ozanna + Sol + Splendor + Gloria + Lux + panis + fons + vitis + manus + Ostium + Ianua + Petra + Lapis + Os + verbum + Salus + Angelus + Sponsus + Sacerdos + pastor + propheta + mediator + Ouis + Vitulus + Serpens + Aries + Leo + Vermis + Athanathos + yskyros + Agyos + Otheos + By these moste holy names & all other names which ar not to be spoken, I humbly beseache ye that theese Ora-cyons Consecratyons & inuocayons of sprites, bandes, & experimentes, which ar conteyned in this booke, maye haue vertue and power (by thy dyuyne vertue), to consecrate all Experimentes, Inuocations of devels,[99] & bondes, yat when-soeuer sprites shalbe shalbe called & coinured by ye vertue of thy holy names, yat forthwith they maye cum from euery parte of ye worlde & diligently fulfyll ye will of the Exorcysor, Neyther hurtynge nor brynginge terroure but rather obey-inge & mynystrynge, And being Bounde by [23r] The vertue of thy holy Name, maye obeye my commaundment, fiat, fiat, fiat. Amen our ffather etc.

[Prayer 6][100]

Oh Omnipotente & euerlastynge God which from ye begynnynge madest all thynges of Naughte, to whome all creatures obey, & euery knee bendeth,[101] celestytall, terrestryall and infernall, whom ye angelles & Archangelles ffeare, domynatyons & Potestates worshippe & trymble,[102] which houldest all thynges in thy hande, And madeste man accordinge to thy lykenes, And dyddest caste donne ye wycked into hell, I moste humbly beseache the Omnipotent ffather, by our Lorde Ihesus Chryste thy Sonne, in whose power ar all thynges, who sytteth on thy ryghte hande Oh omnipotent ffather, who also shall cum to iudge ye quycke & ye deade & ye worlde by ffyar. Amen. Oure ffather etc.

Oh father of heauen, one in substance and thre in person, whyche dyddest suffer Adam and Heaue & many other to synne, and yen to be crucyfyed for their synnes, most ientle father I desyre ye meakely by thy name alpha & Omega, & in the name of thy sonne Iesus Chryste, yat thow wylte suffer thy Angelles to healpe me, which sumtyme [23v] weare incredulous, & yat I maye speake with them, & to doe what I will with them, withoughte hurtynge me or any creature, Cummaunde oh Lorde you which haste geuen vertue to stones hearbes & wordes[103] And to thy holy Names, yat by them I may bynde & Lose Sprites, by thy helpe, wonderfull vertue and power. Amen. Our ffather etc.

[Prayer 7][104]

O Greate & eternall deytye & moste hyghe vertue which is spreade dyspersed & dysposed by ye callynge on of these thy holy names, yat is to saye + Onotheon + Stymulamathon + Elioram + Elzephares + Tetragramaton + Elyoram + Egirion + Eriona + vriorucat + Onoebesonn + Noym + Ioseph + messias + Sother + Emanuel + Sabaoth + Adonay + I call vpon y^e, I worshipp the with all my mynde & strengthe, yat by these presente Oratyons, consecratyons, inuocatyons, bondes of Sprites and Exerimentes which ar in this booke, may be consecrated & prepared accordingely, That when soeuer euill or goode sprites shalbe called & bounde by the vertue of thy holy name, that forthwith they maye cum from euery part of ye worlde, & fulfyll diligently ye will of ye Exarsysor, neyther hurtinge nor fearynge any creature, But [24r] Rather Obedyent & mynystrynge (& by thy dyuyne vertue), fulfyllying the vertu of ye Exorcysors wordes and cumaundmentes. fiat, fiat, fiat. Amen. Our Father etc.

[Prayer 8][105]

In the name of our Lord Ihesus Christe ye father ye sonne & ye holy Ghoste, ye holy trynytye and inseperable vnytie, I call vpon ye that thow mayste be my health & defence and protectyon of my soule now & for euer by ye vertue & power of thy holy crosse I desyer ye Oh Lord Iesus Chryste ye sonne of ye Lyuynge God, & by ye merytes & intercessyons of our blessed virgyn Mary thy mother, & in ye name of all thy sanctes, yat you wouldeste gyue me thy grace & dyuyne power ageynst all naughtye sprites, that whensoeuer I shall call them, by ye vertue of thy holy names, yat forthwith they maye cum from euery parte of the worlde, & fulfyll ye will of ye Exorsysor neyther hurtyne nor fearynge any creature, but rather obedyent and mynystrynge, And by the dyuyne vertue maye fulfyll my commaundment & Soe be yt Amen. Our ffather which arte in heaven etc. [24v]

[Prayer 9][106]

O Lord Ihesus Christ by thy infallyble mercye, haue mercye vpon me, & heare my prayer, yat[107] call vpon thy moste holy name, by god ye father, ye sonne and the holy Ghoste, & I desyre the moste mightie Lorde yat ye prayer & ye wordes of my mouthe, may please y^{e108} the trewe and Lyuying God, & yat thow wouldest gyue me power (althoughe vnworthye and A myserable synnar) yat by thy moste holy names + Iesus + Christus + Alpha et + omega, El + Eloy + Emanuell + Sabaoth + Adonay + And by all other thy secreate & dyuyne names, which ar conteyned in thys booke, yat by ye vertue sanctymony & force of ye seyde names, & by thy vertue and dyuyne power this booke may be consecrated, blessed & confyrmed, And by ye vertue of ye Sacramente of thy most precyous body & bludde yat ye vertue with yt shoulde obtayne, yt maye effectualy obtayne, withought any fraude or decepte to consecrate ye bandes of sprites & all other Experimentes, in notatyons, & coniuracions & yat yt may obtayne & haue, an holye vertue and power, wherunto yt is apoynted you Lorde Iesus Chryste grauntynge yt which syttest in ye moste higheste, to whome be honour & glory worlde withoughte ende Amen. God ye ffather + bless y^e, God ye Sonne + blesse y^e, God ye holy ghoste blesse the, mary ye most holy mother of owar Lorde Ihesus Chryste + blesse the + [25r] And sanctyfy ye that thow mayste haue ye vertue of A sacrament in y^e,[109] All the Angelles in heauen + blesse the, All ye patryarkes & prophetes + blesse the, All ye Apostles & decyples of our Lorde + blesse the, All martars & confessors + blesse the, And at all tymes, all ye holy & Electe of God, & all caelestyall vertues, blesse the, All angelles Archangelles, vertues, potestates, principates, cherybyn & seraphyn (by authorytye & Licence from god) confyrme & + blesse the, And all merytes, Intercessions, oratyons and invocatyons, of all ye Sainctes of ower Lord Ihesus Christe[110] + bless + sanctifie + consecrate & + confyrme this booke, yat by the omnypotente mighte & powar yt maye obteyne ye effect yat yt is apoynted for, The Almightie Lorde grauntynge yt, who Lyueth and reigneth worlde withoughte ende Amen. Leaue me not oh Lorde God accordinge to thy greate mercye Let thy mercy lighten vpon vs, as we haue trusted, Let me neuer be confounded, Let my prayeres enter into thy Eares oh Lord & inclyne thy Eare to my prayar, Oh Lord heare my prayar & my crye shall cum to the,[111] Let vs praye[112] [25v]

Except the Lord bylde the howse their Labour is but loste yat buylde yt. Except ye Lorde Keape ye cytye, the wachmen watch but in vayne. yt is but Loste laboure yat now haste to ryse vppe early, & so late take reste and eate ye breade of carefulnes. ffor so he gyueth his beloued sleape. Loe chyldren & ye fruyte of ye wombe are an herytage & gyfte yat cumeth of the Lorde. Lyke as the arowes in ye hande of the Gyaunte, euen so are ye yonge chyldren. Happy is ye man yat hathe hys Quyver full of them. They shall not be ashamed when they speak with their Enemyes in the Gate.[113] Glory be to ye ffather & to ye Sonne and to ye holy ghoste, As yt was in ye begininge is now & euer shallbe world wythought ende Amen.[114]

[20. Instructions for consecrating the book][115]

Nota yat in the concecratynge of the booke ye partie sholde abstayne from venus, nyne dayes,[116] and eate lyttle meate, therefore ye Lente is best,[117] & euery day sayinge these 9 prayers aboue sayde, for ye consecration of ye booke, ouer the booke, being wraped uppe in fyne lane or whighte lynen & sprykelynge yt with holy water & anoyntynge & perfumynge yt, desiring god of his mercy,[118] to consecrate yt, And saye the psalmes miserere deus, videlicet . 51 . 56 . & 57 psalmes, all being miserere[119] [26r] Then Laye yt vpon A cleane table, couered with whighte Lynen, & knelynge doune saye the nyne prayers aboue seyde as ys sayd before, nyne dayes euery daye, yat is to saye in the mornynge none and euenynge, Thy face beinge turned into ye Easte, And at the leaste fayle not mornynge and Eueninge. After thys sorte maye Experimentes also be consecrated.

[21.] The method or order to worke in this arte

Thow which desyrest to work in thys science muste praye to God the father deuoughtelye, yat by his grace thow mayste be made worth, Thow must be cleane in they aperell, as clean shirte, sweate cleane clothes, thy body and feate all washed thy longe heare cut of, thy nayles pard, both of they feate and handes, and all this tyme not to lye with any woman, Ageyne ye place muste be cleane, and in Nature Agreynge to ye place of ye planet or Spyryt, As for Example [26v] To procure love call Die et hora veneris in a Garden or chamber, & the better yt ys yf ♀ be in ♉ ♎ or . ♓ . Eyther for callinge of ♀ Angelles, or for callynge of hir Intelligence Hagiell.

Also ye exorcysor muste stand with his face mostely into ♀ quarter which is South or Southweste. But in any wise in callynge or consecratynge, let ye aperell, both Lynen & wollen, be neate & cleane, & vse fastinge pamperinge not thy self two muche, Ageyne thinges consecrated may be prophaned And in ye oulde lawe in Leuyticus, yt is seyde, The vncleane person yat cometh to consecrated thinges shall perishe.[120] Praye vnto god 9 dayes afore you workeste that thow mayse haue thy desyre, incense the place when thou prayeset, ffor dauyd sayth, O Lord my prayer I shalbe directed vnto the as incence, in thy sight[121] Also fumigacyons & vnctyons, open the Elementes & cause sprites to appeare, which take thereby theyr bodyes,[122] And what soeuer you doest doe yt with a feruente desyre of the harte, & in all thynges yat thow goest abought, haue god before thy Eyes, ffor yt is wrytten yat yf thow seakest ye Lorde you shalt fynde hym, but yt must be with all ye harte [27r] ageyne Saint Mark sayth, whatsoeuer yow doe aske in prayer beleaue & you shall haue yt, and St Mathew saythe yf yow had fayth as much as A grayne of mustsard seade, nothinge should be impossyble vnto yow.[123] The prayer of ye iuste auayleth much; ffor helyas at St Iames seyth, was a man as we ar & he prayed yat yt shoulde not rayne, and yt reigned not in thre yeares & syx monethes And agaeyne he prayed & yt rayned.[124] But take heade yat in all thy prayeres thow requyre no vayne thinge which may be ageynste hys dyuyne will, for God willeth all goodnes, & you must not take hys name in vayne,[125] for such shall not be vnpunyshed. ffaste & gyve almes for ye Angell seyde to Tobyn prayer is good with ffastynge & almes and in ye booke of Iudith yt is seyde ye Lord will heare your prayer with fastinge.[126]

These ar ye principles which aperteyne vnto Magyke, And therfore yf any thorough his owne vnbelef or sluggysh ignorance obteyne not his desyre, let him impute ye faulte to his owne ignoraunce and not to me, yat I shoulde wrighte any false thynge, but let hym condempe him self, for yat he vndersthandeth not ye trewe meanynge of my worke beinge darke and full of mysteries, & may doth soone erre.

And note yat fayer water, [27v] Oyle, paper, parchment, ynke, penne, compasse & fumygatyons, must be consecrated & so must ye Sercle, garment, sworde pentacles Seales, as Also ye place or gounde consecrated[127] And nota yat the ground, ynke, & Sercle is not consecrated vnless in ye tyme of consecratyon yt be sprynkled with holy water & fumygated. & ye paper, parchment, penne, compasse, pentacles, seales, sworde & booked, ar not rightely consecrated, vnlesse in ye consecratyon they be sprynkeled with holy water fumed & annoynted

[22. To make a pentacle, table or lamen]

And nota That to make a pentacle, Table or lamen to call the intelligence or goode angell of any planet, first yow must consyder what mettall yat planet will haue whether lead, brasse, coper, syluer or goulde, yf yow make yt not in metall then must yow make yt in vergyn parchment, with ye colours apropryed to yat planet. This must be doone in ye daye & hower of ye planet. & when he is in his house or Exaltacyon, Then make a round Sercle & in ye Sercle a Square, to make ye Table of intelligence in cyphars of ye intelligence or angell of yat planet, & in the vtter sircle [28r] wright ye caracter of ye intelligence & his hebrue & Latyn name and ye names of god anseringe that intelligence in hebrewe & Latyn & at ech corner in the sqaure one pentagonum, for yf I shoulde call onely hagiell ♀ intelligence, yet must I haue 4 pentagoni, & looke so many sprites as yow call so many pentagoni yow must haue in your lamen or table. This Lamen should be wrapped in fyne lane, consecrated & oyled & sprynkled & fumed with his apropyed fumygacyon, & also in callynge to stande towarde that quarter of ye worlde with thy face yat that Intelligence is in, & laye the lamen afore the, & in apearinge shewe yt hym.

See fol. 50 for ♀ intelligence which sheweth 3 or 4 weyes, therfore not onely to make hagiell apeare to his caracter but also being caryed abought yow to procure loue etc. & thus of all other intelligences of thother planetes mutatis mutandis. Obseruinge ther mettalles, colores, places, houses & exaltacyons, etc. & to procure hatred or to worke contrary, take yᵉ character & name of yᵉ euill intelligence etc. [28v]

[23. To make pentacles by holy scripture][128]

But to make pentacles by holy scripture As in yᵉ first of the Reuelacyon, make a dubble or Tryple Cercle, & within the Sercle wrighte or pycture onely the Maiestie of God, & in yᵉ vtter Sercles the Tenne deuyne names of God and the scripture apropryed therfore, As god syttyinge in his throne, haueinge a sharp sword in his mouth, as yt is pictured in the new Testament and in yᵉ Sercle wright I am Alpha & Omega, The fyrst & yᵉ last, which is, which was, & which is to cum. I am yᵉ fyrst and yᵉ last, being deade and am alyue, & behould I am lyuynge vnto yᵉ end of yᵉ worlde, & I haue yᵉ keyes of death, & of hell, Comaund thy vertu oh Lord, Confyrme thys oh Lord yat thou has wrought in vs, Let them be as duste scattered with yᵉ wynde[129] and yᵉ Angell of yᵉ Lorde dryuynge them, let thear weye be slyppery & darke, and yᵉ Angell of yᵉ Lorde flowynge them, Then wrighte these names in yᵉ extreme Sercle which ar tenne in number, yat is to saye El + Elohim + Elohe + Sabatoh + Elion , Escerchie + Adonay + Iah + Saday + Tetragramaton +

[24. On pentacles]

And nota pentacles ar holy signes, preseruying vs from euyll helpinge vs to bynde euill sprites, to pull them donne, and to allure vnto vs [29r] goode Sprites,[130] & nota planetary pentacles should be made in A new mone yᵉ planet in house or Exaltacyon, & with his proper mettall or colores as is sayde afore in yᵉ tytle of planets And in this tytle.

[25. Rules for Operating][131]

And whosoeuer doth consecrate ringe Ringe, Scepter, sword, book, pentacle, etc. must be in an honest godly, learned & deuoute man, for withought these thinges no man can work to haue hys purpose,[132] & he muste obserue his tymes and howeres, as well by daye as nighte, & specyally to the Age of yᵉ mone, yat she be newe & in euen number after hir change, as 2. 4. 6. 8. 10. 12. 14.[133] ffor after yᵉ ffull yt is no workynge vntyll yᵉ change ageyne Also let his vpper garment, be very whyte cleane & odoryferous, for sprites ar gretly delighted with sweate sauores.

And nota in euery worke, let ye Tyme daye or nighte be fayer & cleare not truble-sum. And yf you calleste easterly sprites turne to ye Easte, yf westorne, weste & yf yt may be worke on Sundaye or at ye leaste when ye sunne shyneth for Spirites desyre much to apeare vnder ye sunne beames.[134]

Also thre dayes afore yow worke, defyle not your self with wemen, neyther vse excesse in meates or drinkes,[135] And yat which you intendest reueale yt to no creature vnlesse yt be to thy sworne frende,[136] And afore you workes wash they handes and [29v] pare thy nayles, & cutte thy bearde, & in euery adiuracyon thow shouldest seuen tymes repeate thy coniuracyon East, West, north, & South etc. in eche quarter .7. tymes, And as often as thow touchest thy lamen, hauynge ye greate names of God in yt & anoynted with oyle of Spyke,[137] shewe yt them reuerently knealynge or bending therunto, And yow shold haue vpon your lefte hande & lytle fynger A rynge, ye makeing therof shalbe seyd hearafter, And when you cumest from werke ought of the Sercle, keape ye thre houres from candle lyght yf you workest in ye nighte yf in ye daye thre houres from ye Sonne lighte, lyinge vpon thy bedd, After thre houres Eate what you wylte,[138] and as you doest soe let thy frende or companyon or felowes doe also, be yt for fastynge, washinge abstinence from ♀, prayer & cleannes in aperell Reueale thy mynde to no person but to they felow or felowes for yf thow doest you shalt haue thy purpose no more.[139]

And nota the sercle shoulde be 15 or 17 foote ouer,[140] But cornelius seyt but 9 foote ouer,[141] & ye names of God therin for thy defence, videlicet + Agla + in ye Easte +Saday + Sabaoth + in the South + Tetragramaton + יהוה + [30r] in the weste + Adonay + Eloy + in the Northe. And nota yat in ye sercle, pentacle, or Experimente these or such lyke dyvyne names must be wrytten in them Elles there is no apparance or affect nor yet any truth. And nota ye dayes & houres of of ⊙, ♀, ☿, & ☽ in ye change & in euen numberes are goode to worke, ♄ & ♂ contrarye. And nota an Experiment is sayde to be made die et hora ♀ yf in hir day and hower ye thinge be begune and wroute vpon, though not ended thre houres or three dayes after for prolyxytie of ye worke, The lyke understande by callinge in a sercle die & hora ♀.

Yf you makest an Experimente for loue or frendshippe, by character or rynge, reveale yt to no creature And yf you workest with a felow or felowes, let him or them, be godly, honeste, chaste, cleane, stronge in fayth & of goode corage desy-ringe ye effecte as well as thy self, & yf you fayleest once or twyse, yet leaue not of, for sum tymes ye vncleanes of the place, ye yll lief of ye master or his felowe, their want of fayth & such lyke, make his worke frustrate [30v] And nota yf yow make your sercle in yᵉ nighte, make yt on Saturday At Sunne settinge which is mercuries night, And nota all sercles must be rounde Sauyinge yᵉ Sercels of Bylet and Amaymon which muste be square.¹⁴² And all sercles must be mayde in a solytary place, as in a woode or elles wheare + wayes crosse, But the Sercle of Amayon & ♀ Sercle for Loue muste be in a greane place And none must speake but yᵉ master, he must stande & they sytte,¹⁴³ but he firste knealynge, Easte, weste North & into yᵉ south, & deoutly adiurynge etc. And nota yt is goode to worke die & hora mercurij with the rysynge of the Sunne, or in the after none in the 8 planetary hower for ☿ is but twyse reynynge in a naturall day, I mean from Sunne to Sunne,¹⁴⁴ videlicet one wednesdaye at yᵉ rysynge of the Sonne & yᵉ 8. planetary hower after none afore sunne settynge, or elles in mercuryes night which is on Saturdaye at yᵉ settinge for then ☿ taketh yᵉ fyrste howerof yᵉ nighte, and ageine reyneth yᵉ 8 planetary hower after sunne setting which is after mydnighte, on Sunday, [31r] mornynge, ffor loue make your Sercle die & hora ☉, or die & hora veneris, ffor hatred, die & hora ♄. ffor experimentes, die & hora ♃.

And nota yf you wilt worke on Sunday Nighte in the first hower of yᵉ Sunne you must worke on wedynsdaye nighte after sunne setting, for wednesday night is yᵉ night of yᵉ sonne, wheroff he is Lorde for yat he reigneth the first hower of yᵉ night, euen as he is Lord on Sunday for raynynge yᵉ fyrste hower of yᵉ daye etc. & yf you wylt worke on munday nighte take thursday night, yf one wedynsday night, take saturdaye night, yf one fryday nighte take munday nighte. And nota yᵉ Lorde of yᵉ night is easyly known yf yow counte the 3d planet of yᵉ daye inclusiue, Example from Sol to ☿ dessending is 3.¹⁴⁵ Therfor I doe saye wedynsday night is the Sunnes artyfyciall night etc. And nota euery space in yᵉ Sercle shoulde be one hande breade from an other, & cornelius seyth yᵉ hoole cercle should be but 9 foote ouer, sum take 15 or 17 foot ouer

Also deperte not owt of yᵉ Sercle, though [31v] thou hast no aperance, withoughte geuynge of them lycence for by thus doinge many haue bene in daunger, for sprites lye inuisyble, & haue no corporall bodyes, & therfore can not be seene, and many tymes they apeare not, beinge agashed¹⁴⁶ to beholude yᵉ dyuyne names in the sercle thy pentacle or lamen the deuyne names of the sworde thy rynge they cepter,¹⁴⁷ Also many tymes they appeare not for yᵉ unworthines of yᵉ caller or his felowes, yᵉ rudenes of yᵉ place or their mystakinge of their worke or for yᵉ fearfulnes of yᵉ person or persons, leaste they shoulde be ouer much terrible vnto them. Also many tymes horribles sightes will apeare to feare yᵉ from thy worke, as to see thy father or mother slayne afore thy face, or to thinke ye waues of ye Sease shoulde droune the, Or Serpentes, lyons, bulles, beares or dogges to deuour the, Sumtyme ye iudge or mayor of ye Toune to cum vnto the, all which are but illusyons to feare ye from thy worke, and make ye loose thy labour, be stronge in fayth & feare not, and then they can not hurte y^e, but rather obeye the, [32r] for god suffereth none to be confounded yat put their truste in him, he is aboue all devylles sprites, Ageine many tymes they cume laughinge & playinge, to make the laughe also, & take awey they deuotyon, but looke vpon thy book, & not on them

And yf they require sacryfyce giue them none, but force them by the deuyne worde of god, and while you arte master & haue ye staff^148 in thy hande keepe yt, but yf you giueste sacryfyce then are they master & thow thier bonde slaue,^149 which then will fill ye with lyes, doe nothinge for ye but bringe ye beggery & an euill end. fforsake not thy god & maker, for any goulde or syluer, Indeade ye deuill will tempte man, for he was not ashamed to tempte Chryste,^150 And doubtless with sacryfyse, they will quickly cum, & euery simple and ignoraunte person maye so soone haue them, but then to their owne beggary & confusyon.

And nota the sworde should be bright & shynynge,^151 hauyng on, grauen on, thone syde,^152 & agla, on thother syde or elles yt must be made of wyllow & ye names, wrytten on eche syde which myst be consecrated [32v] oyled & anoynted, fumed & sprenkled with holy water, & ye master going to ye place should cary ye sworde in his hand an other should cary ye consecrated fyar & water, ye third should cary his garment, & euer as he goeth ye master should saye lytanias, & his felowes should answeare lytanias. The master should haue a pentacle of defence consecrated, oyled fumed & sprinkled with holy water, & yf ye sprites be dysobedyent shew yt them, which will make them yeld & quake therat,^153 so will they at ye sighte of ye deuyne names in thy sword, & nota summ make the sercle with there sworde, other with a peace of cosecrated chalke^154 haueinge A nauyle or corde nayled in the center & so in circumgiringe, drawe ye thre sercles, also yf sprites be dysobedyent extende to them thy sworde & they shall obeye the. Also ye master shoulde haue A Crowne vpon his head representynge a kynge & therfore to be obeyed,^155 & in the fore parte shoulde hange a lamen, & an other behynde his back also, for defence.^156

In any wyse keape well thy Sercle, And goe not awaye in [33r] a soden after their departure but staye sum while in prayer, for many times they lye hydde pryuately ought of thy sighte, And though they apeare not yet goe not oute of ye Sercle without gyuynge lycence as is seyde before. Nota also sumtyme they apeare not in ye fyrste nor secunde nor third tyme of profe[157] yet giue yt not ouer, Sume haue steyed 14 dayes afore they haue obteyned,[158] yea sum greate learned men as R[159] seyith haue not hadde their purpose afore ye second mone, fore heare note yat after a full mone yt is no workinge vntill y^e nexte change. And thus much as touchinge y^e maner & order of workinge in this arte of secrete magyke

finis [33v]

[26.] A good common figure [for] Any one spirit Baron or any other.

[34r]

[27. Figures for Sunday, Monday, Wednesday, and Friday in each season][160]

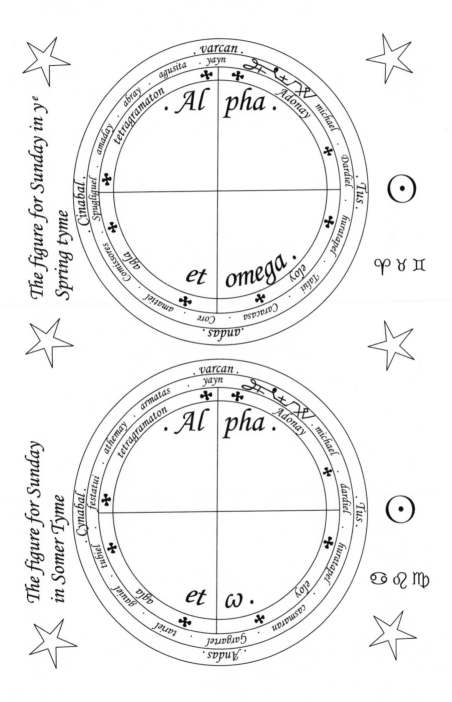

[34v]

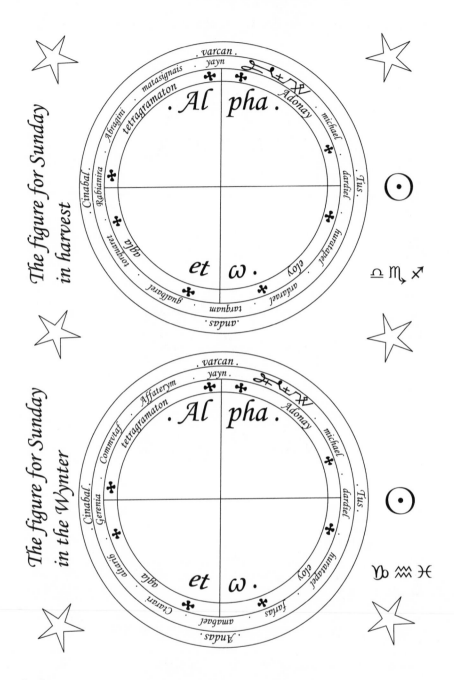

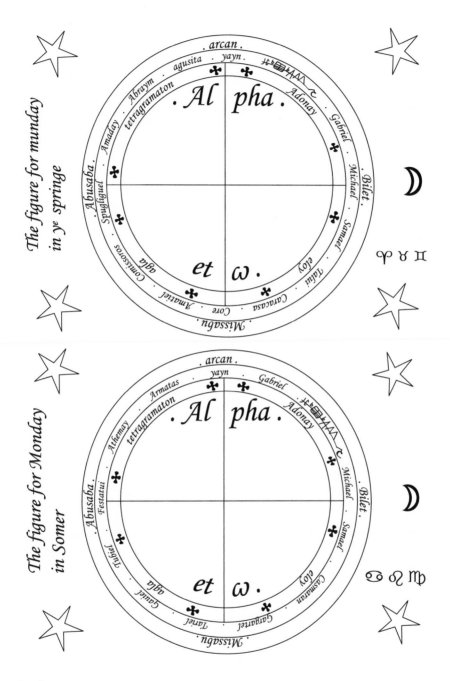

The figure for munday in ye springe

The figure for Monday in Somer

[35v]

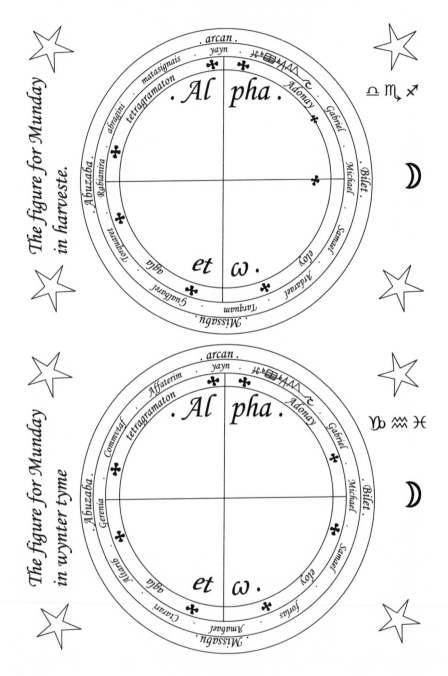

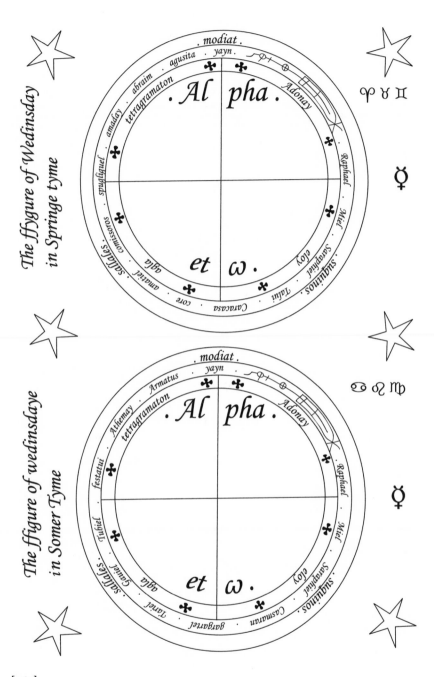

The ffygure of Wedinsday
in Springe tyme

The ffigure of wedinsdaye
in Somer Tyme

[36v]

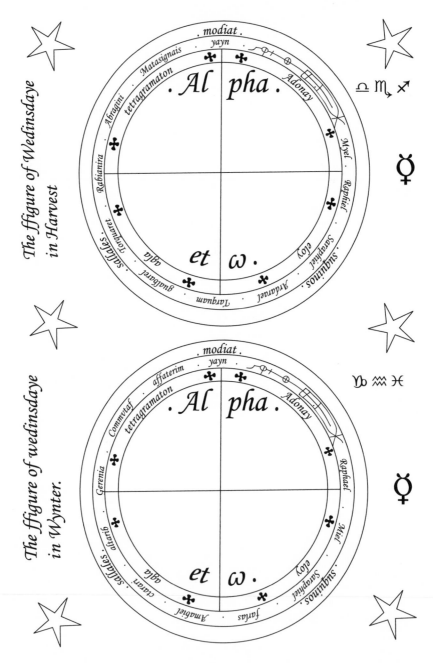

The ffigure of Wedinsdaye in Harvest

The ffigure of wedinsdaye in Wynter.

[37r]

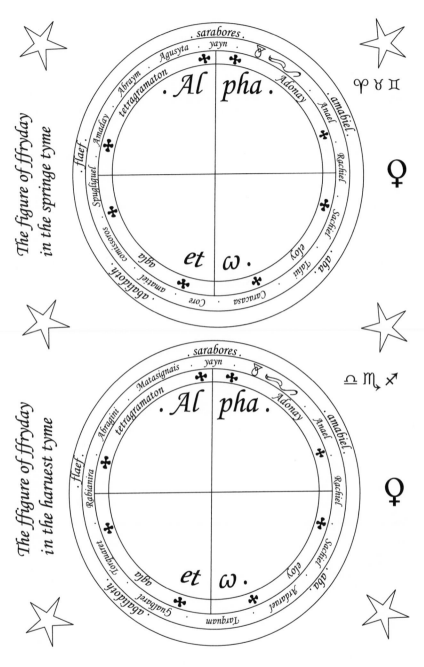

The figure of ffryday in the springe tyme

The ffigure of ffryday in the haruest tyme

[37v]

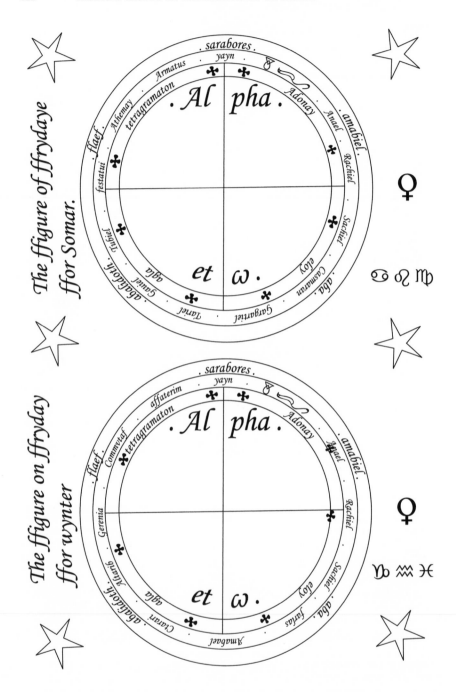

Notes

1. The meaning of this note is not entirely clear. It seems likely that Owen Lording, who was parish clerk of Boxgrove in Sussex, commissioned this manuscript from the anonymous scribe and that George Stent, who was a local notary, witnessed either the request for, or the delivery of, the book. The date is consistent both with what we know of the lives of Lording and Stent. Lording took the Oath of Protestation in 1641 confirming his Protestantism and loyalty to Parliament and administered it to those in his parish. He died on December 3, 1642. For his will see Chichester, West Sussex Record Office, B. Dean 16 (3 December 1642). George Stent was a notary who appears in documents of the first decade of the seventeenth century. See Archdeaconry of Chichester Detection Book: West Sussex Record Office, EP 1/17/13 fol. 8v (7 October) and EP 4/3/2 (8 March 1625/6, sic). See also West Sussex Record Office, Add MSS 6926, 6927, 4 June 1605.

2. In the figure below, אגלא is the original Hebrew notarikon or acronym rendered in Latin letters as AGLA. The letters stand for the four words in the Hebrew phrase *Atah Gibor Le-olam Adonai*, "You, O my Lord, are mighty forever." יהשוה (Yehoshua) is one of the common variations of the name Jesus. This magic image is drawn from the *Liber quartus*, which refers to it as the most powerful of images. For a fuller description see below, item 22.

3. This passage alludes to a variety of biblical passages from Revelation. See Revelation 1:8, 1:17–18, and 22:13. It concludes with a quotation from Psalms 35:5–6. Alpha and omega are the first and last letters of the Greek alphabet.

4. The sources for this section are multiple. See appendixes for a full description.

5. In the figure below, a later scribe has corrected the second last number in the uppermost row to 54 from 45, a mistake also occurring in all early printed versions of Agrippa's works. The scribe has also mistranscribed two numbers that were correct in the original: top to bottom, the third column from the left should read 13 / 63 / 23 / 64 / 33 / 74 / 43 / 3 / 53 (emphasis mine). *DOP*, 2:22 (318); Basel 1578, 225. A subsequent scribe notes in the margin: "369 / 9 × 41."

6. A later scribe has made notes beside each table indicating the sum of each side. In the margin beside this number a further calculation has been made (slashes indicate line breaks): "ם / 3321 / 9 × 369 / 81 × 41."
The logic behind this math is as follows. Each column and diagonal in the table for the moon square adds up to 369. This multiplied by 9 (the number of columns or rows) renders 3321. The average of the numbers in the square is 41. This multiplied by the total number of squares (81) also renders 3321. This number is the number of the intelligence. Hence, the later scribe has corrected the number in the text to 3321.

7. This image is slightly different from what is found in Agrippa, who has ⚏. *DOP*, 2:22 (318).

8. This is written at the top in red ink. The meaning is unclear.

9. Next to the figure below, a later scribe notes in left margin: "260 / 8 × 23 ½."

10. = tin.

11. Agrippa has "mercurialis." *DOP*, 1:29 (141–42). This is *mercurialis perennis*, commonly known as "dog's mercury."

12. Also known as cinquefoil.

13. These do not correspond to plants listed by Agrippa. *DOP*, 1:29 (141–42).

14. The circuit of the heavens through which the planets pass is known as the zodiac and is divided into twelve houses or signs. Each planet is associated with a particular house and has its "exaltation" within a particular sign (and technically within one degree of that sign). Mercury's exaltation is the fifteenth degree of Virgo. The instructions here suggest the broader interpretation of the term.

15. The seal is drawn from the *Heptameron*, 581 (Turner, 95). All the other seals for the planets are similarly drawn from this work. Ibid., 575–87 (88–108).

16. The table does not appear on the obverse as this note suggests. This is strong evidence that this manuscript is a copy of an original in which the figure did appear on the next page.

17. The option of using metal, paper, or wax is mentioned in *Liber quartus*, 553 (Turner, 61).

18. = marjoram or cinquefoil.

19. Next to figure below, a marginal note: "175 / 7 × 25."

20. Agrippa has "inter humores pituita cum sanguine, spiritu ac semine genitali" (among humors, phlegm with blood, spirit, and generative seed). *DOP*, 1:28 (140).

21. Agrippa has הגיאל, which is correct. The error appears to result from a simple line skip from the incorrect word to the correct one after the initial letter. The scribe does not make the same error in his illustration of the lamen. *DOP*, 2:22 (313).

22. It is not clear the scribe intended a taw, but the scribe's illustration of the lamen and Agrippa both have this letter.

23. The scribe follows the Basel 1578 and 1550 editions in this figure. See Basel 1578, 223; *DOP*, 2:22 (316).

24. = *ut probatur* [as is proven].

25. = as was said [above].

26. Zephyrus (west wind), according to *Heptameron*, 586 (Turner, 102).

27. = the use.

28. Necromantic manuals consistently anticipate the potentially horrific or otherwise deceptive appearance of demons by insisting that they appear in nonthreatening form or sometimes by proscribing the form in which they will appear. Fictional accounts of necromantic invocations describe demons appearing as voluptuous young women to seduce the magician out of the protective circle. See for example Caesarius of Heisterbach, "Dialogus Miraculorum," in *Caesarius of Heisterbach. Dialogus miraculorum. Textum ad quatuor codicum manuscriptorum editionisque principis fidem accurate*, ed. Joseph Strange (Coloniae: J. M. Heberle, 1851), 279–81.

29. = *Costus speciosus. Costum* in Latin. Also known in English as spiral ginger.

30. The figure below copies an error in fourth row from Basel 1578, 222. This should be written 18 / 20 / 22 / 21 / 17 / 13 (emphasis mine), as in *DOP*, 2:22 (315). Marginal note beside this figure: "111 / 6 × 18 ½."

31. This should be נכיאל. *DOP*, 2:22 (313). The scribe has copied this error from Basel 1578, 220.

32. Next to figure below, a marginal note: "65 / 5 × 13."

33. = bitter.

34. = tin.

35. = in the day and hour of Mars.

36. Marginal note: "34 / 4 × 8 1/2."

37. This should be הסמאל. *DOP*, 2:22 (313). The scribe follows Basel 1578, 219.

38. = in the day and hour of Jupiter.

39. Thursday is the day of Jupiter.

40. = sour flavor.

41. Next to figure below, a marginal note: "15 / 3 × 5."

42. = as said before [above].

43. = the end of [the discussion of] characters, sigils, and tables of good and bad angels.

44. = know.

45. On binding see *DOP*, 1:40 (158–59).

46. In one of the principal theories of vision in the Middle Ages, the eyes were assumed to produce rays that struck objects and reflected back images. This theory was also extended to explain the effects of the evil eye and the power of glances. See David C. Lindberg, *Theories of Vision from Al-Kindi to Kepler* (Chicago: University of Chicago Press, 1976). The scribe, however, appears to be referring to Agrippa, who also discusses the use of ointments to enhance the power of the eye in enchantments. *DOP*, 1:50 (181–82).

47. Some forms of love magic proscribe preparing some sort of image or substance and then kissing the intended object of the magic with this object in the operator's mouth. See for example Cambridge, University Library, Additional 3544, p. 61. The scribe may also have drawn on Agrippa. *DOP*, 1:45 (170).

48. That is, use sweet for good and sour for hatred and evil. For a discussion of imagination and taste as an example of sympathetic magic see *DOP*, 1:64 (222–24).

49. The scribe has added a "y" to the name. See Basel 1578, 219; and *DOP*, 2:22 (313).

50. The figure does not correspond with *DOP*, 2:22 (317). The scribe follows Basel 1578, 229.

51. = changing what needs to be changed.

52. It is common to require that conjurations only be performed in the first half of the lunar month, from the new moon to the full moon: "Debet autem componi haec tabula, luna crescente, diebus & horis, quae tunc spiritui conveniunt." *Liber quartus*, 553 (Turner, 62). In the *Thesaurus spirituum* this idea is expounded at length. See London, British Library, Sloane 3853, 13v. See also below, item 25.

53. In this case meaning a six-pointed star. See the figure of folio 12v.

54. = five-pointed stars.

55. The following list of names, including those in the table below, is drawn from *Heptameron*, 578–81. The scribe has mistakenly written the name "Varcan," who is the ruling angel of the air on Sunday according to *Heptameron*, 575. In the following table, the scribe follows the Basel 1578 edition, writing "Babiel" in place of "Rabiel," as found in most other editions. See for example the 1565 edition published in Köln (VD 16 ZV 272), 144. The spirits associated with the spring are also drawn from *Heptameron*, 564. Here the scribe copies "augusita" rather than "augusia" as found in other editions. See Köln 1565 (VD 16 ZV 272), 103. The numbering of the spirits is original to the Boxgrove Manual.

56. The form of this table or lamina and of the four that follow bear some similarities to what is found in *Heptameron*, 574 (Turner, 87). It also follows some of the suggestions in *Liber quartus*, 540–42 (Turner, 47–48), such as a double circle and five-pointed stars in each of four corners.

57. "Amenn so be it" is written at the top in red ink at a later date by a contemporary hand. Figure 13 is an exact copy of the pentagon in *Heptameron*, 567 (Turner, 80). The instructions written by the scribe are also the same except that he strips out some of the Roman Catholic elements, in particular the priestly garments and the mass of the Holy Spirit. "Vestis sit sacerdotis, si fieri potest: si non possit haberi, sit linea & nitida. Deinde sumat hoc pentaculum factum die & hora Mercurij, crescente luna, in charta membrana hoedi. Sed prius dicatur super illo Missa spiritus sancti, & aspergatur aqua baptismali." *Heptameron*, 566. "Let it be a priest's garment, if it can be: but if it cannot be had, let it be of linen and clean. Then take this pentacle made in the day and hour of Mercury, the moon increasing, in parchment made of a kid's skin. But first let there be said over it the Mass of the Holy Ghost, and let it be sprinkled with the water of baptism." Turner, 79. On the protective qualities of pentagons see *Liber quartus*, 540–41 (Turner, 47).

58. = in a waxing moon.

59. = But let Mercury be in Virgo or Gemini.

60. These correspond to the names and descriptions of these spirits in *DOP*, 2:7 (268), 3, 18 (452–57) and 3:24 (468–71). Agrippa has Vurieus for Oriens in *DOP*, 3:34 (471), but this appears to be a mistake in the original that was duplicated across all subsequent editions. He has Oriens in *DOP*, 2:7 (268). In manuscripts Oriens is also the accepted name. See for example London, British Library, Additional 36674, fol. 51v; London, British Library, Sloane 3853, fol. 138r; London, Wellcome Library, Wellcome 110, fols. 6v and 110v; and Oxford, Bodleian Library, Rawlinson D. 252, fol. 15v.

61. = juggling. The term was often used as a synonym for performance magic involving sleights of hand.

62. Although the scribe's Hebrew characters are barely recognizable, it seems clear he intended the tetragrammaton in the center of this figure (i.e., יהוה).

63. = from manuscript books.

64. The particular source this scribe may have drawn on would be difficult to identify since divine names occur so frequently. The sources for many of these words lie in Christian antiquity, but the more proximate sources are probably liturgical. The ninth-century *Alma chorus domini*, which is employed in all the English usages, contains the following list: Messias, Soter, Emmanuel, Sabaoth, Adonai, unigenitus, via, vita, manus, homousion, principium, primogenitus, sapientia, virtus, alpha, omega, fons, origo boni, paraclitus, mediator, agnus, ovis, vitulus, serpens,

aires, leo, vermis, os, verbum, splendor, sol, gloria, lux, imago, panis, flos, vitis, mons, ianua, petra, lapis, angelus, sponsus, pastor, propheta, sacerdos, athanatos, kyrios, theos, pantocrator, and Iesus. On the *Alma chorus domini*, see G. M. Dreves and C. Blume, eds., *Analecta hymica medii aevii*, 55 vols. (Leipzig, 1886–1922), vol. 25, no. 2, and vol. 53, no. 87. These names recur in many medieval English manuscript sources, including more conventional devotional works such as the *Burnet Psalter* (fol. 66r–v; Arnott et al., "Burnet Psalter") but also in numerous books of magic from charms to necromancy. See for example their appearance in the other text in this volume, the Antiphoner Notebook, in item 56. For an examination of divine names in magic texts see David Porreca, "Divine Names: A Cross-Cultural Comparison (Papyri Graecae Magicae, Picatrix, Munich Handbook)," *Magic, Ritual, and Witchcraft* 5, no. 1 (2010): 17–29; Julien Véronèse, "God's Names and Their Uses in the Books of Magic Attributed to King Solomon," *Magic, Ritual, and Witchcraft* 5, no. 1 (2010): 30–50.

65. Although the note clearly refers to Henry Cornelius Agrippa von Nettesheim, no such list appears in Agrippa, nor do many of these names. All but a few appear in various places in the *Heptameron*, sometimes with slightly modified spellings (e.g., "Zebaoth" for "Sabaoth"). Only Eli, Eloha, Eheye, Esche, helyoren, hod, Jod, Na, Ye, Jhesuh, Sanctus, Benedictus, Ipse, and messyas clearly do not appear there (explicitly as divine names), and the last five would be reasonable ones for the scribe to insert. A small detail tends to confirm the *Heptameron* as the principal source. The scribe writes a number beside some words, indicating that they are to be repeated. For Va, Aye, Ha, Eye, and Ya the respective numbers match the number of repetitions of these words found in incantations in the *Heptameron*. Eye and hau appear repeated three times in that work as well, probably referring to what our scribe has rendered "heye" and "hu." *Heptameron*, 575–88 (Turner, 89–102). The *Heptameron* is clearly attributed to Peter of Abano but only travels with works attributed to Agrippa. This may explain why the scribe suggested Agrippa as the author.

66. This prayer and the instruction to sprinkle with holy water are a direct translation from *Heptameron*, 565–66 (Turner, 79).

67. The phrase "creature of" derives from liturgical sources such as the consecration for salt in the standard Catholic liturgy. See "Exorciso te creatura salis . . . (I exorcize you creature of salt . . .)," in *Manuale ad usum percelebris ecclesie sarisburensis*, ed. Collins, 1. The scribe of this manuscript no doubt drew the phrase from magic manuals where it is regularly used. See for example "Exorcizo vos creaturas planetarum dedicatas eorum spiritibus et in earum horis fabricatas et earum potencia factas per Uryel Salatiel Acoel . . ." Oxford, Bodleian Library, Rawlinson D. 252, fol. 80v. "Exorciso vos creaturas planetarum spiritibus dedicatas horisque eorum fortitudinis fabricatas per uriel salatiel acoel . . ." Copenhagen, Kongelike Bibliotek, Gl. Kgl. S. 1658, fol. 245. See also London, Wellcome Library, Wellcome 110, fol. 65v; and London, British Library, Sloane 3853, fol. 14r.

68. The scribe has created this prayer from instructions for consecrations in the *Liber quartus*. These begin as follows: "Sic in consecratione Aquae commemoramus, quomodo Deus locauerit firmamentum in medio aquarum, quomodo in paradiso terrestri, locauit fontem aquarum, ex quo per quatuor flumina sacra rigatur vniversus orbis terrarum: item, quomodo fecit aquas, iusticiae suae instrumentum, in destructione gigantum, per diluuium generale super omnem terram: & in destructionem exercitus Pharaonis, in mari rubro." *Liber quartus*, 546. "So then, in the consecration of water, we ought to commemorate how that God hath placed the firmament in the midst of the waters, and in what maner that God placed the fountain of waters in the earthly Paradise, from whence sprang four holy rivers, which watered the whole earth. Likewise we are to call to remembrance in what manner God made the water to be the instrument of executing his justice in the destruction of the Gyants in the general deluge over all the earth, and in the overthrow of the host of Pharaoh in the Red-sea." Turner, 53. The same patterns of emulation continue (where possible) with the following consecrations up to the consecration of the book (item 19).

69. The prayer contains a string of allusions to miraculous occurrences of water in the Bible, including well-known stories in Genesis and Exodus. For the four rivers flowing out of paradise see Genesis 2:10–14. The story of the flood starts at Genesis 6:17. Moses brings water from the

desert in Exodus 17:6 and Numbers 20:10–11. "Mylhorse" is an archaic word for an ass; for the story of the water coming from the jawbone of an ass, see Judges 15:15–16. For Jesus's baptism see Matthew 3:13–17.

70. The crosses indicate that the reader should make a gesture in the sign of the cross.

71. = In the name of the Father, and of the Son, and of the Holy Spirit. Amen. Let it be done, let it be done, let it be done. The first portion of this is a standard liturgical phrase; the latter repetition of "fiat" commonly occurs at the end of magic formulae.

72. The scribe had to make a greater effort to create this consecration than he did with the previous ones. The text in the *Liber quartus* reads only "Sic, in consecratione olei & fumigiorum commemoramus sacra ad hoc pertinentia quæ legimus apud Exodum, de oleo vnctionis & nomina diuina, ad hæc conformia, quale est nomen Christus, quod vnctum sonat, & si quid huiusmodi in mysterijs est: quale illud Apocalypsis de duabus oliuis stillantibus oleum sanctum in lampades, ardentes ante faciem Dei, & huiusmodi." *Liber quartus*, 547. "And likewise in the consecration of Oyl and Perfumes, we are to call to remembrance such holy things as are pertinent to this purpose, which we read in Exodus of the holy anoynting oyl, and divine names significant hereunto, such as is the name Christ, which signifies anoynted: and what mysteries there are hereof; as that in the Revelation, of the two Olive-trees distilling holy oyl into the lamps that burn before the face of God: and the like." Turner, 54–55.

73. The scribe intends to say that the original Greek meaning of Christ (Χριστός) in English is "anointed."

74. As above, this prayer alludes to several important scriptural references to oil. God ordains in several places in Exodus the use of oil for sanctifying priests (e.g., Exod. 28:40–41 and 29:7–9) and also relating to ritual places, objects, and implements (Exod. 30:22–33). Inspired by the spirit of God, Samuel anoints David king in 1 Samuel 6:1–13. For the two olive trees and two candles before the face of God, see Revelation 11:4.

75. With the exception of the two sentences noted below, the consecration once again closely follows the model set down in the *Liber quartus*, 546–47 (Turner, 54).

76. This line echoes the first line in the standard Catholic exorcism for salt in the preparation of holy water. Exorciso te creatura salis . . . (I exorcize you creature of salt . . .)," in *Manuale ad usum percelebris ecclesie sarisburensis*, ed. Collins, 1. Whether the scribe was aware of this is unclear, however, as similar formulae are regularly employed in magic manuals. See for example Oxford, Bodleian Library, Rawlinson D. 252., fol. 80r–v.

77. This initial sentence is drawn from the discussion of the exorcism of fire in *Heptameron*, 566 (Turner, 79).

78. God spoke to Moses from a burning bush in Exodus 3:2–3. For the pillar of fire that led the Israelites, see Exodus 3:20–22.

79. = splendor of God, light of God, lamp of God See Psalms 90:17 (89:17 Vulg.).

80. This last sentence is also drawn from *Heptameron*, 566 (Turner, 79).

81. = consecration of the sword. Despite requiring a sword, the *Heptameron* gives no instructions for consecrating one. The *Liber quartus* only mentions the passage from Maccabees and the biblical verse "Take unto you two-edged swords." *Liber quartus*, 548 (Turner, 56). Following this text seems more or less original, although it clearly follows the scriptural focus of the models provided by Agrippa. The ritual performance in this text is thus not merely a slavish rehearsal of that work. The consecration of the sword seems most likely to have been inspired by the use of a sword in the *Thesaurus spirituum*, on which this scribe also drew. Cf. London, Wellcome Library, Wellcome 110, fol. 5v.

82. Judas receives a golden sword 2 Maccabees 15:15. The source of the passage on the two-edged sword is unclear and the scribe evidently found it so as well. Possibilities include Psalms 149:6, Proverbs 5:4, Hebrews, 4:12, and Revelation 1:16. On selling one's garment to buy a sword, see Luke 22:36. David sees an angel with a sword smiting the people of Israel in 2 Samuel 24:17. For examples of the sword, rod, or staff of God see Judges 7:18–20, Exodus 17:9, and Psalms 23:4, respectively. References to God as a consuming fire may be found in Hebrews 12:29, Deuteronomy 4:24, and Deuteronomy 9:3.

83. This may be based on the requirement of a litany of the saints in the *Liber consecratio-num*. Kieckhefer, *Forbidden Rites*, 9.

84. = consecration of the book or parchment.

85. A subsequent scribe notes here "Oratio .1.ᵃ" and has numbered an additional nine prayers. The second section of this prayer, beginning "Oh inuysyble god . . . ," is drawn from the *Liber consecrationum* or a closely related text. See Kieckhefer, *Forbidden Rites*, 264–65. The subsequent scribe regards this as the second prayer, but this renders ten rather than the nine prayers called for in the instructions. As all the other prayers end with the Lord's Prayer, it seems likely that this was intended as the second part of the first prayer.

86. On the delivery of the Ten Commandments see Exodus 34:27–28. The text follows the tradition that the Bible (clearly written over many centuries) was inspired as a whole by the Holy Spirit.

87. = whether willing or not.

88. That is, the tetragrammaton, the four-letter name of God (יהוה).

89. By giving the first words of the Lord's Prayer (Matt. 6:9–13) the text intends the operator to complete the prayer from memory.

90. See the *Liber consecrationum* in Kieckhefer, *Forbidden Rites*, 266–67.

91. The texts compiles various aspects of the first creation story in Genesis 1:1–29 and of the ejection from the Garden of Eden in Genesis 3:2–24.

92. Genesis 6:1–8:15.

93. Abraham was visited by God in the form of three men (understood by Christians to represent the Trinity) in the plain of Mamre and he fed them under a tree. See Genesis 18:1–8.

94. The text alludes to miraculous incidents surrounding Moses's delivery of the Israelites from Egypt in Exodus 3:2, 14:26–30, 34:27–28, and 17:6–7. Continuing on this theme, the text turns to other major stories of delivery from evil by God in Daniel 3:19–30, 6:1–24, and 13 Vulg., as well as Jonah 1:17–2:10.

95. See the *Liber consecrationum* in Kieckhefer, *Forbidden Rites*, 267.

96. See the *Liber consecrationum* in Kieckhefer, *Forbidden Rites*, 267–68. "On pie iuste, Adonay qui es fons misericordie . . ."

97. The employment of psalms is quite common in ritual magic texts. In part this may derive from liturgical uses, particularly the gradual and penitential psalms that were recited on a regular basis. See for example Oxford, Bodleian Library, Rawlinson D. 252, fols. 38v and 63r. On the use of psalms in rituals see also *DOP*, 3:61 (583).

98. See the *Liber consecrationum* in Kieckhefer, *Forbidden Rites*, 268–70.

99. Text has "delues."

100. This corresponds loosely to the *Liber consecrationum* in Kieckhefer, *Forbidden Rites*, 270–74. In most cases, the prayers end with the Lord's Prayer, and so this prayer might conceivably have been intended as two. In fact, an annotating scribe suggests a new prayer begins at that point (i.e., after the Pater Noster). However, the first section does not ask that some aspect of the book be blessed or imbued with power, a formula that takes place in all the other prayers. I suggest, therefore, that despite the Pater Noster in the middle, this is a single unit. Regarding these prayers as one also makes sense of the scribe's insistence that there are nine rather than ten prayers.

101. Isaiah 45:23.

102. A reference to the nine orders of angels as described in the *Celestial Hierarchies* of Pseudo-Dionysius the Areopagite.

103. That is, occult powers or properties. These include the demonstrable properties of the magnet or lodestone but also the supposed magic powers associated with certain plants, stones, or words. See Brian P. Copenhaver, "A Tale of Two Fishes: Magical Objects in Natural History from Antiquity Through the Scientific Revolution," *Journal of the History of Ideas* 52, no. 3 (1991): 373–98. For a classic text detailing the power of stones and herbs circulating in print in England in the sixteenth century see Albertus Magnus, *The Secrets of Albertus Magnus. Of the Vertues of Hearbes, Stones, and Certaine Beasts. Whereunto Is Newly Added, a Short Discourse*

of the Seauen Planets Gouerning the Natiuities of Children. Also a Booke of the Same Author, of the Maruellous Things of the Worlde, and of Certaine Effects Caused by Certaine Beasts (London: W. Iaggard, 1599).

104. See the *Liber consecrationum* in Kieckhefer, *Forbidden Rites*, 274–75.

105. See the *Liber consecrationum* in Kieckhefer, *Forbidden Rites*, 275–76.

106. This prayer is closely related to the *Liber consecrationum* in Kieckhefer, *Forbidden Rites*, 260–64.

107. The hand that has numbered the prayers and made corrections elsewhere in the manuscript inserts "I" before this word for the sake of clarity.

108. Psalms 19:14.

109. Among the various grandiose claims of ritual magic texts, that magic items might have the virtue of a sacrament was perhaps the most dramatic and certainly heretical, but most people recognized its problematic nature. The *Ars notoria* claimed only that its rituals were sacramental, John of Morigny claimed that his system was akin to a sacrament, and even here the text does not claim sacramental status for its consecration, but only requests of God that it confer the *virtue* of a sacrament. On the sacraments and the *Ars notoria* see Véronèse, "Magic, Theurgy and Spirituality in the Medieval Ritual of the *Ars Notoria*." See also John of Morigny, "Prologue to *Liber visionum*," 169. Even if most texts never quite claimed a status akin to one of the seven sacraments, Thomas Aquinas directly condemned this idea, suggesting it was certainly in the minds of users and other readers of magic texts. Aquinas, *Summa theologiae*, IIa, IIae, q. 96, a. 1.

110. The list from the angels to this point reflects the notion of intercession in Catholic theology of the original text. The scribe evidently felt comfortable with this despite the fact that he has clearly chosen to exclude other Roman elements.

111. Psalms 32:22 and 71:1–2.

112. Here the prayer shifts into a more performative mode, suggesting either that the narrator assumed others might be present during the ritual or that the phrases were pillaged directly from liturgical contexts where such phrases were common.

113. This section quotes Psalm 127 in its entirety.

114. This phrase is a very common liturgical convention.

115. This procedure is loosely based on the *Liber consecrationum* but is radically simplified. Notably absent is the requirement that masses be said over it as it lies on the altar in a church, although it does send the operator to his quarters to conclude the operation with rituals and prayers. The use of a table covered in white linen may be an attempt to make up for this loss in a private setting and in a form workable for a Protestant. In place of the masses we have a regime of fasting and private prayers. Rather than concluding with all seven penitential psalms, this operation requires just three, and only one of these is a penitential psalm (Ps. 51, "Miserere mei Deus"). All do, however, begin with the word "miserere" (i.e., have mercy). See Kieckhefer, *Forbidden Rites*, 8–10.

116. = abstain from sexual pollution. On occasion the symbol for Venus was employed to indicate sexual pollution; here the name is simply spelled out.

117. The intent is either that a Lenten fast should be observed or that it is best to do this during Lent.

118. Note that the text demands not only empty ritual, but ritual accompanied by sincere belief, emotion, or religious affect.

119. In the Latin Vulgate Psalms 50, 55, and 56 begin with the word "miserere" (i.e., have mercy). Note that the scribe follows the Protestant numbering system.

120. Leviticus 22:3.

121. Psalms 141:1.

122. Similar ideas about suffumigations and unctions are found in Agrippa, *DOP*, 1:45 (169–72). The *Holy Almandal* is a medieval ritual magic text based on an Arabic and potentially Sanskrit original. After due ritual preparations, an angel spirit will speak with the operator and appear in the smoke of incense passing through the Almandal, a small, specially constructed table or altar. See Jan R. Veenstra, "Venerating and Conjuring Angels: Eiximenis's *Book of the*

Holy Angels and the *Holy Almandal.* Two Case Studies," in *Magic and the Classical Tradition*, Warburg Institute Colloquia, ed. Charles Burnett and W. F. Ryan (London: Warburg Institute, 2006), 119–34; and Veenstra, "Holy Almandal." It seems likely that the magic practices of Marsilio Ficino involved seeing demons in suffumigations. See Michael J. B. Allen, "Summoning Plotinus: Ficino, Smoke, and the Strangled Chickens," in *Reconsidering the Renaissance*, ed. Mario di Cesare (Binghamton, N.Y.: Medieval and Renaissance Texts and Studies, 1992), 76–85.

123. The scribe cites a range of passages all affirming the efficacy of prayer combined with firm faith. See Matthew 7:7–8 and 17:20, as well as Mark 11:24.

124. James 5:16–18.

125. Such requirements occur in other magic manuals, despite their frequently self-interested goals. See for example the Antiphoner Notebook, item 2. On not taking the Lord's name in vain, see Exodus 20:7.

126. Fasting and alms are recommended in Tobit 12:8. The book of Judith recommends fasting and prayer (4:13).

127. Most texts do not require the consecration of the clothing or the parchment used for books or seals. Instead they tend to insist that the material from which they are made be clean or new (e.g., parchment must nor have been written on before—that is, it is to be "virgin"), and that the finished item be consecrated. There is some precedent for consecrating everything in the magician's toolbox and also the specific items mentioned in this list. For example, the *Clavicula Salomonis* requires specially prepared ink. See London, British Library, Additional 36674, fol. 19r–v.

128. An illustration of this pentacle appears as item 1 above. These instructions are drawn from *Liber quartus*, 542–43 (Turner, 48–49).

129. This duplicates a passage above (item 1), next to which an illustration of this figure may be found.

130. *Liber quartus*, 540–41 (Turner, 47). Agrippa also attributes power over evil spirits to pentacles. *DOP*, 2:23 (319).

131. These rules (including the requirement of the new moon above) roughly replicate the order and contents of the rules in the *Thesaurus spirituum*. The author leaves out masses to Saint Cyprian and another mass of the operator's choice, suggesting that the relatively light use of Roman elements in this work was intentional. The rest of the rules tend to be shortened and reworked somewhat, but the dependence on the *Thesaurus spirituum* is clear. See London, British Library, Sloane 3853, fols. 10r–12r. The inclusion of particular masses may be found in numerous other works of ritual magic as well. In chapter 52, for example, the *Sworn Book of Honorius* requires a mass of the Holy Spirit.

132. The rules in the *Thesaurus spirituum* advise that the operator must work together with a priest. Evidently to accommodate Protestant theology, the priest has become simply an honest, godly, and learned man. Although not explicitly, the operator in the *Liber consecrationum* was probably intended to be a priest, since he is said to have a priestly cincture and stole. Kieckhefer, *Forbidden Rites*, 9.

133. This duplicates the advice given in the *Thesaurus spirituum*. This is to say that the magician should begin working in every even day after the new moon to the middle of the lunar month or the full moon, at which point the moon begins to wane again. Although cited in the initial rules it is repeated again after. See London, British Library, Sloane 3853, fol. 13v.

134. The *Thesaurus spirituum* also says spirits like to appear in the rays of the sun ("spiritus multum appetunt in radiis solariubs operare et appere") and insists therefore that one must operate in clear atmospheric conditions. See London, British Library, Soane 3853, fol. 10v.

135. The rules from this point to the one concerning the ring are more or less the same as what one finds in one section of the *Thesaurus spirituum* and, more crucially, in the same order. See London, British Library, Sloane 3853, fol. 11r; and London, Wellcome Library, Wellcome 110, fols. 52v and 62r. These begin with relatively common requirements of three days of abstinence and the washing and paring of nails. More distinctive are the seven prayers in each of the cardinal directions and the requirement of wearing the consecrated ring on the little finger of the left

hand ("annulum Semper debes portare in minimo digito sinistre manus"). See London, British Library, Sloane 3853, fol. 11r.

136. This does not appear in the Sloane 3853 or Wellcome 110 Latin versions of the *Thesaurus spirituum*. But something like it does appear on the badly damaged first page of an English epitome of the *Thesaurus spirituum*. Angle brackets indicate mutilation and contain suggested readings; punctuation inserted for clarity: "The maister <yn th>is work must have a perfect <&> sure faith in his work, & doubt not. <he> that doubteth to obtain his petition <spea-><ke>th with his lippes & not with his hart. <ye se>cond is that yow must be secret <& t>ake heed that yow bewray not <ye sec>rets of this arte, but only to your <fell>oes, which be of your counsayle." London, Wellcome Library, Wellcome 110, fol. 1r. These kinds of "sworne" friends appear commonly in ritual magic manuals. See for example the brotherhood (literally sworn to loyalty and secrecy) in Hedegård, *Liber iuratus Honorii*, 61 (1:20–20). But references to compatriots operating with the magus are also quite common. See ibid., 129 (1–2), 133.

137. = spikenard.

138. In other words, at this stage the abstinence from food may be broken.

139. Magic texts tend to emphasize the value of secrecy as a way of enhancing the perceived value of the document. Few suggest that the magic will not work if the secrecy is broken. See Boudet and Véronèse, "Le secret dans la magie rituelle médiévale." To this learned discussion I would add that secrets were not held by individuals but groups. Klaassen, *Transformations of Magic*, 120–21.

140. Curiously, manuscripts of the *Thesaurus spirituum* include both measurements. London, British Library, Sloane 3853, fol. 13r, has seventeen feet and London, Wellcome Library, Wellcome 110, fol. 62r, has fifteen. Hedegård, *Liber iuratus Honorii*, 119, 43 (12:4, 35:12).

141. Once again the scribe draws this from the *Heptameron* but attributes it to Agrippa rather than Peter of Abano as the printed book does. *Heptameron*, 556 (Turner, 74).

142. Amaymon is one of the kings of the four cardinal directions. See for example *DOP*, 3:24 (468–73).

143. The *Liber iuratus Honorii* (130:6; Hedegård, 136) advises the compatriots have stools, in part to avoid rubbing out the circles drawn in the ground.

144. For the discussion that follows, see the appendixes, below.

145. That is, one is to count through the week three days from Sunday to Wednesday.

146. = aghast.

147. The *Thesaurus spirituum* includes the ritual use of sword, scepter, and ring, which are to be inscribed with divine names. The conjurations regularly invoke them afterwards. ". . . per illud ineffabile de nomen quod in sceptro meo scupltum est . . ." London, British Library, Sloane 3853, fol. 36v.

148. Presumably "scepter" is intended here as no staff has been mentioned to this point.

149. Conjuring manuals walked a fine line. Antimagic authors claimed that magicians made pacts with the devil, something that was assiduously avoided among ritual magicians up to 1600 and usually beyond. Here the act of sacrifice is characterized as an act of worship or obeisance, a way of recognizing a position of servitude, and hence a kind of pact or bond. In the later Middle Ages, recognizing that texts did not ask magicians to make pacts of this kind and generally avoided making sacrifices, antimagic tracts argued that there were *implicit* pacts made during such magic operations, even when they lacked explicit sacrifices or similar acts. See Jan R. Veenstra, *Magic and Divination at the Courts of Burgundy and France: Text and Context of Laurens Pignon's Contre Les Devineurs (1411)* (New York: Brill, 1998), 343–55; Jean-Patrice Boudet, "Les condamnations de la magie à Paris en 1398," *Revue Mabillon*, n.s., 12, no. 73 (2001): 101–37; Frank Klaassen, "The Middleness of Ritual Magic," in *The Unorthodox Imagination in Medieval Britain*, ed. Sophie Page (Manchester, U.K.: Manchester University Press, 2011), 135–42.

150. Matthew 4:1–11; Mark 1:12–13.

151. The *Thesaurus spirituum* describes the sword in similar terms: "Primus igitur oportet te habere habere gladium splendidum." London, British Library, Sloane 3853, fol. 64r.

152. = having carved "on" on the one side.

153. Evidently the third pentacle in item 11. It may also be a reference to the *Vinculum Salomonis* or *Pentaculum Salomonis* texts of unstable contents, which describes the creation of a pentacle to be employed if spirits do not obey. See for example Oxford, Bodleian Library, Rawlinson D. 252, fol. 87v; London, Wellcome Library, Wellcome 110, fols. 6r–38v; Cambridge, University Library, Ll. i. 12, fol. 9r–9v.

154. The *Thesaurus spirituum* mentions both techniques. See London, Wellcome Library, Wellcome 110, fol. 34v; Cambridge, University Library, Additional 3544, p. 23.

155. This is a common element in conjuring texts. See for example London, Wellcome Library, Wellcome 110, fol. 50v. See also Cambridge, University Library, Additional 3544, p. 7.

156. The *Practica nigromancie*, a text commonly associated with the *Thesaurus spirituum*, advises the operator to hang a protective sigil on your breast. London, British Library, Sloane 3853, fol. 6v. See also London, British Library, Additional 36674, fol. 151.

157. = attempt.

158. It seems likely that a period of acclimatization was necessary before the magic began to be subjectively convincing. See Klaassen, "Subjective Experience of Medieval Ritual Magic."

159. The abbreviation most commonly means *recipe*, meaning "take." Robert the Turk, cited as the teacher of William Bacon, the putative author of the *Thesaurus spirituum*, seems the most likely meaning here.

160. Figure 18 is an almost exact copy of what appears and is described in the *Heptameron*, 574–76 (Turner, 87–89) and to instructions for the composition of the circle in *Heptameron*, 562–63 (Turner, 74–75). All the remaining images are directly modeled on it. The only difference is that the name Michael is repeated on both sides of the seal in the *Heptameron* and does not have a picture of the sun on the right side. The latter was no doubt intended as a finding device indicating the day of the week and not an element in the figure itself. The scribe also mistranscribes "abraym" as "abray." The angel names that appear in this circle are drawn from the lists in the *Heptameron* and are suitable for a figure of the sun to be used in the spring in the first hour of a Sunday. The middle band begins with the seal of the sun, followed by the angels of Sunday (i.e., Michael, Dardiel, and Huratapel). *Heptameron*, 575 (Turner, 88). Following these, Talui to Agusita are angels associated in various ways with the spring (in order of appearance in the *Heptameron*), and the last, Yayn, the angel reigning in the first hour of the day. *Heptameron*, 564 (Turner, 76–77). In the outer circle are Varcan, the king of the angels of the air reigning on a Sunday (logically at the top), and his ministers, Tus, Andas, and Cynabal. *Heptameron*, 575 (Turner, 88). All the remaining images draw in the same fashion using names appropriate to the planet and season from *Heptameron*, 563–65 and 574–89 (Turner, 76–78 and 88–103).

Note that in figure 19, the scribe copies "Torquaret" as opposed to "Tolquaret" from Basel 1578. *Heptameron*, 565 (Turner, 77). Cf. Basel 1550, 559. In figure 20, the scribe has "Abusaba" rather than "Abuzaha." *Heptameron*, 577 (Turner, 90). In figure 21, the scribe has "forlas" for "farlas." *Heptameron*, 564 (Turner, 76). The scribe mistakenly wrote "Adonay" and a cross in the outer circle in the upper right quadrant. This was clearly intended for the inner circle. In figure 22, the scribe discovered that "gargatel" has been omitted and inserted the name. In figure 23, the scribe has "Amabiel" for "Amabael." *Heptameron*, 565. Finally, in figure 25, the scribe mistranscribes "Gargatel" as "Gargatiel." *Heptameron*, 558 (Turner, 77).

APPENDIXES

Overview of Sources Used in Boxgrove Manual

This table provides an overview of the sources used in the Boxgrove Manual. For full details, see the notes in the relevant section.

Item(s)	Folios	Contents	Source(s)
1		Sigil of the Apocalyptic Christ	*Liber quartus*
2–8	1v–10v	Things that are "attributed to the planets" and planetary tables	*DOP* *Liber quartus* *Heptameron* (For specific details, see below.)
9	11r	On Binding	*DOP*
10	11v–14r	Making Lamens or Pentacles to Call Good Spirits	*Heptameron* *Liber quartus*
11	14v	The Names of Evil Spirits	*DOP*
12	15v	Divine Names According to a Manuscript	An unidentified manuscript, perhaps the one containing the *Liber consecrationum* or *Thesaurus spirituum*
13	16r	Divine Names According to Agrippa	*Heptameron*
14	16v	Consecration of Suffumigations	*Heptameron*
15	16v–17r	Consecration of the Water	*Liber quartus*
16	17v–18v	Consecration of the Oil	*Liber quartus*
17	18v–19r	Consecration of the Fire	*Liber quartus* *Heptameron*
18	19r–19v	Consecration of the Sword	*Liber quartus* *Heptameron*
19	19v–25v	Consecration of the Book	*Liber consecrationum*
20	25v–26r	Instructions for Consecrating the Book	*Liber consecrationum*
21	26r–27v	Instructions for Operation	*Thesaurus spirituum*
22–24	27v–29r	Instructions on Making Pentacles, Tables, and Lamens	*Liber quartus Heptameron?*
25	29r–33r	Rules for Operating	*Thesaurus spirituum* *Heptameron*
26–27	33v–37v	Figures	*Heptameron*

Details on Sources for Boxgrove Manual, Items 2–8

In the Boxgrove Manual, items 2–8 (fols. 2r–10v), the author drew on a variety of sources and locations within those sources. In order to reduce the complexity of the notes, the details are provided here.

Subject	Details	Source
Colors and planets		*DOP*, 1:49 (177–80)
Places and planets		*DOP*, 1:48 (175–77)
Herbs, metals, and planets		*DOP*, 1:23–29 (131–42)
Spices and odiferous woods and planets	These are drawn from the ingredient lists for suffumigations, although sometimes the scribe lists these separately as with the suffumigation for Venus (fol. 6v).	*DOP*, 1:44 (168–72) *Heptameron*, 574–89
The magic squares, spirit names (both in Latin and in Hebrew), and the powers of the squares relative to planets	What Agrippa identifies as a "daemon" of the planet is rendered in the Boxgrove Manual as an "evil angel." Although potentially ambiguous, Agrippa makes clear that the term "daemon" here refers to a demon in the classic sense of the term as opposed to the "intelligence" that is a good spirit. "Et praesunt illi nomina divna cum intelligentia ad bonum et daemonio ad malum et eliciuntur ex ea characteres Lunae et spirituum eius" (*DOP*, 2:22 [312]).	*DOP*, 2:22 (310–18)
Figures of the planets and spirits		*DOP*, 2:22 and 33 (310–18 and 347–50)
Seals		*Heptameron*, 575–87 (Turner, 88–108)
Familiar appearance of demons, their particular forms, and the signs of their arrival	Although the scribe probably drew these from the *Liber quartus* they reflect the influence of the *Liber iuratus Honorii*, 120.	*Liber quartus*, 34–35
The powers ascribed to the fully composed figures	These are summaries of the powers attributed to the numerical squares in Agrippa.	*DOP*, 2:22 (313–18)
Powers of the spirits	Taken from the sections relevant to each planet.	*Heptameron*, 575–87

Planetary Hours and Ruling Planets

The following table illustrates the system for determining planetary hours and the ruling planet for a given day or night. The planet ruling the first hour of a given day or night is said to rule that entire twelve-hour period. Note that the planets simply repeat the order in which they appear in the first seven hours on Sunday continuing the next day, and that the cycles end evenly on the last planet in that series (Mars) on the last hour of Saturday.

		Sunday	Monday	Tuesday	Wednesday	Thursday	Friday	Saturday
HOURS OF THE DAY (starting at sunrise and dividing the day in twelve equal parts)	1	Sun	Moon	Mars	Mercury	Jupiter	Venus	Saturn
	2	Venus	Saturn	Sun	Moon	Mars	Mercury	Jupiter
	3	Mercury	Jupiter	Venus	Saturn	Sun	Moon	Mars
	4	Moon	Mars	Mercury	Jupiter	Venus	Saturn	Sun
	5	Saturn	Sun	Moon	Mars	Mercury	Jupiter	Venus
	6	Jupiter	Venus	Saturn	Sun	Moon	Mars	Mercury
	7	Mars	Mercury	Jupiter	Venus	Saturn	Sun	Moon
	8	Sun	Moon	Mars	Mercury	Jupiter	Venus	Saturn
	9	Venus	Saturn	Sun	Moon	Mars	Mercury	Jupiter
	10	Mercury	Jupiter	Venus	Saturn	Sun	Moon	Mars
	11	Moon	Mars	Mercury	Jupiter	Venus	Saturn	Sun
	12	Saturn	Sun	Moon	Mars	Mercury	Jupiter	Venus
HOURS OF THE NIGHT (starting at sunset and dividing the night in twelve equal parts)	1	Jupiter	Venus	Saturn	Sun	Moon	Mars	Mercury
	2	Mars	Mercury	Jupiter	Venus	Saturn	Sun	Moon
	3	Sun	Moon	Mars	Mercury	Jupiter	Venus	Saturn
	4	Venus	Saturn	Sun	Moon	Mars	Mercury	Jupiter
	5	Mercury	Jupiter	Venus	Saturn	Sun	Moon	Mars
	6	Moon	Mars	Mercury	Jupiter	Venus	Saturn	Sun
	7	Saturn	Sun	Moon	Mars	Mercury	Jupiter	Venus
	8	Jupiter	Venus	Saturn	Sun	Moon	Mars	Mercury
	9	Mars	Mercury	Jupiter	Venus	Saturn	Sun	Moon
	10	Sun	Moon	Mars	Mercury	Jupiter	Venus	Saturn
	11	Venus	Saturn	Sun	Moon	Mars	Mercury	Jupiter
	12	Mercury	Jupiter	Venus	Saturn	Sun	Moon	Mars

BIBLIOGRAPHY

MANUSCRIPTS

Cambridge, University Library
    Additional 3544
    Additional 9308
    D.5.76
    Ll. i. 12
Chichester, West Sussex Record Office
    Add MSS 6926, 6927
    B. Dean 16
    EP 1/17/13
    EP 4/3/2
Copenhagen, Kongelike Bibliotek
    Gl. Kgl. S. 1658
London, British Library
    Additional 34111
    Additional 36674
    Additional 37787
    Harley 425
    Harley 2267
    Sloane 121
    Sloane 3542
    Sloane 3846
    Sloane 3849
    Sloane 3853
    Sloane 3854
London, Wellcome Library
    Wellcome 110
Oxford, Bodleian Library
    Additional B. 1
    Ashmole 1378
    eMus 238
    Rawlinson D. 252

PRIMARY SOURCES

Agrippa von Nettesheim, Heinrich Cornelius. *De occulta philosophia lib. iii. Item spurius liber de caeremoniis magicis, qui quartus Agrippae habetur.* Lugduni, per Beringos fratres. Basel, 1550 (VD 16 ZV 265).
————. *De occulta philosophia libri tres.* Edited by V. Perrone Compagni. Leiden: Brill, 1992.

————. *Opera.* Basel: Thomas Guarin, 1578 (VD 16 ZV 263).

————. *Three Books of Occult Philosophy.* Translated by John French. London: Printed by R. W. for Gregory Moul, 1651.

Agrippa von Nettesheim, Heinrich Cornelius, pseud. *Henry Cornelius Agrippa HIS Fourth BOOK of Occult Philosophy. Of Geomancy. Magical Elements of Peter de Abano. Astronomical Geomancy. The Nature of Spirits. Arbatel of Magick.* Translated by Robert Turner. London, 1655.

————. *Liber quartus de occulta philosophia, seu de cerimoniis magicis. Cui accesserunt, elementa magica Petri De Abano, Philosophi.* Marburg, [1559?].

————. *Liber quartus de occulta philosophia seu de cæremoniis magicis.* In *Opera,* by Heinrich Cornelius Agrippa von Nettesheim, 562–83. Basel: Thomas Guarin, 1578 (VD 16 ZV 263).

————. *Liber quartus de occulta philosophia, seu de cerimoniis magicis.* Köln, 1565 (VD 16 ZV 272).

Albertus Magnus. *The Secrets of Albertus Magnus. Of the Vertues of Hearbes, Stones, and Certaine Beasts. Whereunto Is Newly Added, a Short Discourse of the Seauen Planets Gouerning the Natiuities of Children. Also a Booke of the Same Author, of the Maruellous Things of the Worlde, and of Certaine Effects Caused by Certaine Beasts.* London: W. Iaggard, 1599.

Ars notoria: The Notory Art of Solomon, Shewing the Cabalistical Key of Magical Operations. . . . Translated by Robert Turner. London: J. Cotrell, 1657.

Bailey, Terence. *The Processions of Sarum and the Western Church.* Studies and Texts. Toronto: Pontifical Institute Publications, 1971.

Blundeville, Thomas. *The Fower Chiefyst Offices Belongyng to Horsemanshippe. . . .* London: By VVyllyam Seres dwellyng at the west ende of Paules churche, at the signe of the Hedgehogge, [1566?].

British Museum. "Coventry Ring." AF.897. http://www.britishmuseum.org/.

Caesarius of Heisterbach. *Dialogus miraculorum. Textum ad quatuor codicum manuscriptorum editionisque principis fidem accurate.* Edited by Joseph Strange. Coloniae: J. M. Heberle, 1851.

Clay, William Keatinge, ed. *Liturgical Services: Liturgies and Occasional Forms of Prayer Set Forth in the Reign of Queen Elizabeth.* Cambridge, U.K.: Cambridge University Press, 1847.

Collins, A. Jefferies, ed. *Manuale ad usum percelebris ecclesie Sarisburiensis.* London: Henry Bradshaw Society, 1960.

Dickinson, Francis Henry, ed. *Missale ad usum insignis et præclaræ ecclesiæ Sarum.* 4 vols. Burntisland: E prelo de Pitsligo, 1861.

Dreves, G. M., and C. Blume, eds. *Analecta hymica medii aevii.* 55 vols. Leipzig, 1886–1922.

The Examination of John Walsh Before Maister Thomas Williams, Commissary to the Reuerend Father in God William Bishop of Excester, Vpon Certayne Interrogatories Touchyng Wytchcrafte and Sorcerye, in the Presence of Diuers Ge[n]tlemen and Others. The .xxiii. of August. 1566. London: Iohn Awdely, 1566.

Favent, Thomas. *Historia siue narracio de modo et forma mirabilis parliamenti apud Westmonasterium anno domini millesimo CCCLXXXVI regni vero regis Ricardi secundi post conquestum anno decimo, per Thomam Fauent clericum indicata.* Camden Miscellany 14. Camden 3rd ser. 37. London: Offices of the Royal Historical Society, 1926.

Harms, Daniel, James R. Clark, and Joseph H. Peterson. *The Book of Oberon: A Sourcebook of Elizabethan Magic.* Woodbury, Mich.: Llewellyn Publications, 2015.

Hedegård, Gösta, ed. *Liber iuratus Honorii: A Critical Edition of the Latin Version of the Sworn Book of Honorius.* Stockholm: Almovist & Wiksell International, 2002.

Howell, Thomas Bayly, Thomas Jones Howell, William Cobbett, and David Jardine, eds. *Cobbett's Complete Collection of State Trials and Proceedings for High Treason and Other Crimes and Misdemeanors from the Earliest Period to the Present Time.* 33 vols. London: R. Bagshaw, 1809.

Lawley, Stephen W., ed. *Breviarium ad usum insignis ecclesie Eboracensis.* 2 vols. Edinburgh: Surtees Society, 1880–82.

Manuale ad usum percelebris ecclesie sarisburensis. Edited by A. Jeffries Collins. London: Henry Bradshaw Society, 1960.

Mooney, Linne R., Daniel W. Mosser, Elizabeth Solopova, Deborah Thorpe, and David Hill Radcliffe. "The *DIMEV*: An Open-Access, Digital Edition of the *Index of Middle English Verse*. Based on the *Index of Middle English Verse* (1943) and Its *Supplement* (1965)." http://www.dimev.net/.

Morigny, John of. *Liber florum celestis doctrine / The Flowers of Heavenly Teaching.* Edited by Nicholas Watson and Claire Fanger. Toronto: Pontifical Institute of Mediaeval Studies, 2015.

Nichols, John Gough, ed. *Narratives of the Days of the Reformation: Chiefly from the Manuscripts of John Foxe the Martyrologist.* London: Camden Society, 1859.

Peter of Abano, pseud. *Heptameron, seu elementa magica.* In *Opera*, by Heinrich Cornelius Agrippa von Nettesheim, 527–61. Basel: Thomas Guarin, 1578 (VD 16 ZV 263).

Procter, Francis, and Christopher Wordsworth, eds. *Breviarium ad usum insignis ecclesiae Sarum.* 3 vols. Cambridge, U.K.: Alma Mater Academia, 1879–86.

Reformatio legum ecclesiasticarum, ex authoritate primum regis Henrici. 8. inchoata: Deinde per regem Edouardum 6. prouecta, adauctaque in hunc modum, atque nunc ad pleniorem ipsarum reformationem in lucem ædita. London, 1641.

Scot, Reginald. *The Discouerie of Witchcraft.* London: W. Brome, 1584.Wordsworth, Christopher, ed. *Horae Eboracenses: The Prymer or Hours of the Blessed Virgin Mary According to the Use of the Illustrious Church of York.* Publications of the Surtees Society 132. Durham, U.K.: Andrews & Co., 1920.

Young, Francis, ed. *The Cambridge Book of Magic: A Tudor Necromancer's Manual.* Ely, U.K.: Francis Young, 2015.

SECONDARY SOURCES

Allen, Michael J. B. "Summoning Plotinus: Ficino, Smoke, and the Strangled Chickens." In *Reconsidering the Renaissance*, edited by Mario di Cesare, 76–85. Binghamton, N.Y.: Medieval and Renaissance Texts and Studies, 1992.

Alonso-Almeida, Francisco, and Mercedes Cabrera-Abreu. "The Formulation of Promise in Medieval English Medical Recipes: A Relevance-Theoretic Approach." *Neophilologus* 86, no. 1 (2002): 137–54.

Arnott, Michael, Iain Beavan, Michael Craig, Morton Gauld, and Colin McLaren. "The Burnet Psalter." University of Aberdeen Special Collections. http://www.abdn.ac.uk/.

Ash, Eric H. *Power, Knowledge, and Expertise in Elizabethan England.* Baltimore: Johns Hopkins University Press, 2004.

Bader, Richard-Ernst. "Sator Arepo: Magie in der Volksmedizin." *Medizin-Historisches Journal* 22 (1987): 115–34.

Boudet, Jean-Patrice. "Les condamnations de la magie à Paris en 1398." *Revue Mabillon*, n.s., 12, no. 73 (2001): 101–37.

———. *Entre science et nigromance: Astrologie, divination et magie dans l'Occident médiéval, xiie–xve siècle.* Paris: Publications de la Sorbonne, 2006.

———. "Les who's who démonologiques de la renaissance et leurs ancêtres médiévaux." *Médiévales* 44 (Spring 2003): 117–39.

Boudet, Jean-Patrice, and Julien Véronèse. "Le secret dans la magie rituelle médiévale." *Micrologus* 14 (2006): 101–50.

Bremmer, Jan N., and Jan R. Veenstra. *The Metamorphosis of Magic from Late Antiquity to the Early Modern Period.* Leuven: Peeters, 2002.

Burnett, Charles. *Magic and Divination in the Middle Ages: Texts and Techniques in the Islamic and Christian Worlds.* Aldershot, U.K.: Variorum, 1996.

Burnett, Charles, and W. F. Ryan. *Magic and the Classical Tradition.* London: Warburg Institute, 2006.

Chardonnens, László Sándor, and Rosanne Hebing. "Two Charms in a Late Medieval English Manuscript at Nijmegen University Library." *Review of English Studies* 62, no. 245 (2011): 181–92.

Clucas, Stephen. "John Dee's Angelic Conversations and the *Ars Notoria*." In *John Dee: Interdisciplinary Studies in English Renaissance Thought*, edited by Stephen Clucas, 231–73. Dordrecht: Springer, 2006.

———. "'Non est legendum sed inspicendum solum': Inspectival Knowledge and the Visual Logic of John Dee's *Liber Mysteriorum*." In *Emblems and Alchemy*, edited by Alison Adams and Stanton J. Linden, 109–32. Glasgow Emblem Studies 3. Glasgow: Glasgow Emblem Studies, 1998.

———. "*Regimen Animarum et Corporum*: The Body and Spatial Practice in Medieval and Renaissance Magic." In *The Body in Late Medieval and Early Modern Culture*, edited by Darryll Grantley and Nina Taunton, 113–29. Aldershot, U.K.: Ashgate, 1999.

Clulee, Nicholas H. *John Dee's Natural Philosophy: Between Science and Religion*. London: Routledge, 1988.

Copenhaver, Brian P. "A Tale of Two Fishes: Magical Objects in Natural History from Antiquity Through the Scientific Revolution." *Journal of the History of Ideas* 52, no. 3 (1991): 373–98.

Davies, Owen. *Cunning-Folk: Popular Magic in English History*. London: Hambledon and London, 2003.

Devine, Michael. "John Prestall: A Complex Relationship with the Elizabethan Regime." Master's thesis, Victoria University of Wellington, 2010.

———. "Treasonous Catholic Magic and the 1563 Witchcraft Legislation: The English State's Response to Catholic Conjuring in the Early Years of Elizabeth I's Reign." In *Supernatural and Secular Power in Early Modern England*, edited by Marcus K. Harmes, 67–91. Burlington, Vt.: Ashgate, 2015.

Dillinger, Johannes. *Magical Treasure Hunting in Europe and North America: A History*. New York: Palgrave Macmillan, 2012.

Duffy, Eamon. *Marking the Hours: English People and Their Prayers, 1240–1570*. New Haven, Conn.: Yale University Press, 2006.

———. *The Stripping of the Altars: Traditional Religion in England, c. 1400—c. 1580*. New Haven, Conn.: Yale University Press, 1992.

Eamon, William. *Science and the Secrets of Nature: Books of Secrets in Medieval and Early Modern Culture*. Princeton, N.J.: Princeton University Press, 1994.

Edsall, Mary Agnes. "*Arma Christi* Rolls or Textual Amulets? The Narrow Roll Format Manuscripts of 'O Vernicle.'" *Magic, Ritual, and Witchcraft* 9, no. 2 (2014): 178–209.

Fanger, Claire, ed. *Conjuring Spirits: Texts and Traditions of Medieval Ritual Magic*. Magic in History. University Park: Pennsylvania State University Press, 1998.

———. "Divine Dreamwork: Confluence of Visionary Traditions in John of Morigny's *Flowers of Heavenly Teaching*." *Magic, Ritual, and Witchcraft* 13, no. 1 (2018): 1–39.

———, ed. *Invoking Angels: Theurgic Ideas and Practices, Thirteenth to Sixteenth Centuries*. University Park: Pennsylvania State University Press, 2012.

———. *Rewriting Magic: An Exegesis of the Visionary Autobiography of a Fourteenth-Century French Monk*. Magic in History. University Park: Pennsylvania State University Press, 2015.

———. "Virgin Territory: Purity and Divine Knowledge in Late Medieval Catoptromantic Texts." *Aries* 5, no. 2 (2005): 200–225.

Favreau, Robert. *Etudes d'épigraphie médiévale: Recueil d'articles de Robert Favreau*. Vol. 2. Limoges: Presses Universitaires de Limoges, 1995.

Feingold, Mordechai. "The Occult Tradition in the English Universities of the Renaissance: A Reassessment." In *Occult and Scientific Mentalities in the Renaissance*, edited by Brian Vickers, 73–94. Cambridge, U.K.: Cambridge University Press, 1984.

Giralt, Sebastià. "Magic in Romance Languages." In *The Routledge History of Medieval Magic*, edited by Sophie Page and Catherine Rider. Turnhout: Routledge, forthcoming.

Gray, Douglas. "Notes on Some Middle English Charms." In *Chaucer and Middle English Studies in Honour of Rossell Hope Robbins*, edited by Beryl Rowland, 56–71. London: Allen and Unwin, 1974.

Griffiths, J. Gwyn. "'Arepo' in the Magic 'Sator' Square." *Classical Review*, n.s., 21, no. 1 (1971): 6–8.

Harkness, Deborah E. *The Jewel House: Elizabethan London and the Scientific Revolution*. New Haven, Conn.: Yale University Press, 2007.

———. *John Dee's Conversations with Angels: Cabala, Alchemy, and the End of Nature*. Cambridge, U.K.: Cambridge University Press, 1999.

Hunt, Tony. *Popular Medicine in Thirteenth-Century England: Introduction and Texts*. Cambridge, U.K.: D. S. Brewer, 1990.

John of Moringy. *Liber Florum Celestis Doctrine: The Flowers of Heavenly Teaching*. Edited by Claire Fanger and Nicholas Watson. Toronto: Pontifical Institute of Mediaeval Studies, 2015.

———. "Prologue to *Liber visionum*." Edited and translated by Claire Fanger and Nicholas Watson. *Esoterica* 3 (2001): 108–217.

Jones, Claire. "Formula and Formulation: 'Efficacy Phrases' in Medieval English Medical Manuscripts." *Neuphilologische Mitteilungen* 99, no. 2 (1998): 199–209.

Jones, Peter, and Lea Olsan. "Middleham Jewel: Ritual, Power, and Devotion." *Viator* 31 (2000): 249–90.

Kassell, Lauren. "'All This Land Full Fill'd of Faerie,' or Magic and the Past in Early Modern England." *Journal of the History of Ideas* 67, no. 1 (2006): 107–22.

———. "The Economy of Magic in Early Modern England." In *The Practice of Reform in Health, Medicine, and Science, 1500–2000: Essays for Charles Webster*, edited by Margaret Pelling and Scott Mandelbrote, 43–57. Aldershot, U.K.: Ashgate, 2005.

———. *Medicine and Magic in Elizabethan London: Simon Forman: Astrologer, Alchemist, and Physician*. Oxford Historical Monographs. Oxford, U.K.: Clarendon Press, 2005.

———. "Reading for the Philosopher's Stone." In *Books and the Sciences in History*, edited by Marina Frasca-Spada and Nicholas Jardine, 13–34. Cambridge, U.K.: Cambridge University Press, 2000.

Kieckhefer, Richard. *Forbidden Rites: A Necromancer's Manual of the Fifteenth Century*. Stroud, U.K.: Sutton, 1997.

———. *Magic in the Middle Ages*. Cambridge Medieval Textbooks. Cambridge, U.K.: Cambridge University Press, 1989.

Kittredge, George Lyman. *Witchcraft in Old and New England*. New York: Russell & Russell, 1956.

Klaassen, Frank. "Learning and Masculinity in Manuscripts of Ritual Magic of the Later Middle Ages and Renaissance." *Sixteenth Century Journal* 38, no. 1 (2007): 49–76.

———. "Medieval Ritual Magic in the Renaissance." *Aries* 3, no. 2 (2003): 166–99.

———. "The Middleness of Ritual Magic." In *The Unorthodox Imagination in Medieval Britain*, edited by Sophie Page, 131–65. Manchester, U.K.: Manchester University Press, 2011.

———. "The Return of Stolen Goods: Reginald Scot, Religious Controversy, and a Late Sixteenth-Century Manuscript of Magic." *Magic, Ritual, and Witchcraft* 1, no. 2 (2006): 135–77.

———. "Ritual Invocation and Early Modern Science: The Skrying Experiments of Humphrey Gilbert." In *Invoking Angels*, edited by Claire Fanger, 341–66: University Park: Pennsylvania State University Press, 2011.

———. "The Subjective Experience of Medieval Ritual Magic." *Magic, Ritual, and Witchcraft* 7, no. 1 (2012): 19–51.

———. "Three Magic Rituals to Spoil Witches." *Opuscula: Short Texts of the Middle Ages and Renaissance* 1 (2011): 1–10.

———. *The Transformations of Magic: Illicit Learned Magic in the Later Middle Ages and Renaissance*. University Park: Pennsylvania State University Press, 2013.

Lidaka, Juris. "*The Book of Angels, Rings, Characters and Images of the Planets:* Attributed to Osbern Bokenham." In *Conjuring Spirits: Texts and Traditions of Medieval Ritual Magic,* edited by Claire Fanger, 32–75. University Park: Pennsylvania State University Press, 1998.

Lindberg, David C. *Theories of Vision from Al-Kindi to Kepler.* Chicago: University of Chicago Press, 1976.

Luhrmann, T. M. "The Art of Hearing God: Absorption, Dissociation, and Contemporary American Spirituality." *Spiritus: A Journal of Christian Spirituality* 5, no. 2 (2005): 133–57.

———. "The Magic of Secrecy." *Ethos* 2 (1989): 131–65.

———. *Persuasions of the Witch's Craft: Ritual Magic in Contemporary England.* Cambridge, Mass.: Harvard University Press, 1989.

———. *When God Talks Back: Understanding the American Evangelical Relationship with God.* New York: Alfred A. Knopf, 2012.

MacFarlane, Alan. *Witchcraft in Tudor and Stuart England: A Regional and Comparative Study.* London: Routledge & K. Paul, 1970.

Marsh, Christopher W. *Popular Religion in Sixteenth-Century England: Holding Their Peace.* Social History in Perspective. New York: St. Martin's Press, 1998.

McNamara, Jo Ann, John E. Halborg, and E. Gordon Whatley. *Sainted Women of the Dark Ages.* Durham, N.C.: Duke University Press, 1992.

Mesler, Katelyn. "The Three Magi and Other Christian Motifs in Medieval Hebrew Medical Incantations: A Study in the Limits of Faithful Translation." In *Latin into Hebrew: Texts and Studies. Volume I: Studies,* edited by Resianne Fontaine and Gad Freudenthal, 164–66. Leiden: Brill, 2013.

Mitchell, Stephen A. *Witchcraft and Magic in the Nordic Middle Ages.* Middle Ages Series. Philadelphia: University of Pennsylvania Press, 2011.

Nowotny, K. A. "The Construction of Certain Seals and Characters in the Work of Agrippa of Nettesheim." *Journal of the Warburg and Courtauld Institutes* 12 (1949): 46–57.

Oikonomakou, Mary, Herman Mussche, Doris Vanhove, and Thilo Rehren. "Litharge from Laurion: A Medical and Metallurgical Commodity from South Attika." *L'antiquité classique* 68 (1999): 299–308.

Olsan, Lea. "Charms and Prayers in Medieval Medical Theory and Practice." *Social History of Medicine* 16 (2003): 343–66.

———. "Charms in Medieval Memory." In *Charms and Charming in Europe,* edited by Jonathan Roper, 59–87. New York: Palgrave, 2004.

———. "The Corpus of Charms in the Middle English Leechcraft Remedy Books." In *Charms, Charmers and Charming: International Research on Verbal Magic,* edited by Jonathan Roper, 214–37. New York: Palgrave Macmillan, 2009.

———. "Latin Charms of Medieval England: Verbal Healing in a Christian Oral Tradition." *Oral Tradition* 7 (1992): 116–42.

———. "The Marginality of Charms in Medieval England." In *The Power of Words: Studies on Charms and Charming in Europe,* edited by James Alexander Kapaló, Éva Pócs, and William Ryan, 135–64. New York: CEU Press, 2013.

———. "The Three Good Brothers Charm: Some Historical Points." *Incantatio* 1 (2011): 48–78.

Orht, Ferdinand. "Über Alter und Ursprung der Begegnungssegen." *Hessische Blätter für Volkskunde* 35 (1937): 49–58.

Page, Sophie. *Magic in the Cloister: Pious Motives, Illicit Interests, and Occult Approaches to the Medieval Universe.* University Park: Pennsylvania State University Press, 2013.

Parry, G. J. R. *The Arch-Conjuror of England: John Dee.* New Haven, Conn.: Yale University Press, 2011.

Porreca, David. "Divine Names: A Cross-Cultural Comparison (Papyri Graecae Magicae, Picatrix, Munich Handbook)." *Magic, Ritual, and Witchcraft* 5, no. 1 (2010): 17–29.

Procter, Francis. *A History of the Book of Common Prayer.* New York: Macmillan, 1907.

Raine, James. "Proceedings Connected with a Remarkable Charge of Sorcery, Brought Against James Richardson and Others, in the Diocese of York, AD 1510." *Archaeological Journal* 16 (1859): 71–81.

Roper, Jonathan. *English Verbal Charms*. Helsinki: Suomalainen Tiedeakatemia, 2005.

Roper, Lyndal. "Stealing Manhood: Capitalism and Magic in Early Modern Germany." *Gender & History* 3 (March 1991): 4–22.

Ryrie, Alec. *A Sorcerer's Tale: Faith and Fraud in Tudor England*. Oxford, U.K.: Oxford University Press, 2008.

Scribner, Robert W. "The Reformation, Popular Magic, and the 'Disenchantment of the World.'" *Journal of Interdisciplinary History* 23, no. 3 (1993): 475–94.

Skemer, Don C. *Binding Words: Textual Amulets in the Middle Ages*. University Park: Pennsylvania State University Press, 2006.

Stallcup, Stephen. "The 'Eye of Abraham' Charm for Thieves: Versions in Middle and Early Modern English." *Magic, Ritual, and Witchcraft* 10, no. 1 (2015): 23–40.

Thomas, Keith Vivian. *Religion and the Decline of Magic*. New York: Scribner, 1971.

Timbers, Frances. *Magic and Masculinity: Ritual Magic and Gender in the Early Modern Era*. London: Taurus, 2014.

Tuomi, Ilona. "Parchment, Praxis and Performance of Charms in Early Medieval Ireland." *Incantatio* 3 (2013): 60–85.

Veenstra, Jan R. "The Holy Almandal." In *The Metamorphosis of Magic*, edited by Jan N. Bremmer and Jan R. Veenstra, 189–229. Leuven: Peeters, 2002.

———. *Magic and Divination at the Courts of Burgundy and France: Text and Context of Laurens Pignon's Contre Les Devineurs (1411)*. New York: Brill, 1998.

———. "Venerating and Conjuring Angels: Eiximenis's *Book of the Holy Angels* and the *Holy Almandal*. Two Case Studies." In *Magic and the Classical Tradition*, edited by Charles Burnett and W. F. Ryan, 119–34. Warburg Institute Colloquia. London: Warburg Institute, 2006.

Véronèse, Julien. *L'ars notoria au Moyen Âge: Introduction et édition critique*. Micrologus Library. Florence: SISMEL edizioni del Galluzzo, 2007.

———. "God's Names and Their Uses in the Books of Magic Attributed to King Solomon." *Magic, Ritual, and Witchcraft* 5, no. 1 (2010): 30–50.

———. "Magic, Theurgy, and Spirituality in the Medieval Ritual of the *Ars Notoria*." In *Invoking Angels*, edited by Claire Fanger, 37–78. University Park: Pennsylvania State University Press, 2012.

———. "La notion d''auteur-magicien' à la fin du Moyen Âge: Le cas de l'ermite Pelagius de Majorque." *Médiévales* 51 (2006): 119–38.

Weill-Parot, Nicolas. *Les "images astrologiques" au Moyen Âge et a la Renaissance*. Paris: Honoré Champion, 2002.

Wooley, Benjamin. *The Queen's Conjurer: The Science and Magic of Dr. John Dee, Adviser to Queen Elizabeth I*. New York: Henry Holt, 2001.

Young, Francis. *The Cambridge Book of Magic: A Tudor Necromancer's Manual*. Ely, U.K.: Francis Young, 2015.

———. *Magic as a Political Crime in Early Modern England*. London: Taurus, 2018.

INDEX

women
   as cunning folk, 20, 83n4
   exclusion of from medieval ritual magic, 77
   healing magic for childbirth, 45, 49–50, 53–54
   as skryers, 16n11

Three Biters Charm for, 62
   See also feminization of magic
words of power, 21–22, 29, 38–39, 75
   See also divine names

Yates, Frances, 1–2